THE PATRIOT ACT

ABOUT THE AUTHORS

Cary Stacy Smith is a Ph.D. candidate in psychology at Mississippi State University. His primary research interests include adolescent and adult psychopathy, as well as autism. He has over 50 publications and plans to work as a forensic psychologist upon graduation. He and Dr. Hung have been married for nine years.

Li-Ching Hung, Ph.D. is a professor at the Overseas Institute of Technology, located in Taijung, Taiwan, and an adjunct faculty at Kaplan and Walden Universities in the United States. Her primary research interests include counseling Taiwanese women considering divorce or those already divorced. She earned her Ph.D. in Education at Mississippi State and is working on her dissertation for her second doctorate in Counselor Education.

THE PATRIOT ACT

Issues and Controversies

By

CARY STACY SMITH, Ph.D.

Department of Psychology
Mississippi State University
Mississippi State, Mississippi

and

LI-CHING HUNG, Ph.D.

Professor
Overseas Institute of Technology
Taijung, Taiwan

CHARLES C THOMAS • PUBLISHER, LTD.
Springfield • Illinois • U.S.A.

Published and Distributed Throughout the World by

CHARLES C THOMAS • PUBLISHER, LTD.
2600 South First Street
Springfield, Illinois 62794-9265

© 2010 by CHARLES C THOMAS • PUBLISHER, LTD.

ISBN 978-0-398-07912-3 (hard)
ISBN 978-0-398-07913-0 (paper)

Library of Congress Catalog Card Number: 2009034768

With THOMAS BOOKS *careful attention is given to all details of manufacturing
and design. It is the Publisher's desire to present books that are satisfactory as to their
physical qualities and artistic possibilities and appropriate for their particular use.*
THOMAS BOOKS *will be true to those laws of quality that assure a good name
and good will.*

Printed in the United States of America
MM-R-3

Library of Congress Cataloging in Publication Data

Smith, Cary Stacy.
 The PATRIOT Act : issues and controversies / by Cary Stacy Smith and Li-
Ching Hung.
  p. cm.
 Includes bibliographical references and index.
 ISBN 978-0-398-07912-3 (hard)–ISBN 978-0-398-07913-0 (pbk.)
 1. National security–Law and legislation–United States. 2. Terrorism–
United States. 3. Terrorism–United States–Prevention. 4. War on
Terrorism, 2001– I. Hung, Li-Ching. II. Title.

KF4850.S63 2010
345.73'02–dc22   2009034768

This book is dedicated in loving memory of Elmer Smith.
I miss you, Daddy.

PREFACE

Few legislative acts in American history have caused polarization, as did the United and Strengthening America by Providing Appropriate Tools Required to Intercept and Obstruct Terrorism, more commonly known as The Patriot Act. Depending upon which side of the aisle one leans toward, an American might have thought that the Patriot Act was the opening salvo of a plan to drive the country in the direction of a fascist dictatorship where civil liberties were withheld at gunpoint. On the other hand, if a person leaned in the opposite political direction, he/she might have seen The Patriot Act as a godsend in the fight against international terrorism, especially since al-Qaeda and other such groups did not fight by recognized rules; thus, the only way to win was to combat terrorists in a manner far removed from "acceptable" practices. Practices such as right to legal counsel and freedom from torture were only valid for American citizens, not aliens.

When writing this book, we strove to maintain a moderate tone, free from political bias, and the reader can judge for himself/herself to see if we succeeded. In the Introduction, we speak about the events that transpired on 9/11 and how we, as Americans, responded. Chapter 1 deals with the state of America before 9/11; Chapter 2 centers on how the U.S. changed due to 9/11, along with detail about the Foreign Intelligence Service Act of 1978; and Chapter 3 focuses how we, as Americans, view terrorism, and how similar legislative acts in American history were also full of controversy. Chapter 4 is the longest chapter in the book, and it is where we discuss the Patriot Act itself, with more detail for Titles 1 and 2 than the remaining Titles primarily because the first two Titles were the most contentious. Chapter 5 looks at how various groups and individuals viewed the Patriot Act and their means of changing it so America's civil liberties remain a hallmark of the United States, while Chapter 6 looks at Constitutional law to gauge whether the Patriot Act is legal or not. As the Patriot Act changed many existing laws, we have included a Glossary of Statutes that should help the reader if he/she sees something like 8 CFR Part 287.3(d) and is unfamiliar with Federal Law.

The Patriot Act has lost much of its "teeth" due to judicial intervention. It would be a mistake, however, to assume that it will not rise again. If America suffers from no more terrorist attacks, the Act will stay on the books, but will remain below the radar screen. If we are attacked again and Americans are killed, a recrudescence will occur and many of the arguments presented herein will likely occur again.

C.S.S.
L.C.H.

INTRODUCTION

On September 11, 2001, during the wee hours of the morning, nineteen individuals, each connected intimately with al-Qaeda,[1] hijacked four commercial jet airliners with the intent of killing Americans. Each individual team of terrorists included an individual who had received pilot training within the U.S. After boarding, the individuals smashed two of the airliners (American Airlines Flight 11 and United Airlines Flight 175) into the World Trade Center in New York City, both structures symbolic of American strength. Each tower (1 WTC and 2 WTC) had a jet career into it, thus causing the complete disintegration of both buildings soon thereafter, with widespread destruction to nearby buildings.[2]

The captors smashed the third plane (American Airlines Flight 77) into the Pentagon (another edifice symbolic of American power), located in Arlington County, Virginia. On the fourth aircraft, both passengers and flight crew (United Airlines Flight 93) tried to regain control of their plane from the terrorists,[3] resulting in the craft's crashing in a barren field in rural Somerset County, Pennsylvania.[4]

In addition to the 19 terrorists, 2,974 Americans perished as a consequence of the attacks, with one individual dying as a direct result of inhaling dust from the WTC collapse.[5] As their bodies were never found, an additional 24 people were presumed dead, bringing the overall tally to 2,998, with the vast majority being nonmilitary personnel. The deceased were not only Americans; included in the dead were individuals from over 80 countries scattered around the globe.[6]

---

1. See "Bin Laden claims responsibility for 9/11," *CBC News* (2004–10–29). Retrieved on 2008–01–08.
2. See Neilan, Terence (2001–09–11). "2 Planes Crash Into World Trade Center," *The New York Times.*
3. See "The Attack Looms," *9/11 Commission Report.* National Commission on Terrorist Attacks Upon the United States (2004).
4. Ibid.
5. See Flight 93 Hijacker: 'We Have a Bomb on Board.'" *Fox News* (2006–04–13). Retrieved on 2008–02–23.
6. See Hijacked Planes Used in Coordinated Attacks Upon New York, Washington." *Fox News* (2001–09–11). Retrieved on 2008–2–24.

The National Institute of Standards and Technology (NIST) stated that roughly 17,400 civilians were in the Twin Towers when the terrorists attacked; however, turnstile counts issues by the Port Authority suggested that 14,154 people were usually in the WTC by 8:45 a.m.[7] Most of the individuals beneath the area of contact escaped before the buildings collapsed, along with 18 people that were directly stationed in the impact zone in the south tower.[8] One thousand three hundred and sixty-six people perished that were located either on the floors, or directly above in the North Tower.[9] The 9/11 Commission Report indicated that hundreds were killed at the moment of impact, whereas others were trapped, dying after the structures collapsed.[10] In the South Towers, roughly 600 people were killed instantly, or were trapped at or above the floors of collision in the South Tower.[11]

In addition to the 19 terrorists, 2,974 Americans perished as a consequence of the attacks, with one individual dying as a direct result of inhaling dust from the WTC collapse. As their bodies were never found, an additional 24 people were presumed dead, bringing the overall tally to 2,998, with the vast majority being nonmilitary personnel.

Approximately 200 people ended their lives by leaping from the towers as they burned, crashing onto the asphalt streets below and the rooftops of nearby buildings, hundreds of feet below.[12] Within each tower, some individuals above the point of impact struggled upwards, hoping to make it the roof, as they thought a helicopter might save them; sadly, once they made it, they found the doors solidly locked. Before 9/11, no plans existed for helicopter rescues for one reason: no one had ever crashed a commercial airliner into a building before. In addition, even if such plans had existed, smoke and ash prevented helicopters from rescuing anyone.[13]

The men and women in the Twin Towers were not the only ones killed; hundreds of fire and rescue workers died as well. The New York City Fire

---

7. See Jason D Averill et al. (2005). "Occupant Behavior, Egress, and Emergency Communications," *Final Reports of the Federal Building and Fire Investigation of the World Trade Center Disaster* (PDF), National Institute of Standards and Technology (NIST). Retrieved on 2008–05–20.

8. See Jim Dwyer et al. (2002–05–26). "Last Words at the Trade Center; Fighting to Live as the Towers Die." *The New York Times.*

9. See Eric Lipton, (2004–07–22). "Study Maps the Location of Deaths in the Twin Towers," *The New York Times.* Retrieved on 2008–2–11.

10. See Heroism and Honor." *National Commission on Terrorist Attacks upon the United States.* U.S. Congress. (2004–08–21). Retrieved on 2008–05–20.

11. See "9/11 Death Toll," CNN (2006, April 26). Retrieved on 2008–02–07.

12. See Dennis Cauchon & Martha Moore (September 2, 2002). "Desperation forced a horrific decision," *USA Today.*

13. See "Poor Info Hindered 9/11 Rescue," CBS News (May 18, 2004). Retrieved on 2008–2–22.

Department lost 341 firefighters, as well as two paramedics.[14] The New York City Police Department was also hurt: they lost 23 officers.[15] The Port Authority Police Department lost 37 officers,[16] whereas EMS companies lost additional EMTs and paramedics as well.[17]

> The rules of engagement that existed on 9/11 were woefully inadequate in practically every aspect, but then, the idea that someone would fly a passenger airliner sounded more like a Hollywood epic of the Arnold Schwarzenegger type.

On September 11, the safety of American air space hinged on the cooperation of two vastly different agencies: the Federal Aviation Administration (FAA) and North American Aerospace Defense Command (NORAD)–the former being civilian and the latter being military. The rules of engagement that existed on 9/11 were woefully inadequate in practically every aspect, but then, the idea that someone would fly a passenger airliner sounded more like a Hollywood epic of the Arnold Schwarzenegger type. In reality, what occurred after the attacks illustrated the fact that the FAA had never handled hijackers that wanted to destroy themselves, while NORAD had little idea how to handle commercial airliners that had been turned into weapons capable of killing thousands.[18]

NORAD did not receive confirmation to shoot down any other possible attackers until exactly 28 minutes after United 93 had crashed in Pennsylvania. Fighter jets raced into the air, but the operation, for the most part, was completely ineffective. The pilots had no idea regarding where to go or who their targets were, and though the shoot-down order had been received, the pilots were not informed. In any other circumstances, the situation would seem comical. Our elected leaders in Washington thought that F16s were circling the nation's capital, with specific instruction to obliterate any "hostile" fighters that might approach. The pilots were instructed to "take down" only the "ID type and tail" of any aircraft.[19]

---

14. See Denise Grady & Andrew C. Revkin, "Threats and Responses: Rescuer's Health; Lung Ailments May Force 500 Firefighters Off Job," *The New York Times,* 2002–09–10.

15. See Post-9/11 report recommends police, fire response changes. Associated Press. (2002-08-19). *USA Today.*

16. See Police back on day-to-day beat after 9/11 nightmare, (2002–07–21). *CNN.* Retrieved on 2008–03–03.

17. See Joshi Pradnya (2005–09–08). Port Authority workers to be honored. *Newsday.* Retrieved on 2008–02–20.

18. See op cit, Averill No. 7.

19. Op cit Dwyer, No. 8.

NORAD did not receive confirmation to shoot down any other possible attackers until exactly 28 minutes after United 93 had crashed in Pennsylvania. Fighter jets raced into the air, but the operation, for the most part, was completely ineffective.

The emergency response delivered on September 11 was strikingly similar to the one given by the national defense—it was a hodgepodge of improvisation. In New York City, various civil agencies attempted to keep some semblance of order. The New York City Fire Department, the New York City Police Department, the Port Authority of New York and New Jersey, the employees and occupants of the buildings did their utmost to handle the results of something completely unimaginable occurring over a grand total of 102 minutes. Near the impact zones, the casualty rates approached 100 percent. Many individuals quick to arrive at the scene lost their lives trying to save others. Although no plans or preparations for such an event had been formulated, and while a unified command structure was not achieved, in many ways, the response to September 11 was a success. Communications among the agencies responding to the crisis was practically nil, but even so, approximately 100 of the thousands of individuals working below the impact zone made it out, though aided by emergency personnel.[20]

The Pentagon experienced problems as well, especially in terms of command and control, but in general, the response there was effectual. In the nation's capital, an emergency response system entitled "The Incident Command System" prevailed over the intrinsic difficulties of a response across local, state, and federal jurisdictions.[21]

The United States responded by initiating the War on Terrorism, attacking and deposing the ruling junta in Afghanistan, the Taliban, due to their harboring al-Qaeda terrorists. More importantly, and the subject of this book, the U.S. enacted the Uniting and Strengthening America by Proving Appropriate Tools Required to Intercept and Obstruct Terrorism Act—the Patriot Act. Other countries commiserated with America and they, too, initiated increased antiterrorism legislation and increasing law enforcement powers. Major financial centers, like the various stock exchanges shut down for almost a week, posting gigantic losses upon reopening, no more so than in the airlines and insurance industries. The city of New York's economy, espe-

---

20. See Eric Lipton (2004–07–22). "Study Maps the Location of Deaths in the Twin Towers," *The New York Times*. Retrieved on 2008–1–15.
21. See Heroism and Honor." *National Commission on Terrorist Attacks upon the United States*. U.S. Congress (2004–08–21). Retrieved on 2008–01–30.

cially that of Lower Manhattan, ceased to function, as untold billions of dollars in office space was annihilated or damaged beyond repair.[22]

The attacks not only affected the U.S.; the effects were felt worldwide. All across the globe, 9/11 was condemned, even from countries usually not on America's side. For instance, in France, America's most vitriolic ally in NATO, the nation's top newspapers and news organization wrote: "We Are All Americans" (Nous sommes tous Américains).[23] This good feeling of sympathy and understanding was not shared by everyone, however. In the Middle East, Palestinians danced in the streets upon word that America had suffered great losses due to the attacks.[24] Reports indicated that in China, communal displays of fervor for the attacks erupted spontaneously by Chinese students in Beijing, though it should be mentioned that the journalist writing the report was not in Beijing the day the demonstrations occurred; rather, he based his report on information gathered from his sources; moreover, the report was not filed until 2006.[25] Interestingly, most political leaders throughout the Middle East, including Afghanistan, denounced the attacks. Iraq was a prominent exception, stating publicly that "the American cowboys are reaping the fruit of their crimes against humanity."[26]

> In the Middle East, Palestinians danced in the streets upon word that America had suffered great losses due to the attacks.

The 9/11 Commission Report concluded that the hostility towards America, as exhibited by Khalid Sheikh Mohammed, the "principal architect" of the 9/11 attacks, originated "not from his experiences there as a student, but rather from his violent disagreement with U.S. foreign policy favoring Israel."[27] Similar rationale was shared by the two terrorists that rammed their respective planes into the World Trade Center: Mohamed Atta was portrayed as an individual who was "most imbued actually about . . . U.S. protection of these Israeli politics in the region." When someone asked Marwan al-Shehhi, the suicide pilot that flew into the second Tower, why he and Atta never laughed, he replied, ". . . How can you laugh when people are dying

---

22. See Michael L Dolfman & Solidelle F. Wasser (2004), "9/11 and the New York City Economy," *Monthly Labor Review*, 127.

23. International Reaction. September11News.com. Retrieved on 2008-02-08.

24. See Mixed Response from Arab World (2001-9-11). BBC. Retrieved from http://news.bbc.co.uk/2/hi/americas/1538861.stm on 2008-01-03.

25. See S. P. Jehangir, R. Ciesinger, & M. Young (2006-9-10). 9/11: Five years later. World views of attacks varied. *San Francisco Chronicle*. Retrieved 02-02-08.

26. See Hendrik Hertzberg, (2006-09-11). "Lost love." *The New Yorker*. Retrieved on 2008-02-02.

27. See National Commission on Terrorist Attacks Upon the United States (2004). "Chapter 5," 9/11 Commission Report, Government Printing Office. Retrieved on 2008-03-08.

in Palestine?"[28] In one account, Atta became a martyr as a response to the Israeli Defense Force striking at the beginning of Operation Grapes of Wrath.[29]

Abdulaziz al-Omari, one of the terrorists aboard Flight 11 with Atta, stated in a video, "My work is a message to those who heard me and to all those who saw me, at the same time it is a message to the infidels that you should leave the Arabian peninsula defeated and stop giving a hand of help to the coward Jews in Palestine."[30]

Abdulaziz al-Omari, one of the terrorists, said, "My work is a message to those who heard me and to all those who saw me, at the same time it is a message to the infidels that you should leave the Arabian peninsula defeated and stop giving a hand of help to the coward Jews in Palestine."

Law enforcement and intelligence organizations located throughout the world, in an effort of getting "tough" on terrorism, immediately arrested people branded as terrorists or possible terrorists with the express intention of destroying radical cells around the world.[31] In America, this aroused controversy, as civil rights activists argued that customary constraints on federal surveillance, primarily dealing with the Counter Intelligence Program's (COINTELPRO) monitoring of public meetings were destroyed by the USA PATRIOT Act. The American Civil Liberties Union, the preeminent civil libertarian group in the U.S., wrote that specific civil rights guarantees were being abridged and nullified.

Located at Guantanamo Bay, Cuba, the U.S. opened a compound with the express purpose to hold individuals deemed illegal combatants. Various organizations in America and the world (the European Parliament,[32] Amnesty International,[33] etc.) have difficulties regarding the legality of these detentions. After the attacks, more than 80,000 people, primarily Arab and Muslim immigrants, had biometric data taken and were registered due to the Alien Registration Act of 1940. More than 8,000 Islamic men were questioned closely, with 5,000 foreign nationals being held under Joint Congressional Resolution 107–40, which authorized military force "to deter and

---

28. Ibid.
29. Ibid.
30. See "Al-Qaeda tape finally claims responsibility for attacks." *The Guardian* (2002-09-10). Retrieved on 2008-01-18.
31. See "SE Asia unites to smash militant cells." CNN (May 8, 2002). Retrieved on 2008-03-10.
32. See "Euro MPs urge Guantanamo closure" (2006-06-13). *BBC News.* Retrieved on 2008-01-18.
33. See "USA: Release or fair trials for all remaining Guantánamo detainees" (2008-05-02). Amnesty International. Retrieved on 2008-7-09.

prevent acts of international terrorism against the United States."[34]

All action taken by the government in the days following 9/11 were eventually allowed under the USA Patriot Act, which is the subject of the present book.

34. See "Authorization for Use of Military Force: Authorization for Use of Military Force (Enrolled Bill) *S.J.Res.23 One Hundred Seventh Congress of the United States of America*" (2001–09–21). Retrieved on 2008–04–03.

CONTENTS

THE PATRIOT ACT

Chapter 1

THE U.S. BEFORE 9/11

In order to understand the reasons for the Patriot Act, information concerning the months, weeks, and days leading up to 9/11 is required. One primary reason for the Act was the belief that the traditional way of conducting business had failed; thus, the need for the Patriot Act.

While what transpired on September 11 was a shock to most, it could not have been a surprise to everyone. Islamist extremists had stated many times their intent to kill as many Americans as humanly possible.[35] While the leader of al-Qaeda, Osama bin Laden, would not become the FBI's most wanted individual until the late 1990s, ample warnings from Islamists concerning what they would do had become commonplace.[36]

> While what transpired on September 11 was a shock to most, it could not have been a surprise to everyone. Islamist extremists had stated many times their intent to kill as many Americans as humanly possible.

As early as February, 1993, the World Trade Center was attacked by a group of individuals led by Ramzi Yousef, who tried to bring the WTC down by a truck loaded with explosives. Instead of the mass murder they planned, only six people were killed, though a thousand were wounded. Other plans included those devised by Omar Abdel Rahman, who planned to destroy both the Holland and Lincoln tunnels, as well as other famous landmarks; however, these plans never materialized due to the terrorists' being caught.[37]

One famous incident, made into a famous Hollywood movie, occurred in October, 1993, when Somali tribesmen brought down several U.S. helicop-

---

35. See Text of Fatwah Urging Jihad Against Americans. Retrieved on 2007–11–02.
36. See Understanding Islamism, International Crisis Group, retrieved on 2008–04–08.
37. See Simon Reeve (2002–06–27). *The New Jackals: Ramzi Yousef, Osama bin Laden and the future of terrorism.* Northeastern University Press.

ters, killing 18 soldiers and wounding 73, which is now known as "Black Hawk Down."[38] It later became known that the tribesman received substantial help and guidance from a very well-funded al-Qaeda.[39]

In 1995, legal authorities in Manila found out that Ramzi Yousef planned on destroying approximately one dozen U.S. airliners as they flew over the Pacific.[40] In November, 1995, a car bomb detonated outside the building housing U.S. program director for the Saudi National Guard in Riyadh–five Americans were killed.[41] In June, 1996, a truck bomb flattened Khobar Towers, an apartment complex home to many U.S. soldiers stationed in Dhahran, Saudi Arabia. Nineteen Americans were killed, but hundreds were wounded. Saudi Hezbollah, a terrorist organization that regularly received funds from Iran, were the culprits.[42]

For many years, up until 1997, American intelligence saw bin Laden as a financier of terrorist acts, not a leader.[43] In February, 1998, bin Laden, along with four other individuals, issued a fatwa to the Islamic masses, stating that it was Allah's will for every Muslim to kill all Americans, because of their "occupation" of Muslim holy sites and their untoward aggression against Islam. Six months later, al-Qaeda carried out an operation of brilliance (and a precursor to 9/11). Two simultaneous (or almost so) truck bomb attacks on the U.S. embassies in Nairobi, Kenya, and Dar es Salaam, Tanzania. Twelve Americans were killed, but thousands more were wounded.[44]

In December 1999, Jordanian police thwarted a scheme to bomb popular locales frequented by American tourists.[45] Moreover, at the border separating the U.S. and Canada, a U.S. Customs agent arrested Ahmed Ressam, as he attempted to smuggle into the U.S. explosives earmarked for an assault on Los Angeles International Airport.[46] In October 2000, an al-Qaeda team in Aden, Yemen, rammed a small boat, fitted with an outboard motor and

---

38. See Mark Bowden (1997–11–16). "Black Hawk Down," *The Philadelphia Inquirer.* Retrieved on 2008–01–11.
39. See Peter Berger (2001). *Holy War, Inc. Inside the Secret World of Bin Laden.* New York: Free Press.
40. See Matthew Brezinski (2002–01–02). "Operation Bojinka's bombshell." *Toronto Star.* Retrieved on 2007–12–20.
41. See Special Report of the Select Committee on Intelligence, United States Senate, January 4, 1995 to October 3, 1996. (1997–02–28). Retrieved on 2007–12–20.
42. See Press Release: Federal Bureau of Investigation, 2001–06–21. Retrieved on 2007–12–26.
43. See Martin Sieff, "Experts See Saudi as Broker, Not Author, of Terrorist Acts," *The Washington Times,* 14 August 1998, p. A7.
44. See Associated Press (2007–05–19). "List of Attacks on U.S. Embassies" *USA Today.* Retrieved on 2008–01–06.
45. See Jordan Attacks are likely to Backfire (2005–05–21). *Intelligence Briefing.* Retrieved on 2008–01–06.
46. See Canadian Security Intelligence Service (CSIS), Security Intelligence Report concerning Mohamed Harkat, 2008–2–22.

explosive, blew a hole in the *USS Cole,* almost causing the destroyer to sink, while killing 17 American sailors.[47]

These acts were all precursors to the far more elaborate, and deadly, 9/11 attacks on the World Trade Center and the Pentagon. Even so, by September 11, 2001, President George W. Bush, along with the Legislative Branch, the various news organizations, and the American general public, knew that American was targeted by Islamist extremists that vowed to kill thousands of Americans.

COUNTERTERRORISM BEFORE 9/11

Before proceeding, a short history of counterterrorism before 9/11 is warranted, as one aspect of the imbroglio surrounding the Patriot Act are the titles dealing with this issue. Prior to the Patriot Act, a "legal wall" surrounded intelligence agents and criminal investigators working on a terrorist target, and both had to proceed without knowing what the other may have been doing about the same target.[48] Many federal agencies felt hampered because agents working on intelligence matters could not communicate with agents involved in criminal justice; thus, information that could have been crucial in stopping 9/11 was never properly distributed.[49]

As mentioned earlier, the WTC attack in 1993 was a precursor for 9/11; however, it was also an example of how ineffective America was in dealing with terrorism. On February 26, 1993, a 1200-pound bomb detonated in the parking garage beneath the two towers of the World Trade Center. The resulting explosion was powerful enough to create a hole seven stories up, and in the aftermath, six people died and many more wounded.[50]

President Bill Clinton commanded his National Security Council to organize the rejoinder. Governmental organizations quickly sprang into action to locate the wrongdoers. The Counterterrorist Center, established in 1986 and located in Langley, Virginia at the CIA, scoured its data and sources across the globe. The National Security Agency (NSA), the largest intelligence gathering organization in the United States, searched its communications files and databases for hints.[51] The New York Field Office of the FBI seized power

47. See Lawrence Wright, Looming Tower, Knopf, (2006), p. 322–331.
48. See John. S. Pistole (2004-4-14). Federal Bureau of Investigation: *Congressional Testimony.* Retrieved on 2007-12-20.
49. Ibid.
50. See Charles E. Schumer (2002-05-23). Press Release: Schumer announces agreement to include families of 1993 of WTC bombing in Victim's Compensation Fund. Retrieved 2007-11-5.
51. See Chapter 3: Counterterrorism Evolves. *The 9/11 Commission Report,* Retrieved on 2007-12-20.

away from the local authorities, setting a blueprint for future administration of terrorist incidents.

Four facets regarding the '93 WTC attacks have great importance for the events that occurred on 9/11. First, the attack indicated that Islamic terrorists were bent on destroying Americans and symbols of American power. Ramzi Yousef, the Sunni fanatic who parked the truck in the WTC garage, stated that he had hoped to kill 250,000 people.[52] Second, the Department of Justice performed magnificently during their investigation. Shortly thereafter, the FBI traced a piece of the exploded truck as part of a Ryder rental van that was stolen approximately 24 hours earlier in New Jersey. Mohammed Salameh, who had leased the vehicle and then stated it was stolen, called the rental office numerous times, trying vainly to retrieve his $400.00 security deposit. Within days of the bombing, the FBI had arrested several of the terrorists.[53]

According to the FBI, another terrorist, Ahmad Ajaj, was caught by immigration officials at John F. Kennedy International Airport in September 1992 and charged with document fraud. The person traveling with him was none other than Ramzi Yousef, who had gained entrance into the U.S. with forged papers but asked for political asylum and was admitted. It did not take the FBI long to realize that Yousef had been a primary component in the bombing. He ran to Pakistan straight away after the attack and remained free for almost 24 months.[54]

After arresting Salameh, Abouhalima, and Ayyad, the FBI made its way to the Farouq mosque in Brooklyn, where Sheikh Omar Abdel Rahman stayed. The Sheikh was a fanatic Sunni Muslim cleric who arrived in the United States, from Egypt, in 1990.

Rahman asserted that a Muslim's basic duty to God was to fight God's enemies, especially the behemoth called the United States.

In public utterances, Rahman, nicknamed the "Blind Sheikh," due to his inability to see, preached a sermon taken from Sayyid Qutb's *Milestones*, which stated that the United States was a tyrant, mistreating Muslims around the world. In addition, Rahman asserted that a Muslim's basic duty to God was to fight God's enemies, especially the behemoth called the United

---

52. See Simon Reeve (1999). *The New Jackals: Ramzi Yousef, Osama bin Laden, and the future of terrorism.* London: Andre Deutschland, LTD.
53. See The Keystone Terrorists (2005-7-21). Flynn Files, Retrieved on 2007-12-08.
54. See Laurie Mylroie (Winter, 1995–1996). The World Trade Center Bomb: Who is Ramzi Yousef and why it matters. *The National Interest.*

States.[55] The FBI had an informant in Rahman's organization, and he learned of a series of major attacks to take place at major New York locales, including the Holland and Lincoln tunnels. The FBI immediately arrested Rahman and several of his associates in June, 1993. These arrests led to the prosecution and conviction of multiple people, including Ajaj, Salameh, Ayyad, Abouhalima, the Blind Sheikh, and Ramzi Yousef–all for felonies related to the WTC attack, as well as other plots.[56]

Unfortunately, this instilled a "can do" attitude in the highest levels of government that the outstanding detective and legal skills exhibited by everyone involved in the capture of Rahman was enough to deal with any future terrorist threat. No one in government questioned whether investigative zeal was enough to protect American citizens against Islamist fanatics whose primary goal was to kill Americans and destroy America's symbols of strength.[57]

Third, due to the success of our legal system in the arrest and prosecution of individuals involved in the first WTC bombing, a much needed evaluation regarding the nature and level of the new, possibly lethal menace facing the U.S. was missed. The publicity of the prosecutions did not bring al-Qaeda to the forefront of the public and political leaders.[58]

The U.S. Attorney's office stated during the trial that the men arrested for the bombing were not the only individuals involved; rather, they were the ones unfortunate enough to get caught. The FBI had retrieved various materials from Ajaj indicating that the conspiracy was envisioned at or near the Khaldan camp, a fairly well-known terrorist training camp on the Afghanistan-Pakistan border. In April, 1992, Ajaj flew from Texas to the camp in order to receive education concerning the construction of bombs. While visiting Pakistan, he met Ramzi Yousef, where they chatted about bombing high visibility sites (like the World Trade Center) in the U.S., and designed a "terrorist kit" that included materials such as how-to manuals covering topics like constructing explosives, operations guidance, videotapes espousing the death and destruction of Americans, and false identification documents.[59]

As mentioned earlier in the chapter, Yousef was arrested in Pakistan in January 1995 after the legal authorities in the Philippines uncovered the Manila air plot, an intricate plan for planting explosives on a dozen trans-Pacific airliners and detonating them simultaneously.[60] Khalid Sheikh

---

55. See Evan F. Kohlmann (2004–11–25). *Al-Qaida's Jihad in Europe.* Berg Publishers.
56. See USA v. Omar Ahmad Ali Rahman et al. 1995. U.S. Southern District of New York, 1995–07–13.
57. See The 9/11 Commission Report. p. 72. Retrieved on 2008–04–08.
58. Ibid.
59. Ibid.
60. Op. cit. 6.

Mohammed (KSM), Yousef's uncle, who resided in Qatar at that time, helped Yousef plan the Manila operation and had sent needed funds before the WTC bombing. The U.S. Attorney acquired an indictment against KSM in January, 1996, but someone (like a government official in the Qatari government) tipped him off; thus, Khalid Sheikh Mohammed escaped, and played a primary role in 9/11.[61] Now we will turn toward the role of law enforcement in fighting terrorism.

> The American system of jurisprudence centers on cases that are completed, not in progress; hence, it was not designed to question if the past might fore-shadow events of the future.

One major emphasis of law enforcement is finding guilty the individuals arrested and charged with crimes, which entails making sensitive information open for public consumption. It was impossible for investigators and prosecutors to present everything they had, as it would have alerted others involved in the crime; likewise, if government authorities had released all of their information, ongoing operations against terrorists would have been curtailed. The American system of jurisprudence centers on cases that are completed, not in progress; hence, it was not designed to question if the past might foreshadow events of the future. Moreover, America's system of justice did not permit in-depth analysis to supply clues to terrorist methods in general, i.e., how their operations are funded and how they operate in the United States. The United States is an open society, whereas terrorism inhabits the darkness. Trying to find a way to join the two in an effort to eradicate the latter has proved difficult.[62]

While the bombing increased awareness of the terrorist threat, victorious criminal prosecutions helped spread the belief that the threat could be successfully handled without any major changes. U.S. attorneys emphasized the significance of the acts, and introduced tangible proof of Yousef's technological resourcefulness; however, John Q. Public felt that the terrorists were imbeciles, remembering Salameh's stupidity trying to regain his $400.00 truck deposit. Going to court and prosecuting was the method of dealing with terrorists whose goal was to slap America in the face.[63]

---

61. See Lawrence Wright (2006). *The Looming Tower: Al-Qaeda and the Road to 9/11*. New York: Knopf.
62. See *9/11 Commission Report*, Chapter 3. Retrieved 2007–12–09.
63. Ibid.

FEDERAL LAW ENFORCEMENT

In terms of federal law enforcement, the primary organization is the Department of Justice, and counterterrorism was (and is) handled by the FBI. The majority of agents are not stationed in Washington, as many think, but are located at 56 different field offices scattered about the nation. Before September 11, each special agent in charge was allowed to set the agenda for his/her office.[64]

Each individual field office had two principal issues with which they were concerned. First, the standards by which the offices were judged came from statistical charts concerned with the numbers of arrests, indictments, prosecutions, and convictions. Work aimed at counterterrorism proceeded at a snail's pace, often taking years for any results (and even, the results might not be positive) and was thus, not a popular option for field officers intending to climb up the career ladder. In general, most agents who became managers had almost no familiarity with counterterrorism. Second, FBI field offices tended to decide what issues were priorities; however, most special agents in charge aimed their manpower toward seizing white-collar criminals, disbanding organized crime, as well as infiltrating drug cartels and gangs. In general, field offices usually looked at local problems, not focusing on national issues.[65]

In order to avoid problems, the FBI has what's called an "office of origin" system, in which a single office takes command of an entire investigation. The New York Field Office was given the job of collaring bin Laden, as it was they that had indicted him due to the East Africa bombings, as well as the bombing of the *USS Cole*. The FBI possessed scant knowledge of bin Laden, but what they did have was located in the New York Field Office, and so the office worked directly with the U.S. Attorney for the Southern District of New York to ID, detain, indict, and convict many of the individuals involved in the various attacks and plots. As credit for any arrests and convictions would go to the specific Field Office of origin, other Field Offices had little incentive to become involved in the hunt for al-Qaeda operatives.[66]

The FBI apparatus for domestic intelligence began in the 1930s. Hitler and Tojo loomed on the horizon, and FDR commanded J. Edgar Hoover to scrutinize carefully both foreign and foreign-inspired sedition. In addition, Hoover wanted his agents to search for any probable spying, sabotage, or sedition. In 1948, the investigation of foreign intelligence was given to the

---

64. Ibid. p. 74.
65. Ibid.
66. See FBI Report; *Counterterrorism Progress since September 2001,* April 14, 2004 p. 20. Retrieved 2008–12–20.

recently created Central Intelligence Agency, the successor to the wartime Office of Strategic Services. Hoover protectively safeguarded the FBI against all possible competitors, and as in thinking, he was answerable only to the president; thus, FBI's domestic intelligence gathering continued to grow.[67] During the 1960s, the Bureau received noteworthy aid within the U.S. from the CIA and Army Intelligence.

> The FBI had secretly watched a broad array of political figures, particularly individuals Hoover planned to disgrace (primarily Dr. Martin Luther King, Jr. as Hoover had tapes of King involved in sexual acts with women other than his wife), and had sanctioned illegal wiretaps and surveillance.

Hoover passed away in 1972, and the push toward the FBI performing as a domestic CIA died with him. In 1974, the America public heard firsthand knowledge about Watergate and Richard M. Nixon's faux pas as a president; in conjunction, a general investigative expansion also occurred concerning foreign and domestic intelligence, as detailed by the Church and Pike committees.[68] They released national intelligence attempts to the public, including information about a clandestine program that, during the years 1956 to 1971, spied on various American organizations and, ultimately, American dissenters. The FBI had secretly watched a broad array of political figures, particularly individuals Hoover planned to disgrace (primarily Dr. Martin Luther King, Jr. as Hoover had tapes of King involved in sexual acts with women other than his wife),[69] and had sanctioned illegal wiretaps and surveillance. The knowledge stunned the American public, as indicated by opinion polls, where the proportion of American citizens stating a "highly favorable" view of the Bureau plummeted from 84 percent to 37 percent. This caused the demise of the FBI's Domestic Intelligence Division.[70]

In 1976, Edward Levi, Attorney General under Gerald Ford, approved internal safety regulations to standardize intelligence gathering within the United States and to redirect requests for stronger rules.[71] In 1983, William French Smith, Attorney General under Ronald Reagan, adjusted Levi's regulations to support quicker studies of probable terrorism. He also relaxed the

---

67. See Robert L. Benson. *The Venona Story*. National Security Agency. Retrieved on 2007–12–20.

68. See Seymour Hersh (1974–12–22). "Huge C.I.A. operation reported in U.S. against antiwar forces, other dissidents in Nixon years," *New York Times*, p. 1. Retrieved on 2008–01–22.

69. See Cecil M. Adams (2003–05–02). "Was Martin Luther King, Jr. a plagiarist?" *Washington Post*. Retrieved on 2008–01–22.

70. See David M. Alpern with Anthony Marro and Stephan Lesher, "This Is Your New FBI," *Newsweek*, Jan. 5, 1976, p. 14.

71. See The Federal Bureau of Investigation's Compliance with the Attorney General's Investigative Guidelines (Redacted). *Special Report*, September 2005. Retrieved on 2008–01–22.

guidelines regarding permission for conducting investigations and their length. However, Smith's rules (like Levi's) and regulations realized the relative certainty that the hint of "terrorism," like the hint of "sedition," could show the way to targeting individuals for investigations, primarily due to their beliefs rather than any overt behavior. Smith also acknowledged the truth that prospective terrorists often came from fanatic religious groups and that investigating terrorism could transgress the separation of church and state.[72,73]

In 1986, Congress sanctioned the Bureau to explore terrorist depredations against Americans taking place outside the U.S. Three years later, additional power was given to the FBI in order to arrest individuals overseas without approval from the host country.[74] Back in 1986, a commission chaired by George H. W. Bush had agreed to an idea already recommended by William Casey (Director of Central Intelligence under Ronald Reagan)–a Counterterrorist Center, where the CIA, FBI, and other government agencies could join forces to destroy global terrorism. Although it was primarily a CIA child, the Bureau installed various representatives at the Center and gathered clues that aided in the arrest of individuals wanted for trial in America.[75]

That the FBI conveyed both vigor and professionalism in the pursuit of terrorists is undeniable. One specific example shows the Bureau's credibility: the case of Pan American Flight 103, a plane headed from London to New York, that exploded over Lockerbie, Scotland, in December, 1988, killing all 270 passengers. Preliminary data indicated Syria and, later, Iran as the culprits. The Counterterrorist Center withheld their opinion regarding the architects of the aggression. During this period, FBI personnel, in tandem with their UK counterparts, collected and examined the extensively dispersed remnants of the airliner. During 1991, with invaluable assistance from the Counterterrorist Center, they categorized a tiny fragment that was part of a timing mechanism that was created in Libya.[76]

In concert with other proof, the Bureau pieced together a legal case that pointed directly at Moammar Gadhafi and the Libyan government. In time, Gadhafi conceded his guilt. One outcome of this successful conclusion was that it showed the investigative brilliance of the FBI.[77]

---

72. See *Center for Democracy and Technology's Guide to the FBI Guidelines: Impact on Civil Liberties and Security–The need for Congressional Oversight.* June 26, 2002. Retrieved on 2008-02-02.
73. See Floyd Abrams, "The First Amendment and the War against Terrorism," *University of Pennsylvania Journal of Constitutional Law,* vol. 5 (Oct. 2002).
74. See *History of the FBI: Rise of International Crimes–1980s.* Federal Bureau of Investigation website. Retrieved on 2008-02-02.
75. See Ron Suskind, *The One Percent Doctrine.* New York: Simon & Schuster, 2006.
76. See *History of the FBI: Byte Out of History–Solving a Complex Case of International Terrorism* (2003-12-19). Retrieved on 2008-02-02.
77. Ibid.

FBI ORGANIZATION AND PRIORITIES

Louis Freeh became the Director of the FBI in 1993, a position he retained until June 2001. Freeh, like his predecessors, felt that the Bureau's efforts should be handled principally by the field offices. To stress his staunch beliefs, he severed headquarters personnel and dispersed operations. The special agents in charge of these field offices attained prestige, authority, and autonomy.

Freeh identified terrorism as a primary hazard for the Bureau. He enlarged the quantity of legal attaché offices overseas, specifically emphasizing the Middle East. He advocated that agents search out terrorists instead of waiting for disasters to occur. After the 1993 WTC bombing, Freeh admitted that "merely solving this type of crime is not enough; it is equally important that the FBI thwart terrorism before such acts can be perpetrated." Within the Bureau, he initiated a Counterterrorism Division that would work hand-in-hand with the CIA's Counterterrorist Center. In order to emphasize the importance of this new division, Freeh agreed for greater interactions between senior FBI and CIA counterterrorism officials. He pushed for more collaboration among legal attachés and CIA stations abroad.[78]

> The Office of Management and Budget stated that FBI management appeared reluctant to transfer assets to terrorism from other sections such as child pornography and drug enforcement.

Freeh's labors did not, however, indicate an allocation of funds to counterterrorism. In essence, the Office of Management and Budget stated that FBI management appeared reluctant to transfer assets to terrorism from other sections such as child pornography and drug enforcement. At the same time, FBI spokespeople censured Congress and the OMB for lacking the foresight to grasp the FBI's badly needed funds for counterterrorism. Moreover, Freeh did not compel the various field offices to follow his lead; rather, most field offices offered little help with terrorism.[79]

During 1998, the Bureau released a five-year strategic plan, with Deputy Director, Robert "Bear" Bryant, in charge. This was the first time in its history that the Bureau stated that henceforward, the protection of the United States was its top priority. Dale Watson, future head of the Counterterrorism

---

78. See Louis Freeh. The Complete Transcript of Louis Freeh's testimony. *The Star Ledger* (2004–04–13). Retrieved on 2008–04–03.
79. Howard M. Shapiro, "The FBI in the 21st Century," *Cornell International Law Journal,* vol. 28 (1994). Retrieved 2007–11–29.

Division, stated that after the East Africa bombings, the FBI realized that it needed a quantum shift in the way it handled terrorists. The plan authorized a robust intelligence collection endeavor, with a national computerized system to assist with information gathering, analysis, and distribution. It envisaged the manufacture of a proficient intelligence clique of knowledgeable and informed operatives and analysts. If effectively executed, this would have been a key move in the direction of dealing with terrorism methodically, rather than as separate, unconnected cases; however, the plan failed.[80]

First, the strategy did not acquire the needed human capital. Although the FBI stated its goals clearly, it did not transfer available resources in a manner showing it was serious. While the Bureau's allocation of funds toward counterterrorism more than doubled during the mid-1990s, real spending stayed somewhat steady between fiscal years 1998 and 2001. As recent as 2,000, the FBI had two times as many personnel working on drug enforcement in comparison to counterterrorism.[81]

Second, while the new section's intent was to reinforce the Bureau's strategic investigative competence, it failed to do so. It never obtained needed funds and faced internecine conflict from other FBI divisions. Several of the new division's primary purposes were to recognize movements in terrorist actions, decide specifically the knowledge that the FBI lacked, and in due course, make collection efforts to gaining new information. At this point, however, the FBI showed little understanding or appreciation concerning the importance of analysis. Analysts were used, but in a tactical manner; that is, they provided help for present cases. The FBI made the problem worse by employing analysts from inside, and did not recruit competent individuals possessing the germane educational background and proficiency.[82]

Before September 11, America had a paucity of trained analysts and consequently, few analytical reports existed. Up until 9/11, the Bureau had never seriously analyzed the terrorist menace facing America.

In addition, analysts frequently encountered problems gaining entry to the Bureau's and CIA data that they were supposed to study. This translated into a situation in which gaining access to needed records often hinged on how well the analyst got along with the individuals possessing the data. For these reasons and more, before September 11, America had a paucity of trained

---

80. See PBS: Frontline—Interview with Robert M. "Bear" Bryant: The Man Who Knew." Retrieved on 2007–12–20.
81. Robert Mulhausen. Finding Funds to Fight Terrorism (2002–10–19). The Heritage Foundation. Retrieved on 2008–02–02.
82. Ibid.

analysts and consequently, few analytical reports existed. Up until 9/11, the Bureau had never seriously analyzed the terrorist menace facing America.[83]

Third, the FBI lacked an efficient intelligence gathering apparatus. Gathering intelligence from human sources was limited (unlike the CIA), and agents were not prepared. A mere 72 hours out of 16 weeks were spent discussing counterintelligence and counterterrorism, while most ensuing education was attained on the job. The Bureau lacked a sufficient method for authenticating source reports; likewise, it lacked the means for effectively locating and distributing source reporting. For whatever reasons, the FBI did not contribute satisfactory funds to the surveillance and translation requirements of counterterrorism agents. The translators it had weren't adequate in translating Arabic proficiently, which resulted in a major accumulation of untranslated messages.[84]

Lastly, the Bureau's information systems were risible in their backwardness; no useful system for securing and/or allocating its organizational data existed. While agents documented their efforts, it was practically impossible to squeeze the data into consequential intelligence that could be recovered and circulated if needed.[85]

In 1999, the Bureau created separate Counterterrorism and Counterintelligence divisions. Dale Watson, the Counterterrorism Division's first chief, understood the pressing necessity of increasing the FBI's counterterrorism ability. He produced a strategy called MAXCAP 05, which was made public in 2000. Its primary aim centered on bringing the organization to its "maximum feasible capacity" in counterterrorism, no later than 2005. Various field offices explained to Watson that they lacked almost everything, including analysts, linguists, or agents trained in carrying out a counterterrorism line of attack. In information supplied to Director Robert Mueller in September, 2001, 12 months after Watson introduced his plan to high ranking FBI personnel, practically every field office throughout the U.S. received an assessment of functioning beneath "maximum capacity." The report affirmed that "the goal to 'prevent terrorism' requires a dramatic shift in emphasis from a reactive capability to highly functioning intelligence capability which provides not only leads and operational support, but clear strategic analysis and direction."[86]

---

83. See Joby Warrick et al. Experts: FBI Lacks Staffing to Combat Terrorists (2001–09–25). *The Seattle Times*. Retrieved on 2007–11–02.
84. See Alfred Cumming & Todd Masse, RL32336: FBI Intelligence Reform since September 11, 2001–Issues and Options for Congress (2004–04–06). Retrieved on 2008–05–24.
85. Ibid.
86. Law Enforcement, Counterterrorism, and Intelligence Collection in the United States Prior to 9/11 National Committee on Terrorist Attacks: Staff Statement No. 9.

"THE WALL"

Prior to 9/11, the Bureau used a number of diverse mechanisms for law enforcement and intelligence. In regards to criminal issues, it applied for and used conventional criminal warrants; however, what was customary did not work when the issue was international terrorism. For a number of years, the attorney general had the statutory power to approve the close watch of foreign states and their agents without any judicial oversight, but in 1978, the Foreign Intelligence Surveillance Act was passed by Congress. (For more detail on FISA, see Chapter 2.)

FISA controlled intelligence compilation aimed at foreign states and their agents while in the U.S. It required a judge to evaluate the planned surveillance and was construed that a search be permitted only if its overriding aim was to acquire foreign intelligence information. In essence, FISA could not be used to evade conventional criminal warrant necessities. The Department of Justice deduced that U.S. Attorneys could be informed of FISA data, but could not order or manage its collection.[87]

Nevertheless, the 1994 criminal trial of Aldrich Ames for spying revitalized anxieties concerning the prosecutors' function in intelligence investigations.[88] DOJ's Office of Intelligence Policy and Review (OIPR) was in charge of evaluating and introducing all FISA requests to the FISA Court. OIPR fretted that due to a large number of consultations between FBI special agents and U.S. attorneys, the judge could say that the FISA warrants had been misrepresented. If that had been the scenario, it was possible that Ames could avoid conviction. Richard Scruggs, the interim chief of OIPR, protested to then Attorney General Janet Reno regarding the paucity of information-sharing controls. Relying on his own initiative, he imposed information-sharing practices for all data concerning FISA. OIPR turned into the caretaker for the stream of FISA data given to U.S. attorneys.[89]

During the summer of 1995, Reno provided official procedures geared toward administering data sharing between U.S. attorneys and the FBI. They were devised in a functioning, operational group headed by the Justice Department's Executive Office of National Security, watched over by Deputy Attorney General Jamie Gorelick. This course of action, while necessitating the distribution of intelligence data with prosecutors, controlled the

---

87. See 50 U.S.C. ch. 36, The complete text of the Foreign Intelligence Surveillance Act.
88. See FISA Applied to Secret Foreign Intelligence Physical Searches in 1994, (Counterintelligence and Security Enhancements Act of 1994, Public Law 103-359, Sec. 9).
89. See FBI Intelligence Investigations: Coordination within Justice on Counterintelligence Matters is Limited. General Accounting Office: Report to the Ranking Minority Member, Committee on Governmental Affairs, U.S. Senate (July 2001). Retrieved 2008-03-22.

way in which such sensitive data could be distributed from the intelligence side to the criminal prosecution side of the Bureau.[90]

Shortly thereafter, the procedures were both misinterpreted and used incorrectly; thus, little data transfer occurred. After awhile, the measures became known as "the wall," though the term "the wall" is deceptive, because a number of things led to hurdles regarding the data sharing that resulted.[91]

Going through OIPR became the only conduit for transferring information to the Criminal Division. While Janet Reno's measures did not contain such stipulations, the Office took on the responsibility, stating that its stance mirrored the apprehension of Judge Royce Lamberth, then Chief Judge of the Foreign Intelligence Surveillance Court. OIPR remarked that if it could not control the amount of information given to criminal prosecutors, it would desist from presenting the Bureau's warrant pleas to the FISA Court. The result? The data no longer flowed.[92]

The 1995 measures centered primarily on data exchange between agents and prosecutors, not between different types of Bureau agents; that is, not between agents laboring on intelligence issues and those on criminal concerns. Nonetheless, demands from OIPR, FBI management, and the FISA Court constructed obstructions between agents–even those working on the same teams. FBI Deputy Director Bryant strengthened the Office's vigilance by telling agents that giving away too much data could injure one's career. Special agents in the field started believing, albeit wrongfully, that no FISA data could be distributed with agents working on criminal cases.[93]

This belief grew into the even more inflated notion that the Bureau could not share any intelligence data with criminal prosecutors, even if FISA had not been utilized. Hence, pertinent data from the National Security Agency (NSA) and the CIA often never made its way to investigators. Different evaluations in 1999, 2000, and 2001 stated that data distribution did not occur, and that the primary aim of the 1995 procedures was often disregarded.[94]

---

90. See http://216.109.125.130/search/cache?ei=UTF-8&p=Slade+Gorton+letter+to+the+editor+in+The+Washington+Times.&y=Search&fr=yfp-t-501&u=www.washtimes.com/op-ed/20050817-101757-6420r.htm&w=slade+gorton+letter+letters+editor+washington+times+time&d=MpOrsOrnO2Tp&icp=1&.intl=us|Slade Gorton - letter to the Editor of the Washington Times August 18, 2005. Retrieved on 2008-3-24.

91. See Andrew C. McCarthy, "The Wall Truth," *National Review Online* (2004-04-19). Retrieved on 2007-12-3.

92. See "An Interview with Judge Royce C. Lamberth," http://www.uscourts.gov/ttb/june 02ttb/interview.html. Retrieved on 2007-01-03.

93. See *9/11 Commission Report,* p. 96.

94. See Ibid. p. 96.

Demands from OIPR, FBI management, and the FISA Court constructed obstructions between agents-even those working on the same teams. FBI Deputy Director Bryant strengthened the Office's vigilance by telling agents that giving away too much data could injure one's career.

Other limitations existed as well. Both prosecutors and special agents disputed whether they were excluded by court regulations from sharing grand jury information–although the exclusion affected only a minute fraction that had been on hand to a grand jury, and even then there were exemptions. FBI field offices inferred that the proscription applied to a great deal of the information discovered in an investigation. In addition, several constraints arose from executive order, discussing the intertwining of national information with foreign intelligence. Finally, the NSA placed stipulations on its Bin Laden statements that needed prior consent before sharing any data with criminal investigators and/or prosecutors, thus another block in data sharing.[95]

OTHER LAW ENFORCEMENT AGENCIES

In most people's mind, the DOJ is primarily the FBI, but it is an incorrect assumption. In addition to the Bureau, there's the U.S. Marshals Service, the oldest criminal justice agency in America and a highly proficient organization at locating fugitives.[96] The Drug Enforcement Administration (DEA) had, as of 2006, more than 10,891 employees, with a yearly budget of 2.145 billion dollars. Several occasions occurred when DEA agents introduced reliable sources to the FBI or CIA for counterterrorism use.[97] The Attorney-General of the United States heads DOJ.

According to the 9/11 Commission Report, the Immigration and Naturalization Service (INS), as of 9/11, had more than 9,000 Border Patrol agents, 4,500 inspectors, and 2,000 immigration special agents; thus, it possessed the most potential in terms of counterterrorism.[98] The problem here is that the INS focused primarily on illegal immigrants traipsing over the border, criminal aliens, and a burgeoning accumulation regarding applications for permanent resident status. Even so, their track record regarding illegal

---

95. 9/11 Commission Report, p. 80.
96. *"Fact Sheet: United States Marshals Service"* www.usmarshals.gov. Retrieved on 2007–11–08.
97. For detailed information, see http://www.usdoj.gov/dea. Retrieved on 2007–11–09.
98. 9/11 Commission Report. p. 80.

aliens was atrocious.[99] The White House, the Justice Department, and the Congress strongly supported these issues. Moreover, when Doris Meissner became INS Commissioner in 1993, the organization was considered nothing more than a backwater agency. It was hindered by out-of-date equipment and inadequate human resources. For example, Border Patrol agents still used manual typewriters; inspectors assigned to America's ports of entry using paper watchlists; the haven and other assistance did not successfully dissuade deceptive applicants.[100]

After the 1993 WTC bombing, Meissner provided needed funds (from a budget of 1.3 billion in 1993 to 3.1 billion in 1998[101] to the State Department's Consular Affairs Bureau to computerize its terrorist watchlist, used by both Department of State personnel and border inspectors. The INS directed each person working in a new "lookout" unit to aid the State Department in developing watchlists of alleged terrorists. Likewise, they were told to aid both the intelligence community and the FBI in finding out the best way to deal with terrorists once they appeared at ports of entry. This drive bore fruit: by 1998, many terrorists had been turned away at American borders due to the watchlist.[102]

Congress, with the full backing of President Bill Clinton, doubled the number of Border Patrol agents necessary alongside the Mexican border to one agent each quarter mile by 1999. It snubbed attempts to move extra resources along the Canadian border, where there was one agent each 13.25 miles. In spite of examples regarding the entry of terrorists at our Northern border, the knowledge of terrorist movement in Canada and its easier immigration laws, and an inspector general's report stating that the Border Patrol needed to improve northern border tactics, the only constructive measure was that the number of agents did not decrease.[103]

Inspectors at their respective ports of entry were not directed to concen-

---

99. The Immigration and Naturalization Service's Removal of Aliens Issued Final Orders (2003–02). According to the DOJ's Office of the Inspector General, INS was successful at deporting detained aliens, but highly unsuccessful with those nondetained. The Office stated that only 13 percent of those aliens that were considered nondetained were deported. Moreover, the INS received poor marks concerning its effectiveness at deporting special subgroups as it only removed 6 percent of the illegal aliens from countries supporting and sponsoring terrorism, deporting a mere 35 percent of nondetained criminal aliens, and only 3 percent of nondetained aliens that were refused asylum within the U.S.
100. "INS Commissioner Doris Meissner Announces Retirement." (2000–10–18). *Immigration and Naturalization Service, News Release.* Retrieved on 2008–01–08.
101. See Louis Freedberg & Ramon G. McLeod, "The Other Side of the Law: Despite all US efforts to curb it, immigration is rising" (1998–10–13). *SF Gate. Com.* Retrieved on 2008–02–19.
102. Margaret D. Stock, "United States Immigration Law in a World of Terror" (2003–12–1). *The Federalist Society for Law and Public Policy Standards.* Retrieved on 2007–11–08.
103. CRS Report for Congress. "Border Security: The Role of the US Border Patrol" (2005–5–10). Retrieved on 2008–02–04.

trate on terrorists. Inspectors basically told the American public that they were incompetent; that is, they did not realize that when they examined the names of all incoming travelers against the automated watchlist, they were on the lookout for possible terrorists. Generally speaking, border inspectors lacked the requisite data required to make fact-based decisions concerning admissibility. The INS tried to complete two tasks that would have given investigators important data pertinent to counterterrorism: (1) a system designed to see if foreign students complied with their visa directions and (2) a plan that would have established a method of tracking each foreign traveler's entrance to and exit from the U.S.[104]

The INS established a new law in 1996 that allowed the agency to enter state and local law enforcement agencies. In essence, INS supplied education and training, whereas local law enforcement personnel applied the rules and regulations of immigration authority; however, they lacked access to terrorist watchlists. Cities with a hefty immigrant populace often made it impossible for city workers to cooperate with federal agents. Congress made sure that the number of INS agents remained the same, regardless of the problem's size.[105]

Another law enforcement agency able to aid in counterterrorism, but not used earnestly, was the Treasury Department, which includes the Secret Service, the Customs Service, and the Bureau of Alcohol, Tobacco, and Firearms (ATF). The Secret Service's primary aim is to shield the President and other important functionaries; thus, its special agents joined in the fray with the FBI whenever terrorist assassination intrigues were uncovered or rumored.

The Customs Services stationed agents at every point of entry within the U.S. In addition, they worked together and cooperated frequently with their counterparts in the INS. During the winter of 1999–2000, questions asked by a skilled Customs agent resulted in the capture of an al-Qaeda operative who planned to bomb Los Angeles International Airport.[106]

The FBI occasionally used ATF agents and their resources when needed. After the 1993 World Trace Center bombing, the ATF and its labs were significant in the Bureau's investigation; likewise, their resources were used to investigate Timothy McVeigh's April, 1995 bombing of the Alfred P. Murrah Federal Building in Oklahoma City.[107]

---

104. Ibid.
105. Ibid.
106. Ibid.
107. Combating Terrorism: Law Enforcement Agencies Lack Directives to Assist Foreign Nations to Identify, Disrupt, and Prosecute Terrorists (2007–06–25). General Accounting Office. Retrieved on 2008–04–05.

Sadly, before the events that transpired on September 11, only the Bureau and one of its departments, investigated terrorism. Furthermore, an agent's effectiveness hinged upon particular people being identified, whether a terrorist conspiracy had been unearthed, or if an attack had already taken place. Those thought responsible for the attack had to be found, arrested, and carried back to a U.S. court for trial. FBI agents told the 9/11 committee that they did not have access to cruise missiles; rather, they declared war by using legal channels. Their primary reason for addressing terrorism was that they were directed to by Congress.[108]

The Joint Terrorism Task Force (JTTF) became the principal medium for INS and state and local authorities in working together against terrorism.[109] The JTTF's pilot run occurred in New York City during 1980 as a means of responding to a number of confrontations entailing domestic terrorist organizations. The Bureau's New York Field Office and the local police jointly managed the JTTF, and its mere existence allowed for a swap of data between federal and local authorities.[110] They placed precedence in accord with local field office interests, and many were undermanned. This caused many state and local authorities to believe it was a waste of time to show interest in the JTTF.

The Foreign Terrorist Tracking Task Force began on October 29, 2001 by President George W. Bush in Homeland Security Presidential Directive-2. The Task Force, "with assistance from the Attorney General (John Ashcroft), the Director of Central Intelligence (George J. Tenet) and other officers of the government, as appropriate, . . . to ensure that, to the maximum extent permitted by law, Federal agencies coordinate programs to accomplish the following: 1) deny entry into the United States of aliens associated with, suspected of being engaged in, or supporting terrorist activity; and 2) locate, detain, prosecute, or deport any such aliens already present in the United States."[111]

Although they helped, the JTTFs had several drawbacks. They placed precedence in accord with local field office interests, and many were undermanned. This caused many state and local authorities to believe it was a waste of time to show interest in the JTTF.

---

108. 9/11 Commission Report on Terrorism. Chapter 3.
109. "Quick Facts." Federal Bureau of Investigation. Retrieved on 2008–09–10.
110. "Protecting America Against Terrorist Attack–A Closer Look at the FBI's Joint Terrorism Task Forces." Federal Bureau of Investigation website. Retrieved on 2008–09–11.
111. Homeland Security Presidential Directive-2 (2001–10–29). Retrieved on 2008–06–09.

The Directive stated that the Task Force should have "expert personnel" from the U.S. Department of State, the Immigration and Naturalization Service, the Federal Bureau of Investigation, the Secret Service, the Customs Service, the Intelligence Community, "military support components, and other Federal agencies as appropriate to accomplish the Task Force's mission."[112]

Former Attorney General John Ashcroft and former Director of Central Intelligence George Tenet stated that "to the maximum extent permitted by law, that the Task Force has access to all available information necessary to perform its mission, and they shall request information from State and local governments, where appropriate." They were to invite "foreign liaison officers from cooperating countries . . . to serve as liaisons to the Task Force, where appropriate, to expedite investigation and data sharing."[113]

"Other Federal entities, such as the Migrant Smuggling and Trafficking in Persons Coordination Center and the Foreign Leads Development Activity, shall provide the Task Force with any relevant information they possess concerning aliens suspected of engaging in or supporting terrorist activity." Item number five in the Directive of the tasks assigned to the Task Force is "Use of Advanced Technologies for Data Sharing and Enforcement Efforts."[114]

Due to public disapproval of domestic surveillance, the Church Commission instated several orders preventing the FBI or any other agency from spying on American citizens. However, during 2002, DOJ eradicated directives established following the Church Commission hearings in the 1970s, which confirmed the act of the Bureau's Counter Intelligence Program (COINTELPRO) division spying on political enemies and obstacles set in place to go around basic, first amendments. Opponents fretted that JTTF behavior may represent contraventions of the First Amendment.[115] Information attained by the ACLU through the Freedom of Information Act indicated that personnel at the Colorado JTTF acquired personal information on nonviolent dissenters.[116] In addition, JTTF agents penetrated protester peace groups using a variety of aliases.[117]

On April 28, 2005, Portland stated its position in regards to the JTTF by withdrawing its support.[118] Recently, in June 2008, news was broadcast across

---

112. Ibid.

113. Ibid.

114. Ibid.

115. Ward Churchill & Jim Vander Wall, (1990). *The COINTELPRO Papers: Documents from the FBI's Secret Wars Against Domestic Dissent.* Boston: South End Press..

116. "Press Release from ACLU of Colorado" (2005–12–08). Retrieved on 2008–02–02.

117. "Peace Group Infiltrated by Government Agent" (2003–10–9). Retrieved on 2007–12–12.

118. Sarah Kershaw, "In Portland Ore., a Bid to Pull out of Terror Task force," *The New York Times* (2005–04–23). Retrieved on 2008–07–23.

America that the Minnesota branch of the JTTF approached a source to gain access to "vegan potlucks." Why? So the agents could tell the authorities about information gleaned on protest groups planning on picketing the 2008 Republican National Convention in Saint Paul.[119]

How did this state of affairs come about? Within the country, the United States Congress passed and President Bush signed into law the Homeland Security Act of 2002, thus creating the Department of Homeland Security. This was the single, largest reshuffle of the U.S. government in contemporary history. However, this was not the only shake-up brought about by 9/11. In order to add depth to the massive changes that occurred, we now turn our focus to a number of areas and organizations that were radically modified.

---

119. Matt Snyders. Moles Wanted: In Preparation for the National Republican Convention, the FBI is soliciting informants to keep tabs on local protest groups. *City Pages* (2008–05–21). Retrieved on 2008–05–28.

Chapter 2

CHANGES BROUGHT ABOUT BY 9/11

IMMIGRATION

Prior to 9/11, whenever foreigners came to America for a visit, immigration personnel stamped their passports for a stay up to six months. After 9/11, before anyone's passport is stamped, an officer asks how long he/she plans on staying in the U.S., as well as where he/she plans to stay. Unlike before, foreign travelers do not have their passports stamped for six months; rather, the stamp is good for 30 days and not a day more.[120] If the tourist wishes to stay longer, he/she must contact an immigration officer, and if this procedure is not followed, the visitor could find himself/herself in trouble, especially if he/she is Arabic from the Middle East.[121]

> Before 9/11, when a foreign visitor made his/her way through U.S. customs, immigration officers stamped passports for a visit for up to six months. Now, before a visitor's passport is stamped, an officer may ask specifically how long the traveler intends to stay in the U.S., and the exact location(s) where he/she will be staying. In addition, he stamp is no longer valid for six months, but usually for no more than 30 days.

On October 18, 2001, *The New York Times* wrote, "At this time, hundreds of Saudi citizens are being detained and questioned with regard to the hijackings. A lot of them are innocent people. That number would probably quadruple if we shared advance information on air passengers with the

---

120. *Temporary Migration to the United States: Nonimmigrant Admissions Under U.S. Immigration Law.* United States Customs and Immigration Service (January, 2006).
121. Ibid.

United States."[122] Saudi citizens were not the only Arabs, however, to experience this. Following the attacks, all aircraft originating from any country that supported terrorism was blocked from landing in America.

> A Saudi embassy spokesman quoted in a *New York Times* piece said, "At this time, hundreds of Saudi citizens are being detained and questioned with regard to the hijackings. A lot of them are innocent people. That number would probably quadruple if we shared advance information on air passengers with the United States."

Another area transformed centered on foreigners staying longer than their visas legally allowed. This received huge press coverage and became a "hot point" for politicians. A major impetus for The Illegal Immigration Reform and Immigrant Responsibility Act of 1996 was that it established a system of coordinating the entries and exits of foreigners. However, the plan never materialized.[123] In American media, when the issue was discussed at all, it emphasized the benign attributes of those overstaying their visa, i.e., an American Immigration Lawyers Association spokesperson stated that overstays were "innocent" people spending "an extra week at Disney World."[124]

Another sphere of major change was an attack upon the relative ease at which illegal immigrants obtained false Social Security numbers–this, too, became a common topic in the American Press after September 11. While no data exists, it is highly likely that the 9/11 terrorists had acquired phony Social Security numbers. In the United States, an SSN is practically mandatory if one wants to move about the country. Once someone has one, he/she can do a number of things, including acquiring a driver's license, obtaining a bank card, etc.–acquisitions that would be impossible without an SSN. Most importantly, a SSN allows someone to build a fake identity, an act carried out by several of the hijackers.[125]

After the attacks, news media reported that Mohammed Atta had his driver's license revoked in Broward County, Florida before the attacks.[126] Many pundits for the Patriot Act stated that if the wall preventing local and state

---

122. Robert Pear. "Egypt, Saudi Airlines won't share passenger list data." *The New York Times* (2001–10–18).

123. See Pub. L. 104-208, Div. C, 110 Stat. 3009–546.

124. See Jeanne A. Butterfield; Executive Director, American Immigration Lawyers Association. "Anti-terrorism border controls," Congressional Hearing, Senate Judiciary, Subcommittee on Immigration (2001–10–17).

125. See Steven A. Camarota, "Use Enforcement to Ease Situation." *The Arizona Republic* (2005–10–23).

126. Ken Thomas-Associated Press, "Fed investigate links in Florida" (2001–9–12). Retrieved on 2007–12–29.

law enforcement personnel from conversing with federal agents had not existed, the attacks might have been prevented.[127] Once Americans found out that several of the hijackers were in the U.S. as students, many around the country demanded a massive change in the law, which is exactly what happened.

> After American citizens were told that some of the suspected terrorists were students, in both legal and expired status, a cry was made for change in immigration laws.

Before September 11, most colleges and universities seldom monitored their foreign students, even ones coming from terrorist countries. Prior to 9/11, more than 500,000 foreign students attended American institutions, but their precise addresses were unknown.[128,129] A government official stated that one of the 9/11 terrorists had acquired a visa for studying at a California Berlitz school but never showed up for class. Many institutions that raised objections to student-visa tracking did so for one good reason—they were afraid they would lose a substantial portion of their yearly revenue if foreign students stopped matriculating (due to their status, many pay full tuition). Moreover, school officials feared that they would be viewed as racists or ethnically biased if foreign students received different treatment than American citizens.[130]

In March, 2002, the INS announced new standards for foreign students hoping to study within the U.S., to travelers planning to visit for either pleasure or business, and to anyone ordered deported. Effective upon publication in the Federal Register, the proposal called for:

> a) Students must present evidence of acceptance from an American school, college, or university, before entering. In addition, students could not apply to school if they were already in the country; rather, he/she had to return to their home country and then apply.[131]

127. Barbara Raymond, Laura J. Hickman, Laura Miller, & Jennifer S. Wong. "Police Personnel Challenges after 9/11: Anticipating Expanded Duties and a Changing Labor Pool. The Rand Corporation (February 2006). Retrieved on 2007–11–07.

128. Tanya Shevitz, Huge drops in foreign students on campus: Post 9/11 security discourages many from coming to the U.S. *The San Francisco Chronicle* (2003-9–01). Retrieved on 2008-04-04.

129. Mike Adams, INS unable to track millions in the U.S. *The Baltimore Sun,* 2001-09-21. Retrieved from www.rense.com on 2008-06-06.

130. Ibid.

131. Office of the Inspector General, DOJ. "The Immigration and Naturalization Service's Contacts with two September 11 Terrorists: A Review of the INS's Admissions of Mohamed Atta and Marwan Alshehhi, its Processing of their Change of Status Applications, and its Effort to Track Foreign Students in the United States." (2002-05-20). Retrieved on 2008-02-08.

b) Tourists and business travelers to be limited to a 30 day stay in the U.S., or to the amount of time definitively required to complete their trip. The maximum extended stay to go from one year to six months with extensions given only under very specific, limited conditions.[132]

c) Individuals to be deported or removed from American borders had to surrender within 30 days or sacrifice all rights to legal remedies.[133]

245(i),[134] an immigration program that allowed some illegal immigrants to amend their category to that of permanent resident if they had a sponsor, was momentarily revitalized during 2007. In May 2007, the House of Representatives approved the border security bill that incorporated this revision,[135] but the Senate allowed the bill to "die."[136]

AMNESTY FOR ILLEGAL MEXICANS

This topic was spoken about between President Bush and Mexican President Vicente Fox in February 2001,[137] approximately 7 months before 9/11. Amnesty basically proffers clemency to certain groups of illegal immigrants, permitting them to alter their status to permanent resident, without any consequences. Also talked about between the two leaders were working visa programs for unskilled Mexican laborers.[138] However, this concern was completely eclipsed by 9/11 events and substituted with the above-mentioned discussions about increased border security. Needless to say, many Mexicans were irate, blaming Islamists for their predicament.

> In Florida, state and local police in Florida were allowed to hold in custody anyone with immigration violations—a job previously held only by federal agents.

State and local police were granted federal power, at least in Florida. After 9/11, they had the authority to hold in custody anyone with immigration vio-

132. Ibid.

133. Ibid.

134. Section 245i permitted individuals possessing an Immigration petition or a Labor Certificate filed on or before January 14, 1998 to apply for a green card in the U.S., even if they entered the U.S. illegally or were out-of-status in the U.S.

135. Brandi Grissom. "Bill to give Sheriffs Bulk of Funds to Fight Border Crime," *El Paso Times* (2007–05–23). Retrieved 2007–12–20.

136. Comprehensive Immigration Reform Act of 2007, S. 1348 (proposed). Council on Foreign Relations, 2008. Retrieved on 2008–06–15.

137. Carla Marinucci. Mexico Prepares for Bush Visit: "Cowboy Summit" to be first trip abroad as President. *The San Francisco Chronicle* (2001–02–16). Retrieved on 2008–01–09.

138. Lindsay Duvall. The Guest Worker Program. Earned Legalization and Reform: The Best Solution. Chicago-Kent College of Law. *Honors Seminar* (Spring 2002). Retrieved on 2008–01–20.

lations—a job previously held only by federal agents. Florida was established as a guinea pig of sorts, with other states following their lead.[139] Case law has been used to support the idea that state and local law enforcement have the right to arrest individuals breaking federal law.[140]

INTERNATIONAL TRACKING SYSTEMS

In the U.S., due to 9/11, the REAL ID Act of 2005 became federal law, mandating that certain standards, substantiation, and issuance measures must be met if someone wants to receive a state driver's licenses and/or state ID cards. Otherwise, the individual's ID will not be regarded as valid by the by the federal government for "official purposes," as defined by the Secretary of Homeland Security. The Secretary of Homeland Security stated that "official purposes" meant a driver's licenses and/or ID badges for getting on commercial flights or walking into any federal buildings and/or nuclear power plants. The idea was added a rider for the the Emergency Supplemental Appropriations Act for Defense, the Global War on Terror, and Tsunami Relief, 2005.[141] The House of Representatives approved HR 1268, 368–58,[142] while the Senate approved the joint House-Senate forum statement on that bill 100–0.[143] It became law when President Bush affixed his signature on May 11, 2005.[144]

On March 2, 2007, it was publicized that enforcing the law would be delayed for two years.[145] Various stipulations will be deferred until December, 2009; however, on January 11, 2008, it was proclaimed that the time limit was lengthened to May 2011, with the express hope that states will back the law.[146] This may be a case of wishful thinking. On April 2, 2008 each state in the Union has either requested extra time beyond that of the initial May 11, 2008 fulfillment cut-off date or established spontaneous additions, which means that the REAL ID Act will not become a point of contention until

---

139. George Coppolo. State Police Arrests of People who Break Federal Law (2005–06–03). Retrieved on 2008–01–20.
140. See *United States v. Salinas-Calderon,* 728 F. 2d 1298 (10th Cir. 1984); *United States v. Vasquez-Alvarez,* 176 F3d 1294 (10th Cir. 1999); and *United States v. Santana-Garcia,* 264 F3d 1188 (10th Cir. 2001).
141. See HR 1268, making emergency supplemental appropriations.
142. Ibid.
143. See Senate.gov for more information.
144. See Pub.L. 109–13.
145. Nicole Gaouette. "States Get more Time on National ID Law." *The LA Times* (2008–01–12). Retrieved on 2008–08–20.
146. DHS REAL ID Final Rule, January 11, 2008. Retrieved on 2008–08–20.

December 31, 2009.[147]

While not part of The Patriot Act, many of its provisions use similar language and, like the Patriot Act, it stems from 9/11. The Act mandates the following regulations:

- Creating new nationwide rules and regulations for state-issued driver licenses and non-driver identification cards.
- Relinquishing laws that impede with the assembly of physical barricades along American borders.
- Modernizing and constricting the regulations regarding applying for political refuge and the expulsion of foreigners for terrorist activity.
- Initiating guidelines pertaining to "delivery bonds."
- Altering visa restrictions for short-term workers, nurses, and Australian citizens.[148]

AUTOMATIC REVALIDATION FOR SOME THIRD COUNTRY NATIONALS WAS CANCELED

For years, individuals with officially recognized visitor status to the U.S. could also travel to Canada, Mexico, or neighboring islands up to one month, and then come back to the U.S. using their current I-94 (federal arrival and departure record). However, after 9/11, anyone from Iraq, Iran, Syria, Libya, Sudan, North Korea, and Cuba (terrorist supporting countries) may not be allowed to enjoy this privilege any longer. Likewise, these individuals cannot apply for a new visa while abroad.[149]

NO MORE J-VISA WAIVER FOR PHYSICIANS

The J waiver program was intended to aid foreign MDs, in that if they agreed to practice medicine in poor areas, it would be relatively simple to obtain permanent resident status, if they received a suitable government sponsorship. This program was discontinued in February, 2002. While this concerned an extremely minute number of immigrants, the timing was suspect and its influence could be overwhelming for locales faced with a scarcity of medical treatment, and for MDs hoping to immigrate to America.[150]

---

147. Ann Broach. Big Brother: Homeland Security Blinks on Read ID: No Hassles on May 11. www.newscom (2008–04–02). Retrieved on 2008–05–11.
148. See Op. cit. Pub.L. 109–13.
149. Visa Stamping from Mexico. Immihelp.com Retrieved on 2008–06–21.
150. "Critical Nature of the J-1 Visa Waiver Program for Foreign Medical Graduates." The American College of Healthcare Executives, 2002.

Foreign students arriving in the U.S. for medical training must return to their home, if they have a J-visa, for two years if they wish to adjust to any other nonimmigrant status or to become a legal permanent resident in the United States.[151]

THE END OF THE IMMIGRATION
AND NATURALIZATION SERVICE

One of the major reactions to 9/11 was the House Judiciary Committee voting 32–2 to advocate a proposal that would dismantle the INS. The bill's basic premise centered on the idea that the almost eight decade-old agency be substituted with a newer Agency for Immigration Affairs under the Department of Justice, to be presided over by an Associate Attorney General for Immigration Affairs. A couple of new bureaus would be set up: (1) The Bureau of Immigration Services and Adjudications would handle all immigrant applicants and records processing, as well as maintaining such records. In addition, (2) The Bureau of Immigration Enforcement would manage and organize any legal actions against immigrants violating the law. The bill supplied money for greater financial support, the improvement of the organization, and a method for taking care of any immigrant crises. The bill passed with a resounding vote in the House of Representatives with a tally of 405–9 on 04/25/02.[152]

Individuals coming into America faced more searches and queries from immigration officers asking why they were in the U.S. Stringent restraints regarding airline passengers and their luggage became customary. Nonimmigrants paying a visit to America had to follow rules established by the National Security Entry-Exit Registration System (NSEERS), also known as Special Registration. NSEERS was established on 9/11/02, with its express goal being to trace foreigners coming and going to safeguard U.S. citizens and America's borders. The Department of Justice, and later the Department of Homeland Security, created NSEERS as method for complying with Congress's rules making the entering and exiting America by foreigners troublesome.[153]

However, NSEERS will become part of the United States Visitor and Immigrant Status Indicator Technology ("US VISIT") program.[154]

---

151. Ibid.
152. Wilson P. Dillard, III. "House Votes to Abolish INS, creates two new agencies." GCN (2002-04-26). Retrieved on 2008-02-02.
153. "Special Registration." United States Immigration and Customs Enforcement (2008-10-08).
154. "U.S. Visit Program." United States Immigration and Customs Enforcement (2003-05-23). Retrieved on 2008-02-02.

According to Congressman Bennie Thompson (D-MS),

. . . 327 official land, air, or sea ports of entry and roughly 440 million total border crossings each year, tracking the entry and exit of foreign nationals is no
small task. While several initiatives were started, in 2003, the Department of
Homeland Security created the United States Visitor and Immigrant Status
Indicator Technology or "US-VISIT," a system to meet the original statutory
mandate, as well as many other laws, including requirements for a biometric
system. US-VISIT is an important part of the Department's layered border
security approach and fight against terrorist travel. In ten years, our nation's
entry-exit system has gone from a mostly paper-based system to an automated
program that now uses biometrics and draws on a number of databases. Since
January 2004, US-VISIT has processed more than 76 million visitors and intercepted approximately 1,800 immigration violators and people with criminal
records.2 ICE apprehended 139 aliens based on overstay records identified by
US-VISIT in FY 2006 and the numbers are anticipated to rise as biometrics
become more prevalent.

US-VISIT uses biometric information–digital fingerprints and photographs–to
verify identity and screen persons against watch lists. The scope of the program
includes the pre-entry, entry, status, and exit of hundreds of millions of foreign
national travelers who enter and leave the United States at air, sea, and land
port of entries (POE). The US-VISIT Program Office was recently moved to
the newly created National Protection and Programs Directorate (NPPD) within the Department. US-VISIT was moved to the NPPD, in part, because the
system engages in the identification of threats and is used across multiple components of the Department and other Federal departments.[155]

- Nonimmigrant alien visitors subject to US-VISIT registration at the Port
  of Entry.
- Certain citizens or nationals of Iran, Iraq, Libya, Sudan, and Syria, as
  designated by the DHA Secretary in the Federal Register.
- Nonimmigrants who have been designated by the State Department.
- Any other nonimmigrant, male or female regardless of nationality,
  identified by immigration officers at airports, seaports and land ports of
  entry in accordance with 8 CFR 264.1(f)(2).[156]

Any change in address, job status, or school should be told to the proper
authorities. All nonimmigrants should contact the authorities in writing with-

---

155. "America's Unfinished Welcome Mat: US-VISIT a Decade later." Bennie Thompson (June
2007). Retrieved on 2008-02-02.
156. Official US-VISIT fact sheet. U.S. Department of Homeland Security (2008–06–05). Retrieved
on 2008– 07–29.

in 10 days of any such changes, if he/she plans on staying in the United States for 30 days or more.[157]

Foreign students studying in America must contend with the Student and Exchange Visitor Program (SEVP), which serves a conduit for various governmental agencies that have curiosity regarding foreign students.[158] SEVP is based on computer technology, and the Student and Exchange Visitor Information System (SEVIS) "tracks and observes learning institutions and their programs, student, exchange visitors and their dependents, throughout the duration of approved participation within the U.S. education system."[159] SEVP gathers, keeps, and distributes the data so that only legal foreign students or exchange visitors can enter the United States. The consequence is a straightforward, easy to access system that supplies needed information to the Department of State, U.S. Customs and Border Protection, U.S. Citizenship and Immigration Services, and U.S. Immigration and Customs Enforcement.[160]

If foreign students need to change their address, it may be done with SEVIS.[161] On December 2, 2003, DHS stopped the habitual 30-day and annual re-registration requirements for US-VISIT. Nonimmigrant foreigners that had to conform with NSEERS and file a request or application with USCIS, may have to offer evidence of NSEERS registration to USCIS. If the individual cannot provide such evidence, then he/she will be referred by USCIS to the proper Immigrations and Customs Enforcement (ICE) office for an meeting to decide whether the individual is compliant or not.[162]

> Nonimmigrant visitors not complying with the special registration requisites or other areas regarding their entrance into the U.S. will be deemed "out of status" and may face arrest, imprisonment, penalties, and/or forced removal from the country.

Nonimmigrant visitors not complying with the special registration requisites or other areas regarding their entrance into the U.S. will be deemed

---

157. Student and Exchange Visitor Program. U.S. Immigrations and Custom Enforcement (2008). Retrieved on 2008–08–20.

158. Ibid.

159. The Student and Exchange Visitor Program. U.S. Department of State (2008 February). Retrieved on 2008–05–14.

160. Op cit. Student and Exchange Visitor Program. U.S. Immigrations and Custom Enforcement (2008).

161. Janis Sposato. "Implementation of the Student and Exchange Visitor Information System. U.S. House of Representatives Committee on the Judiciary Subcommittee on Immigration, Border Security, and Claims." (2002–09–18). Retrieved on 2008–08–12.

162. See Department of Homeland Security. 8 CFR Part 264. (ICE No. 2301-3), RIN 1653-AA29.

"out of status" and may face arrest, imprisonment, penalties, and/or forced removal from the country. Any forthcoming applications for an immigration allowance may also be affected. Judgments in these areas would be made based on a case-by-case basis, and are reliant upon the situation concerning each individual case.[163] Specific foreign laborers, described at section 101(a)(15)(D) of the Patriot Act, who are subject to special registration, are exempted from the departure control requirements of 8 CFR section 264.1(f) (8).

LAW ENFORCEMENT

To say that the terrorist attacks of 9/11 caused a paradigm shift in the way the country viewed foreigners would be something of an understatement. The attacks created a situation in which panic and concern were the mainstay of Mr. and Mrs. John Q. Public, with the result being that the U.S.A. Patriot Act (Uniting and Strengthening America by Providing Adequate Tools Required to Intercept and Obstruct Terrorism) was drafted.

> Once it became statutory, the Patriot Act gave the legal authorities the unfettered right to detain foreigners for an unlimited length of time, based solely on distrust, without the detainees having due process of law.

On October 26, 2001, the Act became the law of the land.[164] Once it became statutory, the Act gave the legal authorities the unfettered right to detain foreigners for an unlimited length of time, based solely on distrust, without the detainees having due process of law. Its redefining of "terrorism" included national organizations (especially Islamic-based groups) that became subject to undercover surveillance and criminal investigation. It permitted the FBI to examine Americans without any credible evidence, if the agents stated it was for "intelligence purposes."[165] Moreover, it allowed state and local law enforcement entities to perform covert searches, including phone and Internet spying, and granted the government the right to check on an individual's medical, banking, employment, library, and other personal records without taking into consideration due process.[166]

---

163. Maintaining Your Immigration Status While a Student or Exchange Visitor. USCIS (2008). Retrieved on 2008–04–08.
164. See H.R. 2975.
165. Ibid.
166. Ibid.

PEN REGISTERS

As pen register is a common staple for law enforcement agencies as it a mechanism that traces all numbers dialed from a specific telephone line. Over the years, "pen register" has grown to include practically any apparatus that carries out similar functions to an original pen register, consisting of programs eyeing Internet contact. Title 18 of the United States Code defines a pen register as:

> a device or process which records or decodes dialing, routing, addressing, or signaling information transmitted by an instrument or facility from which a wire or electronic communication is transmitted, provided, however, that such information shall not include the contents of any communication, but such term does not include any device or process used by a provider or customer of a wire or electronic communication service for billing, or recording as an incident to billing, for communications services provided by such provider or any device or process used by a provider or customer of a wire communication service for cost accounting or other like purposes in the ordinary course of its business.[167]

Therein is the present meaning of a Pen Register, as adjusted by passage of the Patriot Act. The first statutory characterization of a pen register was written in 1986 as an element of the Electronic Communications Privacy Act (ECPA) which stated that a "Pen Register" was: "A device which records or decodes electronic or other impulses which identify the numbers dialed or otherwise transmitted on the telephone line to which such device is dedicated."[168]

A pen register is comparable to a trap and trace device. Trap and trace mechanisms display the numbers calling a particular telephone, i.e., all incoming phone numbers. A pen register, however, displays the numbers a particular phone had called, i.e., all outgoing phone numbers. Both terms are used interchangeably, especially when Internet communications are discussed. They are usually called "Pen Register or Trap and Trace devices," to mirror reality; a similar program would likely perform both functions, and the differences between the two are slight. Thus, the term "pen register" frequently portrays both pen registers and trap and trace devices.

The U.S. Supreme Court in *Katz v. United States*[169] (1967) examined the use of Pen Registers, where it was established its "reasonable expectation of privacy" test. *Katz* overturned *Olmstead v. United States,* stating that wiretaps

---

167. See 18 U.S.C. § 3127(3).
168. See Pub. L. No. 99-508, 100 Stat. 1848.
169. See 389 U.S. 347 (1967).

were unconstitutional searches, as it was reasonable to assume that communication between two parties would remain private. The Court held that government must get a warrant to implement a wiretap.[170]

In 1977, however, the Court ruled that using a pen register was not a search, as the "petitioner voluntarily conveyed numerical information to the telephone company" (*Smith v. Maryland*).[171] The Court reasoned that when the defendant dialed the numbers, he disclosed the information to the telephone company in order to contact the other party. This act showed that he did not have a reasonable expectation that the numbers dialed would remain private. In essence, the Court did not make a distinction between divulging the numbers to a human operator or to any automated apparatus used by the telephone company. With the ruling in *Smith,* pen registers lay beyond constitutional protection. If privacy was to become law, it had to come from Congress, not the Judicial Branch.

In 1986, Congress passed The Electronic Communications Privacy Act (ECPA),[172] which contained three chief stipulations or Titles to the ECPA. The third Title established the Pen Register Act, which contained limitations on private and law enforcement uses of pen registers. Private parties were prohibited from using the devices, unless their circumstances met one of the exemptions. One interesting exception centered on businesses. They could use Pen Registers if the communication was obligatory in order for the business to function.[173]

If law enforcement wanted one, they had to get a court order from a judge. On the other hand, all law enforcement had to do was officially state to the judge that the information to be gathered was pertinent to a criminal investigation.[174] This particular prerequisite for obtaining a court order is simpler than any under ECPA's three titles. This is so because pen registers do not collect the "gist" of information, only the address of the information, which was judged as insignificant regarding privacy interests. Pundits have stated that the government should submit "specific and articulable facts"[175] indicating that the data to be collected is of great importance to any ongoing investigation. This is the criterion Title II of the ECPA uses concerning the contents of stored communications.[176]

---

170. See 277 U.S. 438 (1928).
171. See 442 U.S. 735, 744 (1979).
172. Op. cit. Pub. L. No. 99-508, 100 Stat. 1848.
173. Ibid.
174. Paul Schwartz. "Reviving Telecommunications Surveillance Law." University of Chicago Law School Surveillance Symposium (2007–05–31). Retrieved on 2008–02–02.
175. "Specific and Articulable Facts" is a common phrase in legalese and is used in many situations, usually stating that the legal authorities had good reason to stop someone, issue a warrant, etc.
176. See ECPA Pub. L. 99-508, Oct. 21, 1986, 100 Stat. 1848.

ECPA, Title I, 18 U.S.C. §§ 2510 et seq. ("Wiretap Act") made it illegal to eavesdrop or examine the contents of any confidential communication without the authorization of one participant to the communication; likewise, it controls real-time electronic surveillance in federal criminal investigations.[177]

ECPA Title II, 18 U.S.C. §§ 2701 et seq. ("Stored Communications Act") commonly forbids the revelation concerning the contents of electronically stored communications. The Act does not exclude admission of user data to nongovernment entities.[178] The Stored Communications Act firmly curtails the amount of data that an electronic communication service may give to the authorities. A government body usually must supply a subpoena, warrant, or court order to attain data about someone that is stored by the communication service provider.[179] The Patriot Act modified these stipulations to allow admission of such information to the authorities if the service provider believes that there is an impending threat of death or serious physical injury.[180]

ECPA Title III, 18 U.S.C. §§ 3121 et seq. ("Pen Register Act"): barred any rules regarding information that was exclusionary. It states that while civil solutions exist, evidence acquired in contravention of the Act can be used against a defendant in court. Members of Congress have been asked to include an exclusionary rule to the Pen Register Act, as it would then resemble conventional Fourth Amendment safeguards.[181]

> In a reply to a Justice Department suggestion, legislation was initiated after 9/11 to grant power to judges in one area the right to grant pen register and trap and trace orders to service providers anywhere in the country.

Federal agents perform approximately ten times the number of register and trap and trace surveillances, than they do wiretaps.[182] In 1996, DOJ acquired 4,569 pen register and trap and trace orders, with most covering several phone lines.[183] During 1996, 10,520 lines were watched by pen registers or trap and trace devices.[184] The amount of data gathered by the various DOJ agencies over the years led to a number of technological, computer devices

---

177. ECPA, Title I, 18 U.S.C. §§ 2510.
178. Ibid.
179. Ibid–§§ 2701.
180. HR 2579: Section 212.
181. See ECPA Title III, 18 U.S.C. §§ 3121.
182. "CDT's Analysis of S. 2092: Amending the Pen Register and Trap and Trace Statute in Response to Recent Internet Denial of Service Attacks and to Establish Meaningful Privacy Protections." (2000–04–04). Center of Democracy and Technology. Retrieved on 2008–01–20.
183. Ibid.
184. Ibid.

to develop the scrutiny and joining of transactional information obtained from pen registers and trap and trace devices.[185]

In a reply to a Justice Department suggestion, legislation was initiated after 9/11 to grant power to judges in one area the right to grant pen register and trap and trace orders to service providers anywhere in the country.[186] Other conditions could significantly increase the range of these allegedly partial surveillance mechanisms, permitting the attainment of high personal information while placing costly encumbrances on ISPs, portals, and other service providers.[187]

Three laws primarily set the criterion for governmental interception of communications and admittance to subscriber data:

- The federal wiretap statute ("Title III"), 18 USC 2510 et seq., mandates that a judge issue a probable cause warrant, if law enforcement wants real-time interception of the communicated information. Here, the legal standard is high.[188]
- The Electronic Communications Privacy Act of 1986 ("ECPA"), 18 USC 2701 *et seq.*, set criteria for admittance to accumulated email and additional electronic communications, and to business data (subscriber identifying information, logs, toll records, etc.).[189] It is not easy to gain access to someone's e-mail, though the criteria for accessing business data is.
- The pen register and trap and trace laws, enacted as part of ECPA, 18 USC 3121 *et seq.*, controls the capture of "the numbers dialed or otherwise transmitted on the telephone line to which such device is attached."[190] The criteria for getting a court order for these devices are minimal.

Title III controls the capture of the "contents" of communications, which is defined as "any information concerning the substance, purport, or meaning of that communication" 18 USC 2510(8).[191]

The U.S. Supreme Court issued the statement that the substance of communications is safeguarded by the Fourth Amendment's limits on searches and seizures; thus, Title III compels firm restrictions on the capacity of law

---

185. Ibid.
186. See HR 2579: Section 216.
187. See HR 2579: Section 215.
188. "Internet Denial of Service Attacks and the Federal Response." Center for Democracy and Technology (2007–10–07). Retrieved on 2007–12–20.
189. See The Electronic Communications Privacy Act of 1987, 18 USC 2701 *et seq.*
190. See The Electronic Communications Privacy Act of 1986, 18 USC 3121 *et seq.*
191. See The Electronic Communications Privacy Act of 1986 18 USC 2510(8).

enforcement to acquire call content–restrictions that symbolize the safeguards certified by the Fourth Amendment. Law enforcement may only capture content if they received a warrant from a judge that was based upon the likelihood that the individual in question was carrying out one of a number of specially listed crimes, that communications regarding the particular crime will be intercepted, and that the applicable services are frequently used by the suspected lawbreaker, or are being used in conjunction with the crime.[192]

As mentioned earlier, *Smith v. Maryland* stated that to attain such an order, all the authorities needed to do was to make the claim that "the information likely to be obtained is relevant to an ongoing criminal investigation."[193] The Supreme Court affirmed that the data gathered by pen registers is curbed. "Neither the purport of any communication between the caller and the recipient of the call, their identities, nor whether the call was even completed is disclosed by pen registers."[194] More recently, Supreme Court rulings have stressed that pen registers' "only capability is to intercept" the telephone numbers a person calls.[195]

In terms of the Patriot Act, many issues are created by applying the pen register/trap and trace statutes to the Internet. The decree assuredly applies to e-mail and the Worldwide Web, for it specifically mentions electronic communications. One question centers on the statement, "the numbers dialed or otherwise transmitted"? Is it lawful for the authorities to serve a pen register order on an Internet Service Provider like Yahoo, to acquire the addresses of each individual transmitting a message? Does the legal clout regarding a pen register/trap and trace include only numbers (Internet protocol addresses) or does it comprise private e-mail addresses as well? Does the authority of such mechanisms either apply to a search portal or search engine? Can the law apply to URLs as well? Is it possible for the government to serve a pen register or trap and trace order on organizations such as FOX News or CNN in order to acquire the address of each individual that downloaded or read a specific story? Does a pen register order work when someone uses the Internet for phone calls, and if so, would services like Skype be affected? Are the rules the same if someone uses DSL instead of dial-up?

The significance of these issues is magnified by the fact that daily transactions and/or electronic data (i.e., e-mail and surfing the web) give much more detailed information than mere telephone numbers. First, using an e-mail addresses reveals more potentially private information because an email

---

192. See e 18 USC 2518(3).
193. See 18 USC 3122-23.
194. See *United States v. New York Tel. Co.,* 434 U.S. 159, 167 (1977).
195. See *Brown v. Waddell,* 50 F.3d 285, 292 (4th Cir. 1995).

address is distinctive to each individual. For instance, in one office, there may be only one phone that is used to call "outside," while each employee has an individual email account. During the "old days," a pen register only showed the numbers dialed, but if served on an ISP, the address alone would probably ID the particular addressee of each message; likewise, this is just as true for one's home. In today's world, with the ubiquity of the Internet, how many members of a family have their own unique e-mail address? Thus, information gained from electronic sources could establish who is contacting whom.

> 18 USC 3123(a) affirms that a judge can sanction the putting in place a pen register or trap and trace mechanism "within the jurisdiction of the court." The DOJ argued that this encumbrance harmed its war on terror and posed a heavy weight on agents investigating in cyberspace, since a message may leap from computer to computer.

The law affirms that a judge can sanction the putting in place a pen register or trap and trace mechanism "within the jurisdiction of the court."[196] It should be noted, however, that DOJ argued strenuously against this rule, stating that this encumbrance harmed its ability to wage war on terror and prevented agents from investigating in cyberspace, since a message may leap from computer to computer.[197]

This line of reasoning makes sense, but the changes, if made, could/would include common, everyday telephones. Moreover, it would likely include scenarios where it seemed that communications passed through several different service providers. In essence, it would allow a judge in Los Angeles to approve the use of a pen register in New Hampshire on communications beginning and ending in New Hampshire.

In addition, orders given under the purported change, as introduced, would likely lack any semblance of limits. A normal, everyday subpoena, that covers the entire nation in its scope, is directed to a particular individual possessing the preferred information.[198] If this were allowed, the government would be given a blank check to look at anyone, anywhere, at anytime, without worrying about civil liberties.

---

196. See 18 USC 3123(a).
197. Jim Dempsey. "CDT's Analysis of S. 2092: Amending the Pen Register and Trap and Trace Statute in Response to Recent Internet Denial of Service Attacks and to Establish Meaningful Privacy Protections." Center for Democracy and Technology (2007–10–10). Retrieved on 2008–03–22.
198. See Fed. R. Crim. Proc. 17(c).

SEARCH WARRANTS

When the police execute a search of someone's home, it is considered legal if they obtained judicial permission, commonly referred to as a warrant. This is done by contacting the judge either by phone or in person and giving a sworn statement detailing the specifics they deem indicate that proof of a crime may be found in someone's home, (or other place they want to search). The presiding judge may issue the order only if he or she is persuaded that the information given by the police gives probable cause, which may be defined as the logical conviction that someone has committed a crime or that by searching, proof that the crime was committed will turn up.

Two cases heard by the Kansas Supreme Court illustrate how the obtaining of search warrants actually works. In *State v. Horn,*[199] the police attained a warrant allowing for a search of property and "all persons present." The officers announced their arrival, immediately heard people inside moving as if to hide something, burst open the house's door and saw several individuals running quickly to the back of the house. Scattered about the living room was money and drugs—all in the open for the police to see. The defendant, Horn, was captured, was searched, upon whom the police found cash. He was subsequently tried and convicted of attempted possession of cocaine. The warrant allowed the searching of all bystanders present, but it was unconstitutionally broad since the affidavit did not state that selling drugs was the only activity in the residence; hence, the police could not solely depend upon the warrant to search Horn.[200]

The search was legal under the exigent circumstances exception to the warrant requirement. KSA 22-2509[201] allowed the search of individuals in attendance during the carrying out of search warrants to avert the throwing away or hiding of anything depicted in the warrant. This particular warrant detailed drugs and thus, the police had probable cause that the inhabitants had drugs—exigent circumstances vindicated the search. First, the police executed a valid warrant; the inhabitants of the house ran when police proclaimed their presence; plus, cash and drug paraphernalia were lying in the open. These details signified that the property was a conduit for past and present drug trafficking, and that anyone in attendance was trafficking. The

---

199. *State v. Horn,* 15 Kan. App. 2d 365 (rev. denied 248 Kan. 998 [1991].

200. Ibid.

201. Specifically, KS 22-2509 is "Detention and search of persons on premises. In the execution of a search warrant the person executing the same may reasonably detain and search any person in the place at the time:

(a) To protect himself from attack, or

(b) To prevent the disposal or concealment of any things particularly described in the warrant. History: L. 1970, ch. 129, § 22–2509; July 1.

Court ruled that the police were correct in thinking that the individuals attempting to escape probably had drugs: "Given that drugs are easily concealed and easily disposed of, the police had reasonable cause after entering the residence to search everyone running toward the back of the house."[202]

In *State v. Vandiver*,[203] a police officer went inside a dwelling in accordance with a narcotics search warrant. He immediately arrested the suspect, but then saw six individuals playing video games with a plastic container of marijuana nearby; moreover, he smelled marijuana. The officer patted down each individual, and found a small 35mm film cylinder in a defendant's pants pocket. Although he later admitted that the cylinder did not look like a weapon, the officer took it out and opened it up, finding marijuana, at which time he arrested defendant. The Court stated that obtaining the cylinder was unlawful and was not covered by the warrant. Just because the defendant's happened to be near the marijuana did not create probable cause needed to make an arrest for possession.

The Court ruled that even if the officer had probable cause, no exigent circumstances were present. Unlike *Horn,* no confirmatory evidence sustained the idea that the marijuana might be destroyed, no one tried to escape the premises, and no one attempted to hide anything. In order to validate a search under KSA 22-2509(b),[204] probable cause must exist, as should a discernible situation, such as someone running quickly from the police, or a person behaving in an apprehensive manner, as well as the police making reasonable decisions that the validating proof will be destroyed or hidden before a judicial warrant is acquired.

Any occupants of property searched under a standard warrant are aware of the search, either when it happens or soon afterwards. Simply put, this is because, customarily, search warrants were conducted overtly in plain sight and at a point in time that the occupants of the property were there. Traditional search warrants sanction the taking of material substances (such as narcotics or stolen goods); thus, if such objects are located at the searched property and taken as evidence by police officers, the inhabitants will definitely be aware of it. Moreover, traditional search warrants mandate that the police provide a copy of the search warrant, as well as an acknowledgment regarding anything taken to anyone in attendance at the property, or leave the copy and the receipt on the premises.

If no one is around when the warrant is executed, the inhabitants will, at some point, definitely be cognizant of the search and seizure. Obviously, telltale signs of the police's forcible entry, such as a house that has been rum-

---

202. Ibid.
203. *State v. Vandiver* 19 Kan. App. 2d 786 (1994).
204. Op. cit. KSA 22–2509.

maged through without regard to the care of any items, or property that's missing will normally alert the occupant that his/her house has been searched. If, by some chance, the individual does not realize his/her property has been searched, a copy of the warrant and a receipt will be left in a prominent place letting the inhabitant know a legal search was conducted.

However, the scenario just played out has changed over the past two decades. Americans are now living in an era where the use of "sneak and peek" warrants is accepted, and they are radically unlike traditional search warrants. During the 1980s, the DOJ's main stalwarts, the FBI and the DEA, convinced various federal judges to issue approximately 35 sneak and peek warrants, in spite of the dearth of any constitutional sanction for such warrants at the time.[205]

> Sneak and peek warrants only take place when the inhabitants are away from the site to be searched. The entry, search, and property taken by the authorities is handled in a secret manner; that is, the occupants will not know their domicile, office, etc., was searched.

Sneak and peek warrants only take place when the inhabitants are away from the site to be searched. The entry, search, and property taken by the authorities is handled in a secret manner; that is, the occupants will not know their domicile, office, etc. was searched. The search and seizure centers on things like information regarding what, if anything, has transpired within the property. Pictures may be taken and it's uncommon for anything to be taken from the premises. If anything is taken, it's done in such a manner that the occupant is usually unaware; for instance, something seized might be substituted with a copy that appears identical. The occupant will not find a copy of the warrant anywhere on his/her property. It is possible that many sneak and peek warrants are carried out at the same location. In general, only after the authorities arrest someone or come back with a traditional search warrant will the existence of any secret entries be divulged. This may not occur until several months after the clandestine search or searches. Search warrants will be discussed in more detail in Chapter 3.

---

205. "Sneak and Peek Search Warrants." *Flagpole Magazine,* p. 12. (2002–09–11).

TERRORIST FINANCING/BANKING

After 9/11, U.S. government officials stated that the struggle against al-Qaeda money was as serious as the physical fight against al-Qaeda terrorists.[206] Politicians on both sides of the aisle said many times that if America wants to win the war against terrorism, then the fight must include ways of severing the terrorists' money supply. While this draws praise from many, the basic facts are this: there is little way for America to stop terrorists' money flow, as there are many methods for them to acquire needed funds.[207] On the other hand, following al-Qaeda funding is a very efficient method of locating terrorist fanatics and crippling their schemes.[208,209]

In order to better understand the reasoning behind the Patriot Act, we will now discuss, in a detailed manner, how and why American strategy used immediately after 9/11 regarding terrorist funding changed. In addition, we will discuss Title 3 of the Patriot Act, which deals with banking and money laundering.

Restricting the money supply is still the most evident characteristic of American tactics, but it is not the sole weapon, nor is it the most vital goal in combating terrorism. Eventually, creating difficulties for terrorist fanatics when they attempt to get money is an important factor in our overall strategy, but used by itself is not enough. Chasing the finances to spot terrorists and their adherents affords an exceptionally commanding tool in the war against terrorism. Using this tool almost tends to remain imperceptible to John Q. Public, but it is a decisive component in waging the war against al-Qaeda.

> The 9/11 terrorists used American and foreign banks to keep, move, and reclaim their funds when needed. The hijackers placed great sums of money into American banks, mainly by wire transfers and depositing either cash or travelers checks transported from their home countries.

By 1999, al-Qaeda was a principal adversary concerning American interests around the world.[210] The 9/11 terrorists used American and foreign

206. Prepared Statement of Lee H. Hamilton, Vice Chair National Commission on Terrorist Attacks before the Committee on Financial Services, House of Representatives (2004–08–23).
207. "Al-Qaeda: Funding in Afghanistan." Global Security.org. Retrieved on 2008–07–23. Website: http://www.globalsecurity.org/military/world/para/al-qaida.htm.
208. Victor Comras. Al Qaeda Financing and Funding to Affiliated Groups. *Strategic Insights (4)*, 1, (January 2005). Retrieved on 2007–12–29.
209. Maurice R. Goldberg, William F. Wechsler, & Leo S. Wolosky. "Terrorist Financing: Report of an Independent Task Force Sponsored the Council on Foreign Relations" (2002–11–25).
210. The 9/11 Commission Report, Chapter 5.1.

banks to keep, move, and reclaim their funds when needed. The hijackers placed great sums of money into American banks, mainly by wire transfers and depositing either cash or travelers checks transported from their home countries. In addition, a number of al-Qaeda operatives kept money in foreign banks, which they drew upon in the United States using ATM machines and credit card transactions.[211] The hijackers frequently obtained money from operatives in Germany and the United Arab Emirates or openly from Khalid Sheikh Mohammed (KSM) as they journeyed through Pakistan before entering the U.S.[212] September 11 cost al-Qaeda approximately $500,000 of which roughly $300,000 was deposited in various financial institutions throughout the U.S., to be used as needed. The hijackers gave back something like $26,000 to an operative in the UAE in the days preceding the attacks. While they lived in the U.S., the hijackers used al-Qaeda funds mainly for flight training (mostly done in Florida), travel, and day-to-day living costs.[213]

Neither the terrorists nor their financial backers understood the ins and outs of international banking. They left important documents joining them and their backers together.[214] Even so, they were adequately skilled enough to mix together into the enormous international financial network without exposing themselves as terrorists whose primary goal was to destroy American lives. The money-laundering restraints in position at that time were primarily centered on stopping drug kingpins and large-scale financial deception and lacked the ability to detect the terrorists' transactions. While the restraints were effective in stopping the flow of drug money, it was not set up to discover or disturb the quotidian business transactions of terrorists.[215]

---

al-Qaeda was financed, somewhere in the neighborhood of $30 million per year, primarily from various Islamic charitable trust organizations and the utilization of individuals working at banks within the Middle East.

---

211. Jeffrey Robinson. "The money trail: How petty crime funds terror." *The International Herald Tribune* (2004–08–13). Retrieved on 2008–02–15.

212. Tim McGirk. "Terrorism's Missing Link: Khalid Shaikh Mohammed, al Qaeda's deadliest agent, is still at large–and more threatening than ever." *Time* (2003–1–20).

213. Steven A. Camarota. "The Open Door: How Militant Islamic Terrorists Entered and Remained in the United States, 1993–2001." Center for Immigration Studies (2002). Retrieved on 2008–02–23.

214. John E. Lewis. Statement of John E. Lewis Deputy Assistant Director, Counterterrorism Division Federal Bureau of Investigation Before the Senate Committee on Banking, Housing and Urban Affairs (2004–09–29). Retrieved on 2008–02–23.

215. Peter Reuter & Edwin M. Truman. "Money Laundering Controls and Terrorist Finance." *Financial Regulator (10),* 2, September 2005.

Al-Qaeda and Osama bin Laden attained needed funds from a number of places.[216] While bin Laden's family was rich, he lacked the means to any substantial sums of money (especially following his relocation from Sudan to Afghanistan) and did not individually finance al-Qaeda, either through his inheritance or companies he supposedly possessed in Sudan.[217] Rather, al-Qaeda was financed, somewhere in the neighborhood of $30 million per year, primarily from various Islamic charitable trust organizations and the utilization of individuals working at banks within the Middle East.[218] It should be noted that no conclusive proof was found tying al-Qaeda to the international drug trade or the illegal diamond trade; moreover, the organization was not funded by any specific foreign government. Likewise, the U.S. was never a source of money for bin Laden or his group,[219] though disagreement exists.[220]

At the time of 9/11, terrorist funding was not a main concern for national or international intelligence efforts. Intelligence gathering concerning this issue was intermittent, deficient, and more often than not, highly inaccurate.[221] Though the National Security Council felt al-Qaeda financing was vital in its effort to destroy the organization, other agencies did not take a hefty role, angering the National Security Counsel (NSC). The NSC felt that, due to the lack of an efficient interagency apparatus, blame for the predicament was spread among various agencies involved in terrorist intelligence, each functioning separately.[222]

With knowledge regarding the magnitude and nature of the danger and with a new feeling of necessity, the intelligence community formed new organizations in which to zero in on, bringing knowledge, and know-how to the matter of terrorist fund-raising and the covert trafficking of money.[223] Pundits for the Patriot Act state that many of the impediments that hampered terrorist investigations disappeared after the Act was passed.[224] One common refrain is that now, the intelligence community possesses better tools to focus

---

216. Peter Carbonara. "Following the al-Qaeda Money Trail." Cnn.dom community (2001–12–24). Retrieved on 2008–01–23.

217. Associated Press. "Bin Laden's wealth not the force behind terror attacks." *USA Today* (2004–09–02). Retrieved on 2008–01–23.

218. Carbonara, op. cit.

219. "Monograph on Terrorist Financing." National Commission on Terrorist Attacks upon the United States: Staff Report to the Commission. (2004).

220. See Douglas Farah, *Blood from Stones: The Secret Financial Network of Terror* (2004).

221. Joseph M. Myers. The Silent Struggle against Terrorist Financing. *Georgetown Journal of International Affairs (6.1),* Winter/Spring 2004.

222. See op. cit. "Monograph of Terrorist Financing."

223. Ibid.

224. Sarah B. Miller. "In Defense of the Patriot Act." *Christian Science Monitor* (2003–08–20). Retrieved on 2008–02–23.

upon the terrorist threat. In addition, the harmonization between intelligence agencies and law enforcement helps to ID and follow terrorist organizations.[225]

Before the Patriot Act, the U.S. had the Bank Secrecy Act of 1970 (or BSA, but is also known as the Currency and Foreign Transactions Reporting Act), which mandated that American banks help the myriad U.S. governmental agencies to discover and avert money laundering. Specifically, the BSA calls for banks to keep detailed evidence of cash purchases of negotiable instruments, document all cash transactions $10,000 (daily cumulative sum), and to tell of any suspicious goings-on that could indicate money laundering, tax evasion, or other illegal acts. Since it became law, a number of anti-money laundering acts, and that includes various provisions in title III of the Patriot Act, have been ratified to revise the BSA. Criminal cases involving money laundering can now be heard in the region where the act took place, or where the money laundering transfer was initiated. Foreigners engaged in money laundering are forbidden to enter the U.S.[226]

Title III of the Patriot Act, entitled "International Money Laundering Abatement and Financial Anti-Terrorism Act of 2001," was meant to assist in the deterrence, discovery, and prosecution of international money laundering and terrorist funding. It mainly modifies sections of the *Money Laundering Control Act of 1986* (MLCA) and the BSA, as mentioned in the preceding paragraph. It has three subtitles, with the first dealing mainly with intensifying banking rules in order to curb money laundering, especially internationally. The second tries to progress contact between the various law enforcement agencies and banks. This subtitle also augments the recording of important documents, as well as reporting prerequisites. The third subtitle aims at controlling illegal activities terrorists are notorious for, like smuggling and counterfeiting.[227]

The first subtitle stiffened the document reporting obligations for banks, having them verify the total number of business transactions handled from various world locations where money laundering is rampant. Moreover, institutions had to initiate easy to use procedures in order to recognize possessors of bank accounts and those sanctioned to use or direct money through payable-through accounts.[228] The U.S. Treasury received the authority to formulate rules intended to promote information sharing between banks in order to avoid money laundering.[229]

---

225. Jean Schmidt. "Securing Our Nation." 2006–1–13. Retrieved on 2007–12–20.
226. See 31 USC 5311-5330 and 31 CFR 103.
227. See USA PATRIOT ACT, Public Law Pub.L. 107-56.
228. See USA PATRIOT Act (U.S. H.R. 3162, Public Law 107-56), Title III, Subtitle A, Sec. 311.
229. See USA PATRIOT Act (U.S. H.R. 3162, Public Law 107-56), Title III, Subtitle A, Sec. 314.

In addition to enlarging record keeping prerequisites, the Patriot Act put into place new rules making it simpler for law enforcement to spot money launderers and to make it more difficult for them to shield their identities.[230] If money laundering is revealed, the subtitle states that any and all assets should be forfeited by anyone thought to be laundering money.[231] In an attempt to persuade banks to decrease money laundering, the Treasury received the power to obstruct amalgamations of bank holding companies and banks with any institution possessing a poor record of thwarting money laundering. Likewise, the Treasury could stop mergers between FDIC institutions and non-FDIC institutions that possessed an inadequate record in fighting money laundering.[232]

Limitations were erected on various accounts and foreign banks. Foreign shell banks not associated with institutions located physically in the U.S., or do not have to receive any direction from a banking authority in a non-U.S. country, were strictly forbidden. The subtitle contains a number of segments that exclude or limit the use of specific accounts located at banks.[233] Banks must now assume the duty of identifying the possessor of any secretly owned bank outside America that has a correspondent bank account with them. It is likely that more analysis will be used by any American bank to other banks to make sure that nothing illegal occurs. Financial institutions must locate all ostensible and beneficial proprietors of any private bank account opened and preserved in the U.S. by non-U.S. citizens.[234]

Financial institutions are expected to assume an improved inspection of any account that is owned by, or is being sustained for, any elder political leader when there is a belief that the individual is shady.[235] Moreover, any funds deposited from the United States into banks overseas is now the same as placing the money into any interbank account that the overseas institution may have within American borders. Hence, any legal warrants against any foreign individual, though he/she is not an American citizen, can have his/her money frozen in American banks, up to the sum placed within the account at the overseas institution.[236]

---

230. See USA PATRIOT Act (U.S. H.R. 3162, Public Law 107-56), Title III, Subtitle A, Sec. 317.
231. See USA PATRIOT Act (U.S. H.R. 3162, Public Law 107-56), Title III, Subtitle A, Sec. 312, 313, 319 & 325.
232. See USA PATRIOT Act (U.S. H.R. 3162, Public Law 107-56), Title III, Subtitle A, Sec. 327.
233. See USA PATRIOT Act (U.S. H.R. 3162, Public Law 107-56), Title III, Subtitle A, Sec. 313.
234. See Ibid.
235. See USA PATRIOT Act (U.S. H.R. 3162, Public Law 107-56), Title III, Subtitle A, Sec. 312.
236. See USA PATRIOT Act (U.S. H.R. 3162, Public Law 107-56), Title III, Subtitle A, Sec. 319.

Financial institutions are expected to assume an improved inspection of any account that is owned by, or is being sustained for, any elder political leader when there is a belief that the individual is shady.

Limitations were positioned regarding the use of inner bank concentration accounts since such accounts offer little in case an audit is needed for business dealings; likewise, the concentration accounts could be a means of make it possible to launder money. Banks are forbidden from permitting depositors to expressly tell them to transfer money to or from concentration accounts, and they can no longer inform depositors any information about those accounts. Banks cannot offer any pertinent data to depositors that may name such "inside" accounts.[237] Banks must record and abide by rules that regulate identifying where the money is located for each depositor in concentration accounts that blend the funds that belongs to other depositors as well.[238]

Specifically, what is considered "money laundering" was enlarged to comprise the act of conducting financial transactions in America with the purpose of committing a criminal act.[239] Bribing political leaders and the illegal use of public money, smuggling, or illegally exporting of proscribed weapons[240] and the importing of any gun or ammunition not expressly consented to by the U.S. Attorney General,[241] as well as smuggling anything prohibited under the Export Administration Regulations[242,243] were all added. In addition, any crime where the U.S. would be compelled to hand over a person, or whenever the U.S. would have to initiate legal proceedings against someone for trial due to an international treaty was added; likewise, the importation of misleadingly classified commodities;[244] any criminal acts using a computer;[245] and any criminal infringement concerning the *Foreign Agents Registration Act of 1938*[246] were added. Title III also permits any goods acquired due to a felonious act against a foreign country that involves the manufacturing, importing, selling, or distributing of a prohibited substance to be forfeited.[247]

---

237. See USA PATRIOT Act (U.S. H.R. 3162, Public Law 107-56), Title III, Subtitle A, Sec. 325.
238. Ibid.
239. See 18 U.S.C. § 1956(c)(7)(B)(ii).
240. See United States Munitions List, which is part of the *Arms Export Control Act* (22 U.S.C. § 2778).
241. See 18 U.S.C. § 922(l) and 18 U.S.C. § 925(d).
242. See 15 CFR 730-774.
243. See USA PATRIOT Act (U.S. H.R. 3162, Public Law 107-56), Title III, Subtitle A, Sec. 315.
244. See 18 U.S.C. § 541.
245. See 18 U.S.C. § 1030.
246. see USA PATRIOT Act (U.S. H.R. 3162, Public Law 107-56), Title III, Subtitle A, Sec. 315.
247. See USA PATRIOT Act (U.S. H.R. 3162, Public Law 107-56), Title III, Subtitle A, Sec. 320. Amended 18 U.S.C. § 981(A)(1)(B).

Foreign countries have the right to initiate forfeiture proceedings, of which the verdict is imposed by a U.S. District Court.[248] This has been accomplished by Congressional legislation specifying the procedures regarding how the U.S. government might attain a restraining order[249] to safeguard the availability of assets that are liable for foreign forfeiture or confiscation judgments.[250] When the courts consider such a request, great importance is stressed on the capability of foreign courts to engage in due process.[251] The Secretary of the Treasury is also involved in that he must take all sensible steps to persuade alien governments to make it a condition to consist of the legal name of the instigator in wire transfer instructions entering the U.S. and other countries, with the data to stay with the transfer from its commencement site until the point of payout.[252] In addition, the Secretary received a directive stating he should support international collaboration in all matters involving money laundering, financial crimes, and the finances of terrorist groups.[253]

The Act initiated punishment for dishonest officials. Any individual or government workers who act in an illegal manner—including the individual inducing the felonious act—while working in their official capacity, will be charged with a fine that can not be more than three times the original amount of the bribe. In addition, the individual may be jailed for up to 15 years, or he/she could receive both. Punishment applies to banks that do not obey a directive to cease any consequent accounts inside of 10 days after instructed by either by the Attorney General or the Secretary of Treasury. The bank could receive a monetary penalty up to $10,000 per day the account stays open once the 10-day limit has concluded.[254]

Subtitle II made several changes to the BSA, making it more difficult for criminals (primarily money launderers) to function, while making it simpler for the legal authorities and various agencies to regulate money laundering businesses. One change concerning the BSA allowed for the chosen representative or bureau that collects information about illegal activities to report their findings to U.S. intelligence agencies.[255] Several changes addressed matters connected to document keeping and fiscal reporting. An example was a new condition stating that anyone conducting business transactions must

---

248. See USA PATRIOT Act (U.S. H.R. 3162, Public Law 107-56), Title III, Subtitle A, Sec. 323. Amended 28 U.S.C. § 2467.
249. In accordance with 18 U.S.C. § 983(j).
250. See 28 U.S.C. § 2467(d)(3)(A).
251. See USA PATRIOT Act (U.S. H.R. 3162, Public Law 107-56), Title III, Subtitle A, Sec. 323. Amended 28 U.S.C. § 2467.
252. See USA PATRIOT Act (U.S. H.R. 3162, Public Law 107-56), Title III, Subtitle A, Sec. 328.
253. See USA PATRIOT Act (U.S. H.R. 3162, Public Law 107-56), Title III, Subtitle A, Sec. 330.
254. See USA PATRIOT Act (U.S. H.R. 3162, Public Law 107-56), Title III, Subtitle A, Sec. 319
255. See USA PATRIOT Act (U.S. H.R. 3162, Public Law 107-56), Title III, Subtitle B, Sec. 356.

make a description for any cash/and or foreign money receipts in excess of $10,000 and made it against the law to organize business proceedings in a fashion that attempts to avoid the BSA's reporting requirements.[256]

In order to make life simpler, individuals running unofficial value transfer systems remote of what is considered conventional were incorporated into the classification of "financial institution."[257] The BSA was changed to make it compulsory to account for any suspicious dealings while an effort was made to make such reporting simpler for banks and other institutions.[258] FinCEN became an agency of the Treasury department,[259] while the establishment of a secure system to be used by banks to detail any out of the ordinary or suspicious transactions and to supply warnings of any pertinent apprehensive dealings was ordered.[260] In conjunction with these informing duties, a substantial number of requirements are associated with the deterrence and prosecution of money-laundering.[261] Banks were commanded to initiate an antimoney laundering agenda and the BSA was changed to enhance and define antimoney laundering approaches.[262] In addition, civil and criminal consequences for money laundering were boosted while the establishment of penalties for disobedience regarding geographic targeting guidelines and particular document-keeping requirements was initiated.[263]

Other changes to the BSA were initiated through subtitle B. One such change included vesting the Board of Governors of the Federal Reserve System the authority to allow employees to serve as police officers to defend the property of any U.S. Federal institution and permitting the Board to entrust this influence with U.S. Federal reserve institutions.[264] Moreover, the United States Executive Directors of international financial institutions were allowed to use their influence and could choose to back any nation that supported America's War on Terror. The Executive Directors must make available any current auditing of disbursed funds originating from their banks to make certain no cash is distributed to anyone supporting terrorism.[265]

The third subtitle centers on currency crimes. Due to the efficacy of the BSA, criminals engaged in money laundering avoided conventional banks to "clean" their money and began using cash-based operations to evade the law.

---

256. See USA PATRIOT Act (U.S. H.R. 3162, Public Law 107-56), Title III, Subtitle B, Sec. 365.
257. See USA PATRIOT Act (U.S. H.R. 3162, Public Law 107-56), Title III, Subtitle B, Sec. 359.
258. See USA PATRIOT Act (U.S. H.R. 3162, Public Law 107-56), Title III, Subtitle B, Sec. 352, 354 & 365.
259. See USA PATRIOT Act (U.S. H.R. 3162, Public Law 107-56), Title III, Subtitle B, Sec. 361
260. See USA PATRIOT Act (U.S. H.R. 3162, Public Law 107-56), Title III, Subtitle B, Sec. 362.
261. See USA PATRIOT Act (U.S. H.R. 3162, Public Law 107-56), Title III, Subtitle B, Sec. 352.
262. See USA PATRIOT Act (U.S. H.R. 3162, Public Law 107-56), Title III, Subtitle B, Sec. 354.
263. See USA PATRIOT Act (U.S. H.R. 3162, Public Law 107-56), Title III, Subtitle B, Sec. 353.
264. See USA PATRIOT Act (U.S. H.R. 3162, Public Law 107-56), Title III, Subtitle B, Sec. 364.
265. See USA PATRIOT Act (U.S. H.R. 3162, Public Law 107-56), Title III, Subtitle B, Sec. 360.

An innovative attempt was made to prevent money laundering through bulk currency movements, primarily emphasizing the impounding of illegal income and the augmentation in penalties for money laundering.

> Congress realized that making it against the law to evade the reporting of money transfers was inadequate and determined that the law would be enhanced if smuggling of the bulk currency itself was illegal.

Congress realized that making it against the law to evade the reporting of money transfers was inadequate and determined that the law would be enhanced if smuggling of the bulk currency itself was illegal. Thus, the BSA was changed in order to make it a felony to try and elude currency reporting by hiding more than $10,000 on any individual or through any baggage, goods, or other container that enters and leaves the United States. The consequences are up to five years incarceration and the forfeiture of any land or property up to the amount being smuggled.[266] It also enhanced the civil and criminal penalties of anyone violating currency reporting by[267] stating that an individual would face losing all of his/her property implicated in the crime, as well as any other property shown to be owned by the wrongdoer.[268] The Act forbids and punishes anyone running an illegal money transmitting company.[269]

During 2005, this specific proviso in the Patriot Act brought Yehuda Abraham to trial for helping assemble money transfers for Hemant Lakhani, a well-known arms merchant from Great Britain, who was placed under arrest in August 2003 after finding himself in the middle of a well-planned government sting. Lakhani mistakenly attempted to sell a missile to an undercover FBI special agent that pretended to be a Somali radical.[270] The legal meaning of counterfeiting was enlarged to include analog, digital or electronic image imitations, and it became illegal to possess any machine that had the ability to duplicate such images. If convicted of such an offense, one could spend up to 20 years incarcerated.[271] The phrase "unlawful activities"

---

266. See USA PATRIOT Act (U.S. H.R. 3162, Public Law 107-56), Title III, Subtitle C, Sec. 371.
267. As defined in So defined in 31 U.S.C. § 5313, 31 U.S.C. § 5316 and 31 U.S.C. § 5324.
268. See USA PATRIOT Act (U.S. H.R. 3162, Public Law 107-56), Title III, Subtitle C, Sec. 372. Amended 31 U.S.C. § 5317(c).
269. See USA PATRIOT Act (U.S. H.R. 3162, Public Law 107-56), Title III, Subtitle C, Sec. 371. Amended 18 U.S.C. § 1960.
270. See "The Patriot Act: Justice Department Claims Success," National Public Radio (2005–07–20). Retrieved on 2008–01–20.
271. See USA PATRIOT Act (U.S. H.R. 3162, Public Law 107-56), Title III, Subtitle C, Sec. 374. Amended 18 U.S.C. § 1960.

was enlarged to contain lending significant backing or funds to foreign organizations deemed to be terrorist.[272] The Patriot Act states that any individual committing or conspiring to commence any illegal endeavor outside the authority of the United States, and which would be construed as a crime within American borders, will be faces charges under 18 U.S.C. § 1029 which specifically deals with fraud and all interrelated activities in association with access devices.[273]

THE FOREIGN INTELLIGENCE SURVEILLANCE ACT OF 1978

The Foreign Intelligence Surveillance Act of 1978, better known as FISA,[274] was (is) a Congressional act stipulating that specific methods must be followed regarding the physical and electronic spying of foreign agents operating on American soil. This includes U.S. citizens and permanent residents thought to be spying for foreign countries and thus, breaching American law in any area under American jurisdiction.[275]

The PA changed FISA, so terrorists lacking formal backing from foreign countries could be prosecuted. A complete rewording of the bill, called the Protect America Act of 2007, became federal law on August 5, 2007 and perished on February 17, 2008.[276] On July 9, 2008, Congress passed the FISA Amendments Act of 2008.[277] FISA was created due to the investigations carried Sam Ervin and Frank Church in the 1970s. It became known that President Richard M. Nixon used federal funds to covertly watch American political groups that had stated bluntly they were against him, which expressly contravened the Fourth Amendment.[278]

One aim for FISA was to supply both judicial and congressional supervision of America's covert spying of foreign groups and/or individuals in the U.S., while upholding the requisite secrecy mandated in order to safeguard the country. It permitted surveillance without a warrant within the country up to 12 months. However, if an American citizen is in any way involved, a judge must authorize the act no later than 72 hours once the surveillance is initiated.[279]

---

272. See USA PATRIOT Act (U.S. H.R. 3162, Public Law 107-56), Title III, Subtitle C, Sec. 376. Amended 18 U.S.C. § 1956(c)(7)(D).
273. See USA PATRIOT Act (U.S. H.R. 3162, Public Law 107-56), Title III, Subtitle C, Sec. 377.
274. See Pub.L. 95-511, 92 Stat. 1783, enacted 1978–10–25, 50 U.S.C. ch. 36.
275. Ibid.
276. See Eric Weiner (2007–10–18). "The Foreign Service Intelligence Act: A Primer." Retrieved on 2008–02–02.
277. See U.S. Senate Roll Call Vote Summary, Vote 00168, 100th Congress, 2nd Session.
278. See Kevin Caslava (2008–02–20). FISA Debate Involves more than Terrorism (Daily Nexus, 88 (80).
279. Op. cit. Public Law 95-511.

Usually, the words "foreign powers" mean foreign government, and/or any faction within that country, as well as meaning foreign governments with few Americans. In addition, it usually means any group or individual told by a foreign government what to do while in America.[280] The definition also includes groups engaged in international terrorism and foreign political organizations.[281] The sections of FISA authorizing electronic surveillance and physical searches without a court order specifically exclude their application to groups engaged in international terrorism.[282]

- Federal law restricts FISA's function with regard to American citizens. A U.S. "person" includes citizens, legal permanent residents, and any businesses incorporated within American borders. U.S. Code states that "foreign intelligence information" means any data required to safeguard the U.S. against authentic or likely attacks, sabotage or global terrorists.[283]

FISA created a court that meets secretly. While in session, the judge either consents or refuses the application for any search warrants. The only thing the public knows for sure is how many warrants were applied for, how many were given, and/or the number of rejections. During its first 12 months, the FISA court gave 322 warrants.[284] In 2006, the number had skyrocketed to 2224 warrants.[285] During the years of 1979 to 2006, exactly 22,990 applications for warrants were submitted to the court and all but five were approved.[286]

The President (working through the Attorney General) has the authority to authorize electronic surveillance absent a court's consent up to 12 months, but only if it is for gathering foreign intelligence data.[287] In addition, the President's authority is only valid if the operation being conducted is targeting foreign governments[288] or their operatives; likewise, there should be little chance that the spying will gain the substance of any communication in which an American citizen is involved.[289]

---

280. See §§1801(a)(1)-(3).
281. See §§1801(a)(4) and (5).
282. See §1802(a)(1).
283. See 50 U.S.C. §1801(e).
284. See Foreign Intelligence Surveillance Act 1980 Annual Report.
285. See http://www.fas.org/irp/agency/doj/fisa/2006rept.pdf.
286. See Electronic Privacy Information Center. "Foreign Intelligence Surveillance Act Orders 1979–2007" (2008–05–02). Retrieved on 2008–06–06.
287. See 50 U.S.C. §1801(e).
288. See 50 U.S.C. §1801(a)(1),(2),(3).
289. See 50 U.S.C. § 1802(a)(1).

The Attorney General must certify these circumstances under seal to the FISA Court,[290] and detail their agreement to the House Permanent Select Committee on Intelligence and the Senate Select Committee on Intelligence.[291] FISA expressly limits warrantless surveillance[292] to foreign entities as detailed in the statutes[293] but leaves out a number of definitions specified in the statutes.[294] However, FISA does not sanction the utilization of warrantless surveillance on the following: (1) groups involved in global terrorism or behavior appearing to prepare for a terrorist act; (2) political groups that are foreign in origin, and do not possess a significant number of American citizens; (3) any group ordered by and/or run by a foreign government or governments.[295] Under the FISA act, any individual engaging in electronic spying, unless it is allowed by federal law, is liable for criminal charges and/or[296] and civil liabilities.[297]

The President possesses the authority to approve warrantless surveillance at the initiation of armed conflict.[298] If he chooses, the spying can be no longer than 15 days after war has been declared.[299] On the other hand, the government may petition a court for an order allowing the spying utilizing the FISA court.[300] The authorization of a FISA petition mandates that the court obtain probable cause that the aim of governmental scrutiny either be a foreign government or the foreign government's operative and that the location where the surveillance will take place is asked for is either used or will be at some point by the foreign government or its operative. Moreover, the court must state that the planned spying meets specific requirements for data affecting Americans.[301] FISA also allows for a physical examination of the area used by the foreign government or its operative.[302]

FISA Court

The Act created the Foreign Intelligence Surveillance Court (FISC) and enabled it to oversee requests for surveillance warrants by federal police agencies (primarily the F.B.I.) against suspected foreign intelligence agents

---

290. See 50 U.S.C. § 1802(a)(3).
291. See 50 U.S.C. § 1802(a)(2).
292. See 50 U.S.C. § 1802(a)(1)(A).
293. See 50 U.S.C. §1801(a) (1),(2).
294. See 50 U.S.C. §1801(a) (4),(5),(6).
295. See 50 U.S.C. sect;1802 (a)(1)(A).
296. See 50 U.S.C. §1809.
297. See 50 U.S.C. §1810.
298. See 50 U.S.C. § 1811.
299. Ibid.
300. See 50 U.S.C §1805.
301. See 50 U.S.C. §1801(5).
302. See Section 302 of FISA.

inside the U.S. The court is located within the Department of Justice headquarters building. The court is staffed by 11 judges appointed by the Chief Justice of the United States to serve seven-year terms.

Proceedings before the FISA court are *ex parte* and nonadversarial. The court hears evidence presented solely by the Department of Justice. There is no provision for a release of information regarding such hearings, or for the record of information actually collected. Denials of FISA applications by the FISC may be appealed to the Foreign Intelligence Surveillance Court of Review. The Court of Review is a three-judge panel. Since its creation, the court has only come into session once, in 2002.

Resolving Any Legal Infringements

Built-in safeguards exist so individuals who feel wronged have access to criminal and civil liability for any violations of FISA. Criminal charges are allowed if intentional contraventions of the law have occurred, i.e., data known to be gathered through illegal surveillance is disclosed in a public manner. The possible consequences could be fines up to $10,000, up to five years in jail, or both.[303]

The law constructed a means of "taking on the government" for citizens whose personal communications were illegally examined. The law allows for damages in the sum of no more than $1,000 per day. Moreover, the law allows for punitive damages and for the payment of lawyer's charges.[304] Comparable accountability can be found regarding physical searches. In either scenario, the law established an affirmative defense for any law enforcement officer performing his/her job in accordance with a legitimate judicial command. Apparently, this line of defense is unobtainable for anyone working solely under presidential sanction.

During 2004, FISA was changed to take in a "lone wolf" proviso.[305] A "lone wolf" may be defined as a person who is a non-American and either takes part in or plans international terrorist acts. The provisio changed the meaning of "foreign power" in order to allow the FISA Courts to supply search orders without the added problem of locating a link between the "lone wolf" and a foreign government known to subsidize terrorism and/or terrorist groups.[306]

---

303. See 50 U.S.C. §1809–Criminal sanctions.
304. See 50 U.S.C. §1810–Civil liability.
305. See 50 U.S.C. § 1801(b)(1)(C).
306. See "Lone Wolf" Amendment to the Foreign Intelligence Surveillance Act. Retrieved on 2008–02–02 from www. fas.com.

Terrorist Investigations before FISA

In a landmark case,[307] the U.S. Supreme Court ruled that the legal necessities regarding the Fourth Amendment pertained uniformly to electronic surveillance as it did to physical searches. The Warren Court did not tackle the thorny problem of whether such necessities apply to matters of national security. The Burger Court examined the question in *United States v. United States District Court*,[308] where it ruled that judicial endorsement was needed before law enforcement could engage in domestic surveillance—otherwise the the the Fourth Amendment was abridged. Justice Powell stated that the court's ruling did not deal with whether or not the same issues would apply if the individuals to be surveilled were operatives of a foreign power.

Before FISA, several federal courts examined the problem of "warrantless wiretaps." In both *United States v. Brown*[309] and *United States v. Butenko*,[310] the courts upheld the prevailing views regarding warrantless wiretaps. In *Brown*, an American's dialogue was acquired by a wiretap approved by the Attorney General for foreign intelligence reasons. In *Butenko*, the court ruled that a wiretap was legitimate if the chief rationale was for acquiring foreign intelligence data.

In *Zweibon v. Mitchell*,[311] the judges ruled that in order to engage in domestic surveillance with American citizens, a warrant was mandatory. In *Zweibon*, the court stated that groups located in America were not foreign operatives and thus, unless special circumstances were present, it was illegal to electronically surveil American citizens.

Post FISA

Few cases have been adjudicated regarding whether or not FISA is constitutional; however, two lower courts ruled that FISA was constitutional. In the *United States v. Duggan*,[312] the defendants were not Americans but were "soldiers" in the Irish Republican Army, a terrorist organization located in Ireland. The individuals were found guilty for a number of breaches concerning the delivery of weapons and the court ruled that undeniable differences existed between foreigners and American citizens. In the *United States v. Nicholson*, the defendant attempted to make a motion suppressing all evi-

---

307. See *Katz v. United States*, 389 U.S. 347 (1967).
308. See *United States v. U.S. District Court*, 407 U.S. 297 (1972), also known as the Keith case.
309. See 484 F.2d 418 (5th Cir. 1973).
310. See 494 F.2d 593 (3rd Cir. 1974).
311. See 516 F.2d 594 (D.C. Cir. 1975).
312. See 743 F.2d 59 (2nd Cir., 1984).

dence acquired under the auspices of a FISA order.[313] The court agreed with the original court in denying the motion for suppression, rejecting the assertions that FISA contravened the Fifth Amendment, equal protection, separation of powers, and the right to an attorney as spelled out in the Sixth Amendment. On the other hand, a third case involving the special review court for FISA, the counterpart to an Appeals court, stated that FISA lacks the power to encroach the President's legal power for warrantless searches with regards to foreign intelligence. In the case, *In re Sealed Case,* 310 F.3d 717, 742,[314] the special court ruled that other courts had written that the President had the vested right to engage in warrantless searches in the area of foreign intelligence; thus, FISA lacked the authority to invade upon the President's authority.

Some argued saying that, in essence, FISA needed to be changed as it was likely no longer able to deal with specific problems associated with foreign intelligence.[315,316] The arguments centered on the belief that FISA could not handle twenty-first century technology including new tools such as the automated observational techniques like data mining and traffic analysis.[317]

The legal scholar and esteemed Federal Judge Richard A. Posner opined in the *Wall Street Journal* that while FISA maintained a certain significance in the surveillance of known terrorists, it is was nonetheless incompetent in ferreting out unknown terrorists. Specifically, Judge Posner wrote that FISA warrants are designed in accordance with the belief that probable cause exists that the individual to be surveilled is a terrorist, and while this is important, it is much more important to determine, as of yet unknown terrorists.[318]

Improvements on FISA

The Terrorist Surveillance Act of 2006,[319] introduced into the U.S. Senate by Senators Mike DeWine (R-OH), Lindsey Graham (R-SC), Chuck Hagel (R-NE), and Olympia Snowe (R-ME), provided the President with added, but restricted, legal power to carry out electronic surveillance of assumed

---

313. See 955 F.Supp. 588 (Va. 1997).
314. Argued in the Foreign Intel. Surv. Ct. of Rev. 2002.
315. K A Taipale. Fixing Intelligence (2006–01–24). *The Washington Times.* Retrieved on 2008–05–05.
316. Phillip Bobbitt. Why We Listen (2006–01–30). *The New York Times.* Retrieved on 2008–05–05.
317. K A Taipale. Whispering Wires and Warrantless Wiretaps: Data Mining and Foreign Intelligence Surveillance. *NYU Review of Law & Security, No. 7, Supl. Bull. on L. & Sec., Spring 2006.* Retrieved on 2008–05–05.
318. Richard A. Posner. A New Surveillance Act (2006–02–15). *The Wall Street Journal.* Retrieved on 2008–05–05.
319. See S.2455.

terrorists in the U.S., though Congressional supervision was mandatory. Furthermore, on March 16, 2006, Senator Arlen Specter (R-PA) launched the National Security Surveillance Act of 2006,[320] which was designed to alter FISA in order to permit retroactive forgiveness[321] for warrantless surveillance carried out under presidential sanction and made available FISA court (FISC) authority to evaluate, approve, while overseeing all electronic surveillance programs.

Senators Specter and Dianne Feinstein (D-CA) presented the Foreign Intelligence Surveillance Improvement and Enhancement Act of 2006[322] on May 24, 2006, stating that FISA, and nothing else, was the only channel for conducting foreign intelligence surveillance. Each of the three bills (The Terrorist Surveillance Act of 2006, the National Security Surveillance Act of 2006, and the Foreign Intelligence Surveillance Improvement and Enhancement Act of 2006) was debated a number of times in Judiciary Committee hearings. Finally, on September 13, 2006, the Senate Judiciary Committee voted and endorsed each individual bill and decided to let the entire Senate to determine the outcome.[323]

In the House of Representatives, Congresswoman Heather Wilson (R-NM), on July 18, 2006, commenced discussion regarding the Electronic Surveillance Modernization Act.[324] Her bill would allow the President the power to sanction the electronic surveillance of worldwide phone calls and e-mail associated explicitly with recognized terrorists straight away subsequent to or in the expectation of an armed or terrorist assault on the U.S. Any type of surveillance after the preliminary, sanctioned period would mandate a FISA warrant or a presidential documentation to Congress. The House passed the bill on September 28, 2006 and it was given to the Senate.[325]

On July 28, 2007, President Bush asked Congress to approve legislation to improve and reorganize FISA so limitations regarding the electronic surveillance of possible terrorists could be reduced when one individual, or both, are outside the U.S. when the communication occurs. Moreover, he stressed to Congress that it needed to be handled before they took their August, 2007 recess. On August 3, 2007, the Senate passed a Republicanized

---

320. See S. 2453.
321. Walter Pincus. Specter offers Compromise on NSA Surveillance (2006–06–09). *The Washington Post*. Retrieved on 2008–03–09.
322. See S. 3001.
323. See Steven Aftergood. Conflicting Bills on Warrantless Surveillance Advance in Senate (2006–09–14). *Secrecy News*. Retrieved on 2008–04–12.
324. See H.R. 5825.
325. Elizabeth B. Bazan. *Electronic Surveillance Modernization Act, as Passed by the House of Representatives* (2007–01–28). Retrieved on 2008–05–11.

FISA[326] with a vote of 60 to 28, with the House doing the same with a vote of 227–183. On August 5, 2007, President Bush signed The Protect America Act of 2007[327] and it became law.[328]

The Act stated that communications begining or ending in a country outside the U.S. is subject to being wiretapped by the United States government without oversight by the FISA Court. The Act provided that the surveillance of communications no longer needed to submit an application to, or receive an order from, the FISA Court.

In addition, the Act offered several different methods for the government to gauge the legitimacy of an acquisition program, how Uncle Sam could distribute orders to providers to supply information or aid using a specific program, and for the federal government and beneficiary of an order to ask from the FISA Court, a judicial command to force a provider compliance or relief from an unlawful directive. Providers obtain any expenses, as well as complete protection from lawsuits for complying with any orders issued in accordance to the Act.[329]

Some of the key provisions in the Act are:

Either the Attorney General or Director of National Intelligence can approve, up to a total of 12 months, the acquirement of communications regarding anyone thought to be outside America, if either feels that:

1. logical measures are in position for judging that the attainment centers on individual thought t be outside the U.S.;
2. the attainment does not establish electronic surveillance–that is, the attainment does not entail exclusively local communications;
3. the attainment includes acquiring the communications information through the auspices and the aid of a communications service supplier that has the right of entry to the information;
4. a goal of the attainment is to foreign intelligence data;
5. minimization methods detailed in FISA will be utilized.[330]

This decision by the AG and/or DNI must be attested to in a letter, under oath, and endorsed with an apposite affidavit. If urgent action is mandatory and there is not enough time for standard procedures, either AG or DNI can give the attainment by spoken orders, with certification to occur within three

---

326. See S. 1927.
327. See Pub.L. 110-55, S. 1927.
328. See Elizabeth B. Bazan. "P.L. 110-55, the Protect America Act of 2007: Modifications to the Foreign Intelligence Surveillance Act" (2008–02–14). *Congressional Research Service*. Retrieved on 2008–06–06.
329. Op. cit. 208.
330. Ibid.

days. After that, it is recorded with the FISA Court, at which point, the AG or DNI can command a provider to carry out or aid in the in the attainment. If a provider decides he/she does not want to obey the command, the AG has the authority to seek an order issued from the FISA Court forcing the individual to obey the order. If the provider still refuses, he/she could be arrested and charged with contempt of court.[331]

Any individual getting the order has the right to dispute the order's valid-ity by petitioning the FISA Court. A preliminary assessment must occur within two full days of the filing to decide if the petition is trivial, while a decision for any non-trivial petitions must be made–in writing–within three full days of the petition being filed. Decisions made by the Court can be appealed to the Foreign Intelligence Court of Appeals; likewise, a petition for a writ of certiorari can be made to the U.S. Supreme Court. The Act permits providers compensation, at the current price, for giving aid as ordered by the AG or DNI. In addition, it offers complete protection from lawsuits in both federal and state courts for helping the government.[332]

Within four months, the AG must present to the FISA Court the process by which the federal government will decide whether acquisitions sanctioned by the Act correspond with the Act and do not entail solely communications. It is then up to the FISA Court to decide if the process complies with the Act. After this, the court will deliver an order either approving the process or commanding the government to propose a new process within one month or to stop any and all acquisitions. Uncle Sam has the option of appealing the decision to the FISA Court of Appeals and then to the U.S. Supreme Court.[333]

Each six months, the AG has the responsibility of informing the Intelli-gence and Judiciary Committees within the House and Senate regarding any acts of noncooperation with an an order released by either the AG or the DNI, any occurrences of noncooperation with FISA Court-approved meth-ods within the intelligence community, and the specific total of certifications and orders released issued within the reporting period. The changes made to FISA by the Act terminate after six months after ratification, with the excep-tion of any directive in progress on the day of ratification.[334]

Various scholars knowledgeble in national security disagree with regards to the extent the new statute should be construed or utilized. Some feel that due to the alterations in a number of words, the government might feel sanc-

331. Ibid.
332. Ibid.
333. Ibid.
334. See Michael Sussmann. "FISA Amended to Allow Acquisition of Cross-Border Communications Without a Court Order" (2007–08–06). Retrieved on 2008–02–10.

tioned to carry out searches without warrants, and might capture communications, as well as computer mechanisms and the information they hold. Moreover, the capturing of computer mechanisms belonging to American citizens while they are within their country worries some, but the government stated any searches and/or seizures would only occur due to the spying of individuals outside American jurisdiction. Intelligence pundits stated this was unlikely to occur, but Democratic members of congress were (are) nonetheless worried.[335]

On September 10, 2007, during a seminar on updating FISA for the twenty-first century, Kenneth L. Wainstein, Assistant Attorney General for National Security, stated that the present 180-day sunset proviso in the Protect America Act of 2007 concerning wider latitude surveillance powers for the government should be made permanent.[336] In addition, on September 10, Director of National Intelligence, Mike McConnell, stated under oath to the Senate Committee on Homeland Security and Governmental Affairs that the Protect America Act had already paid dividends as it helped thwart a major terrorist conspiracy that was taking place in Germany. Several individuals affiliated with the U.S. intelligence community had reservation regarding McConnell's statements and recommended he correct it, which he later did on September 12, 2007. Opponents alluded to the episode as a case in point of the Bush administration grossly exaggerating the facts while making incongrous assertions about surveillance actions. Individuals involved in counterterrorism stated that, in their opinion, McConell was not intentionally lying; rather, the amount of data was overpowering and he made a mistake and nothing else.[337]

While speaking at Fort Meade, Maryland on September 19, 2007, President Bush suggested that, in order to make America safe from terrorists, the Senate and the House should make the provisos of the Protect America Act permanent. He also stressed the importance of the freedom from civil liability for telecommunications providers that aided governmental surveillance effort.[338]

On October 4, 2007, David Keene, President of the American Conservative Union, and David D. Cole, a liberal law professor at Georgetown University, in their roles as chairs of the Liberty and Security Committee of the

---

335. See James Risen & Eric Lichtblau. "Concerns Raised on Wider Spying Under New Law" (2007–08–19). *The New York Times*. Retrieved on 2008–02–04.
336. See Ryan Singel. "Government Promises to Self-Audit Spying to Make Powers Permanent" (2007–09–11). *Wired News*. Retrieved on 2008–05–09.
337. See Michael Isikoff & Mark Hosenball. "Spy Master Admits Error" (2007–09–12). *Newsweek*. Retrieved on 2008–01–20.
338. See Anne Broache. "President Bush rallies for immortal spy law changes, telco protection" (2007–09–12). *CNET News.com*. Retrieved on 2008–02–26.

Constitution Project, released the "Statement on the Protect America Act."[339] The Statement advised Congress that reauthorizing the Protect America Act was a mistake and that the language contained therein went against the wishes of the Founding Fathers and had the potential to put democracy at risk.[340]

One group, on scientific grounds, wrote that putting the Protect America Act into practice could weaken security, not strengthen it. In the January/February 2008 issue of *Institute of Electrical and Electronics Engineers Journal of Security and Privacy,* technology professionals found several, noteworthy mitakes regarding the technical implementation of the Act. They stated that implementing the Act would likely have grave consequences, primariy that the surveillance organization could be used by hackers, criminally mistreated by individuals with security clearance, and/or exploited by individuals working within government.[341]

The Washington Post wrote that Democratic Representatives in the House planned on introducing legislation that would offer a 12-month period of "umbrella" warrants, and would mandate that the Justice Department Inspector General to review the utilization of the warrants and release quarterly commentary to be submitted to an exclusive FISA court, as well as the House and Senate. This bill would not contain protection for communications providers faced with civil suits in conjunction with the Bush administration's National Security Agency warrantless surveillance agenda. House Democrats reported that if the Bush Administration continued to deny requests for information accounting for the Protect America Act, then the issue of blanket immunity for communications providers was off the table.[342] Shortly thereafter, President Bush stated he would sign no bill that did not offer retroactive immunity for communications suppliers.[343]

In order to avoid having a similar, Republican bill being heard before the entire House, the Democrats had a vote. During the same period, the Senate Intelligence Committee allegedly reached an agreement with President Bush on a dissimilar plan that would provide legal protection for telephone carri-

---

339. See "The Constitution Project: Statement on the Protect America Act. By the Constitution Project's Liberty and Security Committee." 2004–10–07. Retrieved on 2008–04–24.

340. Ibid.

341. See Steven M. Bellovin et al., "Risking Communications Security: Potential Hazards of the Protect America Act." *Institute of Electrical and Electronics Engineers Security and Privacy* (2008–02–05). Retrieved on 2008–02–05.

342. See Ellen Nakashima "Democrats to Offer New Surveillance Rules," *The Washington Post* (2007–10–07). Retrieved on 2008–02–23.

343. See David Stout. "Bush Presses Congress on New Eavesdropping Law" (2007–10–10). *The New York Times.* Retrieved on 2007–12–20.

ers against civil suits for their part in the NSA's domestic eavesdropping program.[344]

Voting along party lines, the Senate Judiciary Committee voted 10-9 to send a different bill to the full Senate rather than debate on the one written by the intelligence committee with the imprimatur of the White House. The full Senate would decide whether or not retroactive, blanket immunity would apply to any communications suppliers that helped the National Security Agency. Senator Leahy of Vermont, chair of the Judiciary Committee, stated that giving immunity was akin to giving the President a "blank check" to do whatever he wanted. Senator Arlen Specter of Pennsylvania, the ranking Republican on the committee, stated that it was possible that only through going to court would Congress ever know the extent of domestic eavesdropping within the U.S.[345]

It was a busy day for Congress because the House of Representatives voted 227–189 to endorse a Democratic proposal that would increase court oversight of government spying inside the U.S., but rejected blanket immunity to any communications companies. While House Judiciary Committee chairman John Conyers (D-MI) did not automatically rule out immunity for providers in the future, he stated that the President had to hand over classified data detailing what the communications providers did that would have them seeking legal immunity.[346]

During February, 2008, the Senate accepted the new FISA permitting full immunity to telecommunications suppliers. On March 13, 2008, House convened a secret session to thrash out interrelated data. The next day, the House voted 213–197 to support a proposal that did not allow telecommunications immunity from civil suits. While the figure was impressive, it was nonetheless not enough to countermand a Presidential veto.[347]

---

344. See Eric Lichtblau (2007–10–18). "Senate Deal on Immunity for Phone Companies," *The New York Times*. Retrieved on 2008–10–18.

345. Pamela Hess. "Congress Takes Up Terrorist Surveillance" (2007–11–15). *Associated Press*. Retrieved on 2008–01–05.

346. See Pamela Hess. "House OKs Surveillance Oversight Bill" (2007–11–15). *Associated Press*. Retrieved on 2008–01–02.

347. See Jonathan Weisman. "House Passes a Surveillance Bill Not to Bush's Liking" (2008–03–15). *The Washington Post*. Retrieved on 2008–06–06.

Chapter 3

PSYCHOLOGICAL UNDERPINNINGS

The Patriot Act changed the way terrorism is defined within the U.S.[348] In Title IV, under subtitle B, a variety of different meanings regarding terrorism can be found. The Immigration and Nationality Act was retroactively altered to keep out foreigners who represent any group supporting terrorism from coming to America. In addition, family members of terrorist supporters are prohibited from visiting the U.S.[349] The meaning of "terrorist activity" was widened to incorporate acts entailing the utilization of any unsafe apparatus, i.e., more than bombs or guns.[350] The Patriot Act states that engaging in terrorist acts may be understood as perpetrating, developing, and/or arranging to take part in a terrorist act. Integrated into this specific meaning is the covert collection of intelligence data on likely terrorist marks, requesting money for a terrorist group, or asking others to engage in terrorist acts.

Any individual who knowingly provides aid to someone planning to carry out terrorist acts is considered engaging in a terrorist act. This consists of giving significant aid such as providing a haven for rest, providing for transportation, communications, money, the transfer of money or any substantial monetary help, bogus documents or IDs, weapons (which includes biological and chemical devices), bombs, or helping in the preparation for the execution of a terrorist act.[351] The INA standards for deciding whether to label a group or organization as terrorist was altered to contain the meaning of a terrorist act.[352] However, this will not include individuals who were members of

---

348. See USA PATRIOT Act (U.S. H.R. 3162, Public Law 107-56), Title IV, Subtitle B, Sec. 411.
349. Ibid.
350. Ibid.
351. Ibid.
352. As detailed in section 140(d)(2) of the *Foreign Relations Authorization Act,* Fiscal Years 1988 and 1989; see 22 U.S.C. § 2656f(d)(2).

a group, but left before it was assigned terrorist status, as determined under 8 U.S.C. § 1189 by the Secretary of State.

FEAR OF DOMESTIC TERRORISM

The FBI gives the following definition for domestic terrorism: "Domestic Terrorism is the unlawful use, or threatened use, of force or violence by a group or individual based and operating entirely within the United States or its territories without foreign direction committed against persons or property to intimidate or coerce a government, the civilian population, or any segment thereof, in furtherance of political or social objectives."[353]

The legal meaning for domestic terrorism within American borders has changed a number of times over the years; moreover, a historian or political scientist could make the argument that America was established by terrorist actions long before al-Qaeda made terrorism a watch word in the media.[354]

> The legal meaning for domestic terrorism within American borders has changed a number of times over the years; moreover, a historian or political scientist could make the argument that America was established by terrorist actions long before al-Qaeda made terrorism a watch word in the media.

According to the U.S. Code of Federal Regulations, "the unlawful use of force or violence, committed by a group(s) of two or more individuals, against persons or property to intimidate or coerce a government, the civilian population, or any segment thereof, in furtherance of political or social objectives."[355] The U.S. Department of Defense states that terrorism is the "calculated use of unlawful violence to inculcate fear; intended to coerce or intimidate governments or societies in pursuit of goals that are generally political, religious, or ideological."[356] The U.S. Congress described a terrorist act as one that was: "premeditated; perpetrated by a subnational or clandestine agent; politically motivated, potentially including religious, philosophi-

---

353. FBI. "Terrorism." http://denver.fbi.gov/nfip.htm Retrieved on 2008–01–08.
354. Amy Zalman. "1773: Boston Tea Party: Terrorism in the United States." Retrieved on 2008–01–03. http://terrorism.about.com/od/originshistory/p/boston_teaparty.htm.
355. See 28 C.F.R. Section 0.85.
356. See FM 100-20, *Military Operations in Low Intensity Conflict*, 5 December 1990; and Joint Pub 1-02, Department of Defense Dictionary of Military and Associated Terms, 12 April 2001, as amended through 9 June 2004.

cal, or culturally symbolic motivations; violent; and perpetrated against a noncombatant target."[357]

For most of our history, America felt that "terrorism" was something that occurred outside American borders; however, this belief changed on April 19, 1995, the day Timothy McVeigh committed a terrorist attack against the U.S. at the Alfred P. Murrah Federal Building, located in downtown Oklahoma City, Oklahoma. The attack killed 168 people, and injured more than 800. Until 9/11, it was the single, deadliest act of terrorism ever seen in the United States.

Immediately following the bombing, Oklahoma State Trooper Charlie Hanger pulled 26-year-old Timothy McVeigh over for operating a motor vehicle without a proper license plate and unlawfully carrying a weapon.[358] Shortly after the bombing, both Timothy McVeigh and Terry Nichols were apprehended for their part in the Oklahoma tragedy. Law enforcement stated that the two were adherents of a militia group and that the bombing was predicated on "getting back" at the federal government because of what transpired at Waco and Ruby Ridge.[359] McVeigh's life ended due to lethal injection on June 11, 2001, whereas Nichols will spend the remainder of life incarcerated in a federal prison. A third individual, Michael Fortier, who presented evidence against McVeigh and Nichols, received a sentence of 12 years for not warning the federal government. Similar to other large-scale terrorist attacks, armchair conspiracy theorists argued that the real truth is hidden and will remain so due to the machinations of an evil American government.[360]

The bombing led to extensive rescue attempts from many different local agencies, as well as generous aid from individuals scattered across the land. Due to complete decimation of the Alfred P. Murrah Federal Building, the federal government enacted laws calculated to boost security around federal buildings and to foil any potential terrorism. Due to this legislation, law enforcement agencies prevented more than 60 domestic terrorist attacks.[361]

As detailed in the Patriot Act, acts of domestic terrorism are those which: "(A) involve acts dangerous to human life that are a violation of the criminal laws of the United States or of any State; (B) appear to be intended–(i) to intimidate or coerce a civilian population; (ii) to influence the policy of a government by intimidation or coercion; or (iii) to affect the conduct of a gov-

---

357. *Terrorism Act 2000.* Office of Public Sector Information. Retrieved on 2007–12–28.
358. Ted Ottley (2005–04–14). License Tag Snag.
359. Nicole Nichols. "Domestic Terrorism 101: Timothy James McVeigh (The Boy Next Door). http://www.eyeonhate.com/mcveigh/mcveigh6.html Retrieved on 2008–06–29.
360. See "WhatReallyHappened.com." *The Oklahoma City Bombing.* Retrieved on 2008–06–14.
361. See Tim Talley. "Experts fear Oklahoma City bombing lessons forgotten." *The San Diego Union-Tribune* (2006–04–17). Retrieved on 2007–12–20.

ernment by mass destruction, assassination, or kidnapping; and (C) occur primarily within the territorial jurisdiction of the United States."[362]

Americans realize that one primary tool used by terrorists is psychological warfare, intended to create fright among the populace. Thus far, terrorists have succeeded: most Americans feel the country will face a terrorist attack at some point in the future.

PSYCHOLOGICAL RESPONSE TO TERRORISM

Americans realize that one primary tool used by terrorists is psychological warfare, intended to create fright among the populace. Thus far, they have succeeded: most Americans feel the country will face a terrorist attack at some point in the future.[363] In addition, Americans admit knowing that the deliberate character of terrorists and not knowing what the future holds is one reason for their fear.[364] Americans, though new to terrorism (unlike Israel or Great Britain), realize that terrorists win when one's fear becomes so great that he/she refuses to function in daily activities. For example, a man becomes worried that it is dangerous for his son to join a little league baseball team because the coach is of Arabic heritage. A mother refuses to allow her daughter to join Girl Scouts because some of the other girls' parents are originally from Middle Eastern countries like Syria or Iran that strongly support terrorism.

Herewith are statistics gathered by the National Mental Health Association:

Three out of four Americans (75%) feel that generating terror and misery with the "common man and woman" is a crucial aim for terrorists. In general, almost all Americans (93%) concur—69% robustly—with the proclamation, *the primary goal of a terrorist attack is to generate fear and distress.*[365]

Nine out of ten Americans (87%) concur—55% vigorously—with the proclamation, *terrorism is psychological in nature because it is meant to cause psychological suffering.*[366]

Almost nine of ten Americans (88%) concur—44% strongly—with the be-

---

362. Public Law 107-56—Oct. 26, 2001.
363. "Public Perspectives on the on the Mental Health Effects of Terrorism: A National Poll." National Association of State Mental Health and Program Directors, the National Mental Health Association and the Consortium for Risk and Crisis Communications (2003–December).
364. Ibid.
365. Ibid.
366. Ibid.

lief, *the threat of terrorism, in and of itself, creates public fear and distress.*[367]

In addition, most Americans (85%) feel that at some point in the future, the U.S. will experience another terrorist attack. Sixty-two percent state that the attack will occur within the next 12 months.[368]

American citizens stated that individuals undergo more pain and suffering regarding terrorism (61%) than they would if they were part of a natural disaster (33%). The rationale for such fear is:[369]

1. Terrorism is intentional and caused by people (89%);
2. Terrorism is fear of the unknown (84%);
3. People can't comprehend the motivations behind terrorism (69%); and
4. There isn't information available about how to cope with terrorism (53%).

On average, women worried more about terrorist acts than did men (77% of women compared to 62% of men). Women are more likely to exhibit apprehension about close relatives being victims of terrorist attacks than do men (57% compared to 43%). Almost two of every three parents (65%) fret that a family member will suffer fright and agony regarding the possible danger of terrorist acts.[370]

Americans state that "fear of the unknown" is the primary source of fear concerning terrorism. Where they were forced to make a choice, 39 percent of Americans chose fear of the unknown as their largest concern, with the conviction that the U.S. government is wholly ill prepared to handle the threat (21%) with confidence that a future terrorist act will occur close to one's home (18%).[371]

Because of this fear regarding future terrorist acts, 55 percent of Americans state their behavior has changed. Thirty-five percent of Americans said they worry much more about their family's safety. In addition, roughly 1 in 5 Americans state their daily lives were altered in other areas too: 22 percent state they were more apprehensive about strangers; 20 percent stated they tried to avoid traveling; 19 percent said they were vigilant and since 9/11 startled easily.[372]

Table 3.1 below indicates that, on average, women are likelier to have undergone changes in behavior due to the risk of terrorism. In general, females were almost twice as apt to be overprotective regarding their safety

---

367. Ibid.
368. Ibid.
369. Ibid.
370. Ibid.
371. Ibid.
372. Ibid.

and that of their family (46% versus 25%), to reveal uneasiness around indi-viduals thought to be "different" (28% versus 15%), to shun traveling (26% versus 14%) and to frighten easily (25% versus 13%).[373]

- Parents are also likelier than the "regular" American adult to have al-tered their activities due to the belief(s) regarding terrorist hazards.

Table 3.1.

Behaviors people have shown in response to the threat of terrorism	All (%)	Men (%)	Women (%)	Parents (%)
At least one behavior from the list below	55	43	66	63
Being more overprotective of you and your family's safety	35	25	46	52
Being nervous about people who are different	22	15	28	29
Avoiding traveling	20	14	26	24
Being increasingly alert at times and startling easily	19	13	25	22
Being emotionally upset more often for no apparent reason	8	6	9	11
Keeping purposeful busy to avoid thinking about the threat of terrorism	8	3	12	8
Having more problems getting to sleep or staying asleep	7	4	9	9

---

373. Ibid.

Regardless of where an American lives, he/she is likely scared about the threat of terrorism. Beliefs and feelings about terrorism vary to some extent by sex, age, income, and education. However, poll results unmistakably signify that almost all Americans fret about terrorism, believe the country will be attacked at some point, and deem it crucial for citizens to have contact to informational programs on the different ways of dealing with the mental blows that arise after a terrorist act.[374]

As Table 3.2 below illustrates, there are some interesting differences:

- Women (77%) are more likely than men to worry (62%), but both are uniformly likely to believe that the U.S. will be attacked in the near future.

- Younger Americans aged 18 to 34 (63%) worry less about terrorist acts do Americans aged 35 to 54 (74%) and seniors (71%) whereas senior citizens feel that an attack in the near future is unlikely (78% versus 91% and 83%).

- In contrast to lower- and higher-income Americans, middle-class American families, making somewhere between $35,000 and $60,000, per year, worry more about terrorism, are more apt to feel that a new terrorist attack is probable, and tend to think that it is more vital to have a means of accessing informational programs.

Table 3.2.

Demographics	Level of Concern about Terrorism (%)	Likelihood of Another Terrorist Attack Soon (%)	Important to Have Access to Programs (%)
All	69	85	87
Men	62	84	83
Women	77	84	92
Parents	68	91	89
Ages 18-34	63	78	89
Ages 35-54	74	91	88
Ages 55+	71	83	85
Income less than $35,000	69	80	82
Income $35,000-$59,999	73	95	93
Income more than $60,000	67	87	90
No college degree	70	83	88
College degree	67	87	87

374. Ibid.

The survey asked the same individuals from a study conducted six months earlier, right after 9/11. The results indicated that the same preponderant proportion of Americans that stated they would willingly give up basic civil liberties for more security immediately after the 9/11 attacks were willing to do so six months later. An astounding 70 percent of the individuals polled experience little concern giving up personal freedom, if they are guaranteed safety from terrorists. In essence, this means that for every ten people you see on the street, seven are more than happy to give up personal freedom.[375]

After the initial fright of having terrorists use American airliners to destroy the World Trade Center had eased, most Americans grew angry. American citizens found it hard to fathom why anyone would fly a jet into two buildings, killing one's self, in addition to hundreds more. Most people thought two things: (1) the attacks were an act of war and (2) the terrorists were cowards since the people who lost their lives were civilians, not soldiers in the military. Many felt despoiled, similar to a rape victim after being sexually assaulted by a nameless assailant. Accordingly, Americans wanted to find the individuals behind the attacks, despite how long it might take, to make sure that nothing like 9/11 ever happened again; thus, many Americans felt that giving up a measure of personal freedom was OK, if they gained more security in the bargain.[376]

Columnist Llewellyn H. Rockwell, Jr. President of the Ludwig Von Mises Institution in Auburn, Alabama wrote: "Freedom is the source of our security. The institutions of freedom are necessary in times of peace and prosperity, but more so in war, just as the first amendment needs defending more against unpopular than popular speech."[377] Undeniably, the attacks increased our alertness of the vulnerability of America, and this fear pushed politicians to do something to "get back" at terrorists. The late, great columnist William F. Buckley, Jr. wrote, "What ripened in the aftermath of Sept. 11 was a sensibility of the individual citizen's dependence . . . on his own resources."[378]

In a poll taken in June, 2002 by the Colonial Williamsburg Foundation, 1,000 American citizens throughout the country were asked if they were willing to give up civil liberties for national security. Herewith follows is a snippet of the report:

> One outcome of the September 11 tragedies may be the end-at least temporarily-of the self-centered American. Twice as many Americans–60 percent–

375. Ibid.

376. James J. Fotis (2004). *Actions speak louder than words.* Law Enforcement Alliance of America. Retrieved on 2008–05–09.

377. Llewellyn H. Rockwell, Jr. "The Attack and its Aftermath." *The Free Market(19),* 12 (2001–12–19). Retrieved on 2008–01–19.

378. William F. Buckley, Jr. Exit Gun Control. *The National Review* (2002–05–20).

said "fundamental responsibility to society and the role you play as a citizen of this country" is more important than "fundamental freedom as an individual and the ability to do whatever you want," which was endorsed by only 30 percent of respondents.

The survey also examined a number of principles on which the United States has been built. Of six principles surveyed, participants chose freedom of speech as the most important for society as a whole, and second most important to themselves and their families.

Beyond freedom of speech, however, respondents were divided in defining how basic Constitutional freedoms can and should be pursued in a post-September 11 climate. For example, 49 percent agreed with the statement "We are living in dangerous times. If we need to relinquish some of our personal freedoms and privacies to protect our country, we should all be prepared to do that." A total 41 percent supported the statement "Even though we are living in dangerous times, Americans should not be forced to give up personal freedoms."

Similarly, 53 percent agreed that the FBI should be allowed greater monitoring powers, while 43 percent did not. "Our Founding Fathers couldn't have anticipated the FBI or massive terror assaults with airplanes....Nevertheless..., it's remarkable how the issues of 225 years ago continue to shape our public dialogue. The debate over the rights of the individual, radical for its time in the 18th century preoccupies us to this day."[379]

Herewith following is information regarding the average American's views concerning civil rights vs. national security.

As is usually the case, people's opinions regarding civil liberties depends upon external factors. Fifty-one months after 9/11, in December, 2005, President Bush defended a secret domestic electronic surveillance program that included the wiretapping of telephone calls and e-mails of Americans suspected of having terrorist ties. The president's statements were given as a comeback to reports stating that, beginning in 2002, Bush gave the go-ahead to the National Security Agency (NSA) to activate the program, with no one overseeing anything.[380]

On May 11, 2006 a *Gallup/USA Today* poll reported that the NSA program included a database with tens of millions of phone call records.[381] In an earlier statement, President Bush defended the activities, saying, "We're not mining or trolling through the personal lives of millions of innocent Americans. Our efforts are focused on links to al-Qaeda and their known affiliates.

---

379. Tim Andrews. *"Half of Americans are willing to give up personal freedoms guaranteed by the Constitution to protect country, study finds."* Colonial Williamsburg (2002–06–28).

380. Americans ponder censure, impeachment for Bush (2006–05–19). *Angus Reid Global Monitor: Polls and Research.* Retrieved on 2008–02–20.

381. Most Americans decry NSA Surveillance (2006–5–17). *Gallup/USA Today.*

So far we've been very successful in preventing another attack on our soil."[382]

Eight-hundred and nine American adults were polled regarding their opinion. The polls indicated that:

"Based on what you have heard or read about the program to collect phone records, would you say you approve or disapprove of this government program?"[383]

Approve   43%
Disapprove   51%
No opinion   6%

In July, 2006, 1,000 American adults throughout the U.S. felt that detailed measures had to be used when dealing with individuals accused of terrorism, according to a poll by Harris Interactive. Seventy percent of those polled backed the utilization of extended camera surveillance, while 62 percent would give permission to law enforcement personnel to monitor Internet chats.[384]

Moreover, 61 percent of those polled would agree for closer surveillance of banking services (credit card transactions, how often money is deposited to one's account, etc.) in order to determine where the money is coming from, and 52 percent would allow the government to monitor cell phones, as well e-mails. While these acts are supported by most American citizens, the majority feel that the president should seek and gain approval from Congress before initiating such programs.[385]

POLLING DATA

Herewith following are the some of the questions asked:

"Here are some increased powers of investigation that law enforcement agencies might use when dealing with people suspected of terrorist activity, which would also affect our civil liberties. For each, please say if you would favor or oppose it."[386]

---

382. President George W. Bush. "President Bush discusses NSA Surveillance Program." The White House (2006–05–11). Retrieved on 2006–02–20.
383. Ibid.
384. "Americans Consider Powers of Investigation" (2006–08–19). *Angus Reid Global Monitor: Polls & Research.* Retrieved on 2008–04–20.
385 Ibid.
386. Ibid.

	Favor	*Oppose*
Expanded camera surveillance on streets and in public places	70%	28%
Law enforcement monitoring of Internet discussions in chat rooms and other forums	62%	34%
Closer monitoring of banking and credit card transactions, to trace funding sources	61%	37%
Expanded government monitoring of cell phones and email, to intercept communications	52%	46%

"Now, regardless of whether you favour or oppose each of the following powers of investigation, do you think this use of investigative powers by the president should be done under his executive authority without needing congressional authorization, or should this use of investigative power by the president be done only with congressional authorization?"[387]

	Without	*With*
Collecting from telephone companies the records of telephone calls made either in the U.S. or to the U.S. by people suspected of al-Qaeda or terrorist activities	38%	59%
Monitoring of cell phones and e-mail to intercept the content of communications of people suspected of terrorist activity	35%	62%
Monitoring of international financial transactions to trace terrorist funding sources	35%	63%
Monitoring of the content of Internet discussions in chat rooms and other forums	31%	66%

In a poll taken in 2006, 1,479 American adults showed differences of opinion regarding the correct method for fighting terrorism, as well as whether

---

387. Ibid.

the war on terror should affect their daily lives. Forty-eight percent of those polled felt that, as Americans, they should be ready to relegate civil liberties for the U.S. to be safe; however, 44 percent disagreed.[388] In December, it became publicly known that President Bush U.S. ordered the wiretapping of telephones, as well as emails of individuals thought to have links with terrorists. He defended the actions, and said that only people thought to be connected to terrorism were affected. Forty-nine percent of respondents think this practice is acceptable, while 48 percent deem it unacceptable.[389]

Herewith following is the poll:

"Which of the following statements comes closer to your view?–"Americans should be willing to give up some of their civil liberties so the government can keep the country safe from terrorism" or "Americans should not be willing to allow the government to take away their civil liberties in the name of keeping the country safe from terrorism."

Give up civil liberties for safety	48%
Not allow civil liberties to be taken away	44%
Don't know	8%

"As you may know, George W. Bush authorized federal government agencies to use electronic surveillance to monitor phone calls and emails within the United States without first getting a court warrant to do so. Do you consider this an acceptable, or unacceptable way for the federal government to investigate terrorism?"

Acceptable	49%
Unacceptable	48%
Don't know	3%

"As you may know, it was recently revealed that the U.S. government has been monitoring international money transfers, including those originating in the United States. The Bush administration says that the program helps in tracking the movements of terrorists. Critics say it could violate the privacy rights of innocent citizens. Do you consider this to be an acceptable, or unacceptable, way for the government to investigate terrorism?"

Acceptable	65%
Unacceptable	30%
Don't know	5%

---

388. "US divided on Civil Liberties and Terrorism" (2006–08–07). *Angus Reid Global Monitor: Polls and Research.* Retrieved on 2008–02–24.
389. Ibid.

A poll administered in February 2004 showed this:[390]

According to a Feb. 16-17 CNN/*USA Today*/Gallup poll, only one-quarter of Americans (26%) believed that the Patriot Act went too far in restricting people's civil liberties in order to fight terrorism. Nearly as many (21%) think it does not go far enough, while the plurality (43%) believes it is about right. That represents a more than two-to-one balance of opinion against the idea that the act goes too far. Public reaction has changed little since first measured.

Based on what you have read or heard, do you think the Patriot Act goes too far, is about right, or does not go far enough in restricting people's civil liberties in order to fight terrorism?[391]

In response, few Americans had "a great deal" of confidence in either Attorney General Ashcroft or the ACLU to balance the need to protect Americans from terrorist attacks with the need to protect basic civil liberties for Americans. But factoring in the percentage who have "a moderate amount" of confidence, Ashcroft receives higher confidence levels than the ACLU does, 57% to 43%.[392]

The one thing each poll showed was that Americans are not united on the issue of how to fight terrorism. While many adults do not seem to mind giving up civil liberties, there are almost as many who claim that giving up any of their rights as American citizens is anathema. One thing is certain: disagreement will continue regarding these issues.

LEGISLATIVE ACTS SIMILAR
IN SCOPE TO THE PATRIOT ACT

Many Americans unfamiliar with their history think that the Patriot Act was the first time our elected leaders in Washington devised statutes that deprived citizens of their civil liberties. This is far from the truth, and we now look at several acts that did just that.

Alien and Sedition Acts

In 1798, the Federalist Congress, under the tutelage of second President John Adams, passed four bills with the intent (so said its proponents) of protecting the United States from the depredations of foreigners working to libel and sow sedition in the United States. At that time, America was fighting an

---

390. Lydia Saad (2004–03–02). Americans generally comfortable with Patriot Act: Few believe it goes too far in restricting civil liberties. *Gallup.* Retrieved on 2007–12–20.
391. Ibid
392. Ibid.

undeclared war with France and that was the ostensible reason for the acts. However, then and now, the acts were considered unconstitutional and were intended to choke public disapproval of the Adams Administration, as well as violate the rights of individual states. The acts grew to become a key political topic in the 1798 and 1800 elections. One act—the Alien Enemies Act—is still law in the U.S. today and in times of war has been used extensively. The others died out or were rescinded by 1802. President Thomas Jefferson thought all were illegal and invalid, and thus, pardoned and ordered the discharge of each individual found guilty of disobeying them.

The first act, entitled the Alien Enemies Law, gave the Commander-in-Chief an amazing array of powers during wartime. Without Congressional approval, the President could arrest and/or deport citizens of nations with which America was fighting for acting in a suspicious manner. Technically speaking, the U.S. was not at war during the years the bill was extant; thus, Adams was unable to use it during his sojourn in the White House. A second act, the Alien Law, sanctioned the President to oust any alien from the country, simply by decreeing it. The third act, and the most partisan, the Naturalization Law, doubled the seven-year probationary period to 14 years during which time foreigners did not have the constitutional rights of an American citizen. The Sedition Law made it a criminal offense to voice one's disapproval of the government.

Jefferson felt the Sedition Act was phony and a contravention of the First Amendment, which guaranteed each American citizen the right of free speech. The infringement upon the First Amendment, however, was not the primary thrust of his dispute; rather, he centered on the violations of the Tenth Amendment, which reads: "The powers not delegated to the United States by the Constitution, nor prohibited by it to the States, are reserved to the States respectively, or to the people."[393] The Alien and Sedition Acts became law in 1798 and at that point in our history, First Amendment rights did not confine the states, as they do today. In Jefferson's opinion, Washington had disregarded the Constitution as the Alien and Sedition Acts allowed the implementation of undelegated powers. With the exceptions of Virginia (Jefferson's home state) and Kentucky, every other state in the Union was Federalist, and quickly undercut Jefferson's stance by decrees that either sustained the acts, or argued that neither Virginia nor Kentucky had the authority to denounce them.[394]

---

393. See United States Constitution: Tenth Amendment.
394. See http://www.constitution.org/rf/vr_04.htm. A website that specifies what each state had to say.

While not part of Jefferson's arguments, the Acts circumvented the Bill of Rights in an additional manner; the Alien Enemies Law differed with the Sixth Amendment, which reads:

> In all criminal prosecutions, the accused shall enjoy the right to a speedy and public trial, by an impartial jury of the State and district wherein the crime shall have been committed, which district shall have been previously ascertained by law, and to be informed of the nature and cause of the accusation; to be confronted with the witnesses against him; to have compulsory process for obtaining witnesses in his favor, and to have the assistance of Counsel for his defence.[395]

The Sixth Amendment secures seven rights for each American citizen, and the Alien Enemies Law prohibited all but one. During war, any individual charged with suspicious behavior, especially if he/she is originally from the country with which America is fighting, does have assurance of either a speedy or public trial. In addition, he/she would not be given an impartial jury of his/her peers, would not be able to confront his/her accusers, would not receive due process for attaining witnesses, nor legal counsel for a defense. This law gave President Adams the authority to remove political dissidents as he saw fit.

Adams, in no way, signed any of the deportation directives. Even so, his underlings organized a directory of foreigners for deportation, though many aliens escaped out of the country before being arrested. Twenty-five people, mainly important newspaper writers, but also Congressman Matthew Lyon, were arrested. Of these 25, 11 were tried, while 10 were eventually convicted of sedition in trials facing patently partisan Federalist judges. With time, however, the Acts cost Federalists their stranglehold on power. Federalists lost their jobs and, in the successive years, Congress frequently expressed regret for its actions and voted for remuneration to be given to the victims. Thomas Jefferson, the Sage of Monticello, won the 1800 election (in a close race with Aaron Burr) and pardoned all of those who were convicted for crimes under the Alien Enemies Act and the Sedition Act.

Judicial Review, the principle in which the U.S. Supreme Court rules on the constitutionality of Congressional legislation, was not created until 1803 with the seminal case, *Marbury v. Madison*. In 1798, the Supreme Court was heavily Federalist in nature and was candidly antagonistic to the Federalists' rivals. Thus, the Supreme Court did not review the constitutionality, though at that time, individual Supreme Court Justices, who were also "riding the

---

395. See United States Constitution: Sixth Amendment.

circuit," sat as judges in various circuit courts and heard many of the cases arraigning foes of the Federalists.

Both Jefferson and Madison wanted the utter unconstitutionality of the Acts to be addressed, which was impossible due to Federalist power. They felt that by taking their case to the American people, the constitutional violations would be resolved. In an effort to achieve their goals, they composed the Kentucky and Virginia Resolutions, which emphasized that the states should invalidate the federal legislation. These resolutions mirrored what was known as the Compact Theory, which stated that the U.S. was a union of sovereign States that consented to yield some of their rightful power in order to join the union; however, joining the union did not mean the states forfeited their sovereign power.[396] Hence, under the auspices of the Compact Theory, each individual state can decide for itself whether the federal government has dishonored its contract, including the Constitution, and thus, nullify any such infringements, or they could secede from the Union, which is exactly what transpired in 1861 when the South seceded from the Union.

In 1801, the Sedition Act was to terminate, corresponding with the conclusion of the Adams administration. This termination barred its constitutionality from being determined by the Supreme Court, though later statements regarding the Sedition Act in Supreme Court opinions indicated that it would it be judged unconstitutional if ever heard by the Court.[397]

Habeas Corpus in the Civil War

Habeas corpus is a legal term meaning a person who has been jailed illegally can ask for relief from an illegal incarceration. The Constitution, in the Suspension Clause, purposely incorporated the English common law practice in Article One, Section 9 which reads: *The privilege of the writ of habeas corpus shall not be suspended, unless when in cases of rebellion or invasion the public safety may require it.*[398]

Federal statutes allow any person the right to petition for a writ of habeas corpus primarily if he/she is detained by federal law enforcement or for violations expressly stated in the Constitution. Writs of Habeas Corpus are usually disputed as ex parte cases, which may be defined as one side of the case being absent. Individuals may also petition their home state for a writ of habeas corpus, depending upon their respective state constitutions and statutes.

---

396. For an excellent review, see Ronald M. Peters, Jr. (1978). *"The Massachusetts Constitution of 1780: A Social Compact."* University of Massachusetts Press: Amherst.

397. See *New York Times v. Sullivan.* The Court declared, "Although the Sedition Act was never tested in this Court, the attack upon its validity has carried the day in the court of history." 376 U.S. 254, 276 (1964).

398. See United States Constitution: Article 1, Section 9.

During the Civil War and Reconstruction period afterwards, as well as currently with our Global War on Terrorism, the vested right to petition for a writ of habeas corpus was significantly reduced for individuals charged with certain behavior.[399]

President Lincoln, in a move decried at that time, suspended habeas corpus on April 27, 1861, in Maryland, southern Indiana, and a number of other midwestern states. His reasons were simple: riots broke out, Lincoln did so in response to riots, neighborhood militias engaged in aggressive behavior, and the fear that Maryland, a border slave state that did not secede as did other slaveholder states, would leave the Union. Lincoln's military commanders also requested that instead of civilian courts, military courts should be appointed to judge "Copperheads" and/or "Peace Democrats," both of which were considered dangerous for the Union cause.

Even so, his actions were disputed in court and in Ex Parte Merryman, a case heard in Maryland, the court struck down Lincoln's suspension of Habeas Corpus17 F. Cas. 144 (C.C.D. Md. 1861). Lincoln disregarded the judicial command to reinstate Habeas Corpus. Lincoln's southern counterpart, President Jefferson Davis, also shelved habeas corpus as well as enforcing martial law. Jefferson felt he had no choice since the move was designed for two-fold purpose: (1) he wanted to maintain a semblance of order and (2) he hoped to stimulate industrial development in the South to recompense for the huge financial loss imposed upon the region due to its secession.

Approximately one week after Fort Sumter surrendered to the Confederates, Lincoln ordered General Winfield Scott, military commander of all Union forces during the beginning of the War, to apprehend any individual between Washington and Philadelphia who was potentially guilty of either seditious behavior or speech. In addition, Lincoln expressly sanctioned the suspension of the writ of *habeas corpus.* Scott relayed the order to his military commanders, with the result that droves of Southern sympathizers were arrested.

This act occurred at the very beginning of the War, when Lincoln needed soldiers to protect the nation's capitol, and when northern brigades were experiencing trouble going through Maryland which, though it had not seceded, still possessed Confederate attitudes and was openly antagonistic to the suggestion of having the Union army invade. Moreover, Maryland's legislature was set to convene, and Lincoln guessed it would likely move to hamper northern soldiers making their way through the state.

---

399. It should be noted, however, that on On June 12, 2008, the Supreme Court ruled in *Boumediene v. Bush* recognizing habeas corpus rights for Guantanamo prisoners. On October 7, 2008, the first Guantanamo prisoners were ordered released by a court considering a habeus corpus petition.

One of the southern sympathizers was John Merryman, a well-known Marylander from Baltimore. He was president of the Maryland State Agricultural Society and was a vocal critic of Lincoln and the northern interests; likewise, he was an ardent secessionist. Upon his arrest, his attorney immediately filed a petition to the state circuit court, which lay under Chief Justice Roger B. Taney, a man known to dislike Lincoln. Quickly, Taney heard the writ of *habeas corpus* and commanded the military officer holding Merryman to show "the cause, if any, for his arrest and detention."[400]

On May 27, 1861, the specific date appointed for the government to substantiate its incarceration of Merryman or let him go, Gen. George Cadwallader, the military officer in charge, told Taney that he declined to obey. Cadwallader stated he required extra time, as he needed to hear what his higher-ups wanted him to do. In addition, he said more was at stake than just Merryman's right to be heard–public safety was at risk as well.[401]

Taney, who was well-known for his democratic ideals (at least for whites) did not particularly like what Cadwallader said, so he issued a writ of attachment against Cadwallader, to be handed to him the next day. Taney felt he was liable to be imprisoned himself, which was the hope of many, including northern newspaper editor, Horace Greeley.

A U.S. marshal was sent to serve the writ, but was not allowed to enter the fort. Nonetheless, Taney decreed that Merryman should be released at once, censured the concept of capricious military arrests, while supporting the concept of civil liberties. In addition, he stated that only the U.S. Congress possessed the power to suspend habeas corpus; thus, the military had no constitutional right to incarcerate Merryman. Taney never stated he agreed with Merryman; rather, he focused on the President and that he did not exhibit, "a proper respect for the high office he fills. . . . He certainly does not faithfully execute the laws if he takes upon himself the legislative power, by suspending the writ of *habeas corpus,* and the judicial power also, by arresting and imprisoning a person without due process of law."[402]

During 1864, Lambin P. Milligan was sentenced to execution, due to planning the theft of Union weapons for the invasion of Union prison camps. Lambin's execution was scheduled for May, 1865, a lucky break as the war had ended. In the famous case, *Ex Parte Milligan* 71 U.S. 2 (1866), the U.S. Supreme Court ruled that the contravention of habeas corpus did not authorize Lincoln to judge and condemn civilians before military panels. They wrote that the only time it is permissible for the military to try civilians is when civilian courts have shut down. This case was significant in that its rul-

---

400. See Patrick S. Poole. (1994). *An Examination of Ex Parte Merryman.*
401. Ibid.
402. Ibid.

ing dealt with civil liberties during and martial law.

President Ulysses S. Grant, during the early 1870s, shelved habeas corpus in nine counties in the upper region of South Carolina, as it moved against the white supremacist group, the Ku Klux Klan, under the 1870 Force Act and 1871 Ku Klux Klan Act. More recently, on November 13, 2001, President George W. Bush issued the Presidential Military Order, giving him the authority to arrest any noncitizens alleged to have a connection to terrorists and/or terrorism as enemy combatants.[403] In this scenario, an individual could be detained for an indefinite period, without arraignment, without being heard before a judge, and without the right to an attorney. Many scholars assert that this goes against both the writ of habeas corpus, and the U.S. Bill of Rights.

The Patriot Act has brought habeas corpus to the forefront of American consciousness again. In *Hamdi v. Rumsfeld,* 542 U.S. 507 (2004), the U.S. Supreme Court affirmed that American citizens are entitled to habeas corpus, even if they are combatants for a terrorist country. In *Hamdan v. Rumsfeld,* 548 U.S. 557 (2006), Salim Ahmed Hamdan petitioned for a writ of habeas corpus, stating that the military tribunals established by President Bush to put on trial the individuals incarcerated at Guantanamo Bay violated both the Uniform Code of Military Justice and the four Geneva Conventions.

The Court disallowed Congressional efforts to remove from the Court its power over habeas corpus petitions by individuals imprisoned Guantánamo Bay, even though Congress had formerly approved the Department of Defense Appropriations Act, 2006 which stated in Section 1005(e), "Procedures for Status Review of Detaineed Outside the United States."

(1) Except as provided in section 1005 of the Detainee Treatment Act of 2005, no court, justice, or judge shall have jurisdiction to hear or consider an application for a writ of habeas corpus filed by or on behalf of an alien detained by the Department of Defense at Guantanamo Bay, Cuba.

(2) The jurisdiction of the United States Court of Appeals for the District of Columbia Circuit on any claims with respect to an alien under this paragraph shall be limited to the consideration of whether the status determination .. was consistent with the standards and procedures specified by the Secretary of Defense for Combatant Status Review Tribunals (including the requirement that the conclusion of the Tribunal be supported by a preponderance of the evidence and allowing a rebuttable presumption in favor of the Government's evidence), and to the extent the Constitution and laws of the United States are applicable, whether the use of such standards and procedures to make the determination is consistent with the Constitution and laws of the United States.

---

403. Cohen & Wells, *American National Security and Civil Liberties in an Era of Terrorism* (2004).

On September 29, 2006, Congress passed the Military Commissions Act (MCA) of 2006, which did away with the notion regarding habeas corpus for foreigners, primarily those felt to be an "unlawful enemy combatant engaged in hostilities or having supported hostilities against the United States" by a vote of 65–34.[404] This was the consequence regarding the bill to endorse military tribunals for prisoners; an effort to take away the deferment of habeas corpus failed 48–51.[405] The MCA became law on October 17, 2006.

Once the MPA passed, the law modified the words from "alien detained . . . at Guantanamo Bay":

> Except as provided in section 1005 of the Detainee Treatment Act of 2005, no court, justice, or judge shall have jurisdiction to hear or consider an application for a writ of habeas corpus filed by or on behalf of an alien detained by the United States who has been determined by the United States to have been properly detained as an enemy combatant or is awaiting such determination." §1005(e)(1), 119 Stat. 2742.[406]

MCA confines habeas appeals only for individuals incarcerated as enemy combatants, or those pending such a resolution. What stayed the same was the stipulation that, after such a resolution is made, it is subject matter for an appeal in U.S. Courts, comprising of an assessment regarding whether the facts deserve such a ruling. If the ruling is sustained, then their incarceration is judged legal; if not, the government has the right to alter the prisoner's status to something else, at which time the habeas corpus limitations are defunct.[407]

Lincoln had his detractors during the Civil War, as does Bush. The issue goes beyond whether the military should hear civilians since terrorists, as a general rule, are not components of a structured hierarchy, as are military soldiers. Terrorists do not wear uniforms indicating their allegiance, thus they primarily kill citizens, not soldiers. Moreover, they do not carry offensive weapons overtly as would a soldier defending his country. Finally, it is sim-

---

404. See Pub. L. No. 109-366, 120 Stat. 2600 (Oct. 17, 2006), enacting Chapter 47A of title 10 of the United States Code (as well as amending section 2241 of title 28).

405. See Rick Klein. "Senate's passage of detainee bill gives Bush a win: Democrats say Bush capitulated." *The Boston Globe* (2006-09-29). Retrieved on 2007-11-23.

406. Op. cit. *Boumediene v. Bush.*

407. The Supreme Court of the United States ruled in *Boumediene v. Bush* that the MCA constituted an unconstitutional encroachment of habeas corpus rights, and established jurisdiction for federal courts to hear petitions for habeas corpus from Guantanamo detainees tried under the Act. Additionally, a number of legal scholars and Congressional members–including Senate Judiciary Committee Ranking Member Arlen Specter (R-PA)–have said that the habeas provision of the Act violates a clause of the Constitution that says the right to challenge detention "shall not be suspended" except in cases of "rebellion or invasion.

ple to spot soldiers, while it is incredibly difficult (oftentimes impossible without adequate intelligence) to spot terrorists.

For the Geneva Conventions to be relevant, the captives must be associated with an enemy's armed forces or be a member of a recognized group that agrees to fight according to the rules of war. Terrorists in al-Qaeda wear no identifiable uniforms or emblems, nor do they fight like traditional soldiers.

In order to clear up the mess, the Pentagon released a number of rules and regulations to oversee military courts. Under Military Commission Order No. 1, issued in March 2002, the Secretary of Defense was given the authority to "issue orders from time to time appointing one or more military commissions to try individuals subject to the President's Military Order and appointing any other personnel necessary to facilitate such trials."[408]

The military tribunals instituted under President Bush will consist of various military staff acting as triers of both fact and law. During these inquiries, any type of proof or evidence may be submitted as long as, according to "reasonable person" standards, it has material value. Defendants are permitted to an assumption that he/she is innocent, and must be found guilty beyond a "reasonable doubt." Once someone is convicted, the President and Department of Defense have the authority to evaluate the sentence.

Critics of the Bush administration state that while it sounds good in theory, in practice it is unconstitutional. The *New York Times* released an editorial after the regulations had been instated and that, in spite of the reality that the proposal regarding military courts for possible terrorists is less disturbing than it was at its start up, "there is still no practical or legal justification for having the tribunals. The United States has a criminal justice system that is a model for the rest of the world. There is no reason to scrap it in these cases."[409]

During the Civil War, each defendant arrested and tried before a military tribunal was an American citizen; today, most likely defendants are foreigners. At the time this book is being written, Guantanamo Bay housed approximately 600 "enemy combatants." William J. Haynes II, General Counsel of the Department of Defense stated that, "an enemy combatant is an individual who, under the laws and customs of war, may be detained for the duration of an armed conflict."[410]

---

408. See Department of Defense, Military Commission Order No. 1, March 21, 2002.

409. Opinion-Editorial. "Refining Military Tribunals." *The New York Times* (2002–03–22). Retrieved on 2008–02–02.

410. See William J. Haynes II. "Enemy Combatants." Council on Foreign Relations, (2002–12–12). Retrieved on 2008–02–05. www.cfr.org/publication.php?id=5312.

Lawful and Unlawful Combatants

"Enemy combatant" is a term possessing two subcategories: lawful and unlawful combatants.[411] "Lawful combatants," according to Haynes, "receive prisoner of war (POW) status and the protections of the Third Geneva Convention. Unlawful combatants do not receive POW status and do not receive the full protections of the Third Geneva Convention."[412]

The United States takes the stance that, as unlawful combatants, individuals associated with al-Qaeda do not merit the safeguards found within the Geneva Convention. Most of the rules and regulations emanating from the Geneva accords are enjoyed by those incarcerated, which brings up an interesting question: What about the individuals imprisoned who are American citizens? Legal scholars disagree regarding whether an American citizen, held due to terrorist activity, should receive special treatment because of his/her citizenship. Pundits for separate treatment state that Americans should be given each protection within our justice system; i.e., right to legal counsel, right to a quick and speedy trial, etc. On the other hand, foreigners can be incarcerated according to customary practices applied to individuals captured during war.[413]

Japanese-American Internment

Due to this specific incident occurring in the memory of many people still alive, more time will be spent exploring the reasons and rationale for this period in American history. Japanese American Internment relates to the compulsory relocation and imprisonment of roughly 120,000[414] Japanese, Japanese Americans (62% of whom were United States citizens),[415] Chinese-Japanese Americans, Korean-Americans, and any other group racial and/or ethnic group thought to possess Japanese nationality during World War II. This includes Japanese-Hawaiians living on the U.S. mainland, as well as Japanese Latin Americans (or "Japanese Latinos") living on the West Coast, primarily in California. Approximately 110,000 men, women and children were forcibly moved to "War Relocation Centers" in remote areas of the

---

411. Ibid.
412. Ibid.
413. NPR (2008–03–25). "Court weighs rights of Americans arrested in Iraq." Retrieved on 2008–07–23.
414. Depending upon who you read, this figure alternates between 110,000 to 120,000.
415. See The War Relocation Authority and The Incarceration of Japanese Americans During World War II: 1948 Chronology," www.trumanlibrary.org, Retrieved on 2008–02–02.
416. Ibid.

country.[416] Any American citizen thought to have one-eighth Japanese was considered suitable for relocation.[417]

Shortly after the surprise attack on Pearl Harbor, President Franklin D. Roosevelt signed the directive entitled "Executive Order 9066," which gave authority to local military leaders to select "military areas" as "exclusion zones," from which "any or all persons may be excluded."[418] This influence was used to announce that all individuals with Japanese ancestry living anywhere along the Pacific coast, which included all of California and most Oregon and Washington; that is, all but those already incarcerated in the relocation camps.[419] The Supreme Court ruled against the civil libertarians and stated the constitutionality of the exclusion orders.[420] In addition, the Court noted that the requirements singling out individuals with Japanese ancestry was not an issue within the Court; rather, it lay beyond the Court's range for the case at hand.[421]

The Japanese held during this period were paid recompense for property losses in 1948; however, most never recovered the monetary loss associated with their removal to camps.[422] In one of his last acts as President, Ronald Reagan signed legislation apologizing for the forced removal of Japanese-Americans. The act affirmed that the U.S. government actions were wrong and that the internment was due to "race prejudice, war hysteria, and a failure of political leadership."[423] Approximately $1.6 billion dollars in compensation was paid out by the U.S. government to internees still alive and their progeny.

One outcome of Japan's sneak attack on Pearl Harbor was the belief that they planned to invade the West Coast of America. While this might sound farfetched today, for six years (1936 to 1942), Japan's military had conquered a huge portion of Asia and the Pacific islands. Many in the U.S. felt that the Japanese army was unstoppable, and both military and civilian politicos had anxieties regarding the fidelity of Japanese-Americans to the U.S. living on the West Coast. Many in Washington thought the Japanese were grave secu-

---

417. Ibid.
418. See Transcript of Executive Order 9066: Resulting in the Relocation of Japanese (1942). http://www.ourdocuments.gov/doc.php?flash=false&doc=74&page=transcript Retrieved on 2007–12–20.
419. See *Korematsu v. United States* dissent by Justice Owen Josephus Roberts, reproduced at findlaw.com Retrieved on 2008–02–04.
420. See *Korematsu v. United States* majority opinion by Justice Hugo Black, reproduced at findlaw.com, Retrieved on 2008–02–04.
421. Ibid.
422. Op. cit. War Relocation Authority.
423. See 100th Congress, S. 1009, reproduced at internmentarchives.com. Retrieved on 2008–03–21.

rity threats,[424] though this apprehension owed more to racism than anything else.

Lieutenant General John L. DeWitt, who led the Western Defense Command, accountable for the safety of the West Coast, and who managed the internment process, frequently voiced to the American media that "A Jap's a Jap." In testimony given to the U.S. Congress, he claimed, "I don't want any of them [persons of Japanese ancestry] here. They are a dangerous element. There is no way to determine their loyalty. . . . It makes no difference whether he is an American citizen, he is still a Japanese. American citizenship does not necessarily determine loyalty. . . . But we must worry about the Japanese all the time until he is wiped off the map."[425] DeWitt did not work alone. Major Karl Bendetsen was primarily to blame for the excessive military reaction.[426]

The government felt that orphaned babies with "one drop of Japanese blood" or any individual possessing one eighth Japanese heritage, or was a direct descendant of an intermarriage of the races lends credibility to the contention that the actions were racially inspired, and not a military prerequisite for safety.[427] Various political leaders also panicked at the idea of Japanese-Americans possibly committing terrorist acts against military and civilian structures located throughout the U.S. Military leaders voiced worries that violent acts aimed at California's water systems was likely, especially since they were extremely vulnerable; likewise, many worried that Japanese-Americans would set fires throughout California and thus, damaging the state.[428]

On February 19, 1942, Franklin D. Roosevelt signed Executive Order 9066, which permitted duly sanctioned military leaders to assign "military areas" as they wished, and indicated that any individual, as detailed by the commander, could be kept out, or "excluded." These "exclusion zones," dissimilar from the "alien enemy" arrests, were valid for any person the military might select, whether American citizen or not. Ultimately, these "zones" would comprise specific areas on both the East and West Coasts, amounting to approximately one third of the U.S. Unlike the ensuing incarceration and internment programs that pertained to huge numbers of Japanese Americans, imprisonment and various constraints under the "Individual Exclusion

---

424. See Michelle Malkin's, *In Defense of Internment: The Case for Racial Profiling.*
425. See Fred Mullen, "DeWitt Attitude on Japs Upsets Plans," *Watsonville Register-Pajaronian,* April 16, 1943. p.1, reproduced by Santa Cruz Public Library. Retrieved on 2008–06–06.
426. Klancy Clark de Nevers. *Colonel and The Pacifist.* 2004.
427. See United States Executive Order 9066.
428. Op. cit. Klancy Clark de Nevers.

Program" were placed mainly on anyone with either German or Italian ancestry, including American citizens.[429]

A timetable for the Japanese Internment follows:

1. On March 2, 1942, DeWitt released Public Proclamation No. 1, stating that anyone with Japanese ancestry would, at a time to be disclosed, faced exclusion commands from "Military Area No. 1." This "area" covered the length and breadth of the Pacific coast to approximately 100 miles (160.9 km) inland, and anyone with "enemy" lineage was ordered to report a Change of Residence Notice if they wanted to move to a new location.[430] A second exclusion zone was chosen a few months afterwards, which incorporated the areas selected by the majority of Japanese Americans that left the first zone.
2. On March 11, 1942, Roosevelt's Executive Order 9095 established the Office of the Alien Property Custodian, and gave it unrestricted and complete jurisdiction over all alien possessions. Material goods were frozen, producing instant monetary difficulties for the individuals deemed as aliens, prohibiting the majority from relocating away form the exclusion zones.[431]
3. On March 24, 1942, Public Proclamation No. 3 instituted an 8:00 p.m. to 6:00 a.m. curfew for "all enemy aliens and all persons of Japanese ancestry" within the military areas.[432]
4. On March 24, 1942, DeWitt issued Civilian Exclusion Orders for precise locations within "Military Area No. 1."[433]
5. On March 27, 1942, DeWitt issued Public Proclamation No. 4, which disallowed anyone with Japanese ancestors from exiting "Military Area No. 1" for "any purpose until and to the extent that a future proclamation or order of this headquarters shall so permit or direct."[434]
6. On May 3, 1942, DeWitt released Civilian Exclusion Order No. 346, commanding everyone with Japanese heritage, whether Americans or not, to register at assembly centers, which would be their home until they were transferred to permanent "Relocation Centers."[435]

Then and now, the internment of Japanese-Americans had its defenders. David Lowman, Former Special Assistant to the Director of the National

---

429. See *WWII Enemy Alien Control Overview* from archives.gov. Retrieved on 2008-04-29.
430. See *Korematsu v. United States* dissent by Justice Owen Josephus Roberts.
431. Ibid.
432. See *Hirabayashi v. United States*.
433. Ibid.
434. Op. cit. *Korematsu v. United States*.
435. Ibid.

Security Agency, wrote that the internment, while brutal, might have been militarily justified.[436] He stated that information gleaned from the MAGIC intercepts (MAGIC was the code name for intelligence gathered from the Japanese transmissions, called PURPLE), contained decrypted data from the Japanese government and military, some purportedly stating a desire to find Japanese-Americans that were willing to spy for their ancestral country.[437]

Today, many individuals still believe that while the internment was not wanted, it was nonetheless needed, especially since some Japanese-American citizens were treacherous, as evidenced by the roughly 20,000 Japanese-Americans in Japan when Pearl Harbor was bombed who chose to enlist in the Imperial Army.[438] A commonly used case in point is Tomoya Kawakita, a Japanese-American civilian who used his English language skills for the advancement of the Imperial Army in the Pacific. He served as an interpreter and a security guard at prison camps; furthermore, he tortured American servicemen.[439]

A man usually thought to be conservative, FBI Director J. Edgar Hoover was against the internment. He disagreed strenuously with DeWitt's characterization of Japanese-Americans as being treacherous. He complained of the internment to Attorney General Francis Biddle, stating that, "Every complaint in this regard has been investigated, but in no case has any information been obtained which would substantiate the allegation."[440]

---

436. See David Lowman, *"Magic: The Untold Story of U.S. Intelligence and the Evacuation of Japanese Residents from the West Coast during WWII."*
437. Ibid.
438. Ibid.
439. See *Kawakita v. United States,* 343 U.S. 717 (1952).
440. Ray Wannall. *Hoover for the Record.* Turner Publishing Co (2000).

Chapter 4

TITLES OF THE PATRIOT ACT

We now turn to a discussion of the Patriot Act, which consists of 10 Titles, named, aptly, Title I to Title X. We will examine each individual Title, as well as the sections comprising it.

USA PATRIOT Act Titles

Title I: Enhancing Domestic Security against Terrorism
Title II: Enhanced Surveillance Procedures
Title III: International Money Laundering Abatement and Anti-terrorist Financing Act of 2001
Title IV: Protecting the Border
Title V: Removing Obstacles to Investigating Terrorism
Title VI: Providing for Victims of Terrorism, Public Safety Officers and Their Families
Title VII: Increased Information Sharing for Critical Infrastructure Protection
Title VIII: Strengthening the Criminal Laws Against Terrorism
Title IX: Improved Intelligence
Title X: Miscellaneous

TITLE 1: ENHANCING DOMESTIC SECURITY AGAINST TERRORISM

Section 101. Counterterrorism Fund

Congressional legislation produced a "Counterterrorism Fund" to give recompense to the Department of Justice for the expenses of restarting the operational abilities lost as a result of the demolition of the Alfred P. Murrah

Federal Building in Oklahoma City, and for other counterterrorism costs.[441] Section 101 of the Patriot Act proceeds in a similar vein in order to compensate the DOJ for the expenses of (1) restarting the operational ability of buildings shattered or obliterated by terrorists; (2) thwarting, scrutinizing, and prosecuting terrorist acts by any legal means necessary, which includes the doling out of money as an incentive to help law enforcement; and (3) initiating all assessments necessary to determine the relative weakness of federal facilities to terrorist attacks. The Fund is also accessible for the reimbursement of federal agencies regarding the expenses connected with overseas incarceration of anyone blamed for terrorism in contravention of U.S. federal law.

Section 102. Sense of Congress Condemning Discrimination Against Arab and Muslim Americans

Congress, recognizing that the U.S. Constitution mandates the safeguarding of both civil rights and civil liberties of Arab-Americans, Muslim-Americans, and Americans from Southern Asia, should be shielded; thus, any brutality toward and/or prejudice against any American citizen should be reviled, at all costs. Moreover, the loyalty of all Americans, regardless of their ancestry and religious beliefs, should be recognized.

> Section 102 was written as a universal declaration confirming the reality that different racial and ethnic groups perform an essential part in the United States, and warrant full civil rights as any other American.

Section 102 was written as a universal declaration confirming the reality that different racial and ethnic groups perform an essential part in the United States, and warrant full civil rights as any other American. Additionally, this section also censured any deeds of hostility against these groups that might have taken place after 9/11, and indicated that the accountability for 9/11 rested entirely with the individuals that committed them, not racial or ethnic groups.

The section also stated that "Muslim Americans have become so fearful of harassment that many Muslim women are changing the way they dress to avoid becoming targets" and that "many Arab Americans and Muslim Americans have acted heroically during the attacks on the United States." Mohammed Salman Hamdani, a 23-year-old Pakistani-American who lost

---

441. See Public Law 104–19, 109 Stat. 249 (1995).

his life while trying to rescue others after the World Trade Center was attacked, was cited as an example.

Section 103. Increased Funding for the Technical Support Center at the Federal Bureau of Investigation

This section authorized the expenditure of $200 million for each of the fiscal years 2002, 2003, and 2004 for the Technical Support Center, and FBI organization established in section 811 of the Antiterrorism and Effective Death Penalty Act of 1996.[442]

Section 104. Requests for Military Assistance to Enforce Prohibition in Certain Emergencies

The Posse Comitatus Act and its organizational assistants, 18 U.S.C. 1385, 10 U.S.C. 375, forbid making use of the U.S. Armed Forces to carry out civilian statutes, unless directed to do with expressed, statutory permission. Exceptions regarding the Department of Justice include any crisis involving biological, chemical, or nuclear weapons.[443] In addition, section 104 amended section 2332e to incorporate any federal crisis involving any other possible weapons of mass destruction.

Section 104 altered title 18 of the United States Code to permit the Attorney General to seek help from the Department of Defense whenever weapons of mass destruction are utilized illegally inside the U.S., or are illegally utilized outside American borders by U.S. citizens. Chemical weapons are expressly barred from the explanation of Weapons of Mass Destruction within section 104.[444]

Section 105. Expansion of National Electronic Crime Task Force Initiative

In a move to counteract a wide variety of electronic crimes, comprising of those aimed at destroying America's significant infrastructure and financial networks, this segment commands the Director of the United States Secret Service to create a system of electronic crime task forces based primarily on the New York Electronic Crimes Task Force.

This proposed system, aka "the National Electronic Crime Task Force (NECTF)," is accountable for "preventing, detecting, and investigating elec-

---

442. See (Public Law 104–132, 110 Stat. 1314 (1996).
443. See 18 U.S.C. 2332e, 175a, 229E, 831(e), and 10 U.S.C. 382.
444. Ibid.

tronic crime, including potential terrorist attacks against critical infrastructure and financial payment systems."[445]

Section 106. Presidential Authority

Section 106 alters section 703 of the International Emergency Economic
Powers Act[446] allowing the President to commandeer foreign possessions in
response to a foreign attack. The power becomes accessible once the U.S. is
involved in an armed conflict or the nation has been hit by a foreign nation
or its inhabitants. If that situation arises, the possessions of any foreigner,
association, or country that designed, endorsed, or helped initiate the aggression or attack becomes subject to forfeiture. The President or his representative may decide the specifics under which the possessions are impounded,
managed and dispensed with, and/or liable to an innocent owner defense
established by section 316 of the Patriot Act. In addition, the Patriot Act
allows the President to impound the same possessions on comparable
grounds (section 806).

TITLE II: ENHANCED SURVEILLANCE PROCEDURES

Title II established amplified authority for surveillance to a number of
government organizations and groups. This title contains 25 sections, with
one segment (section 224) having a sunset clause with an expiration date of
December 31, 2005 for many of the title's stipulations. This was extended
twice: on December 22, 2005 the sunset clause was extended to February 3,
2006 and on February 2, 2006 it extended a second time, up to March 10,
2006.

The disagreement that many have regarding the Patriot Act has to do with
Title II issues. Pundits for the act state that the provisions are needed if
America wants to win the War on Terrorism, while critics dispute that, say-
ing that several Title II sections contravene the U.S. Constitution.

> Title II permits governmental organizations to collect "foreign intelligence
> information" from both American and non-American citizens.

---

445. See Gretel Johnson. Secret Service expands Cybersecurity task forces. *IDG News Service*
(2002–8–22).
446. See (IEEPA) 50 U.S.C. 1702.

Segments of Title II alter the Foreign Intelligence Surveillance Act (FISA) of 1978[447] and its provisos in 18 U.S.C. that deals with "Crimes and Criminal Procedure."[448] It also changes the Electronic Communications Privacy Act of 1986.[449] In essence, Title II enlarges various federal organizations' authority in seizing, distributing, and using confidential telecommunications, with an emphasis placed on electronic communications like e-mail. Moreover, Title II modernizes the regulations that oversee computer crime investigations. It states the methods and restrictions for anyone who thinks his/her civil rights were violated to seek remedy, and that includes against the U.S. government. There is a segment dealing with trade restrictions against nations with governments' supporting terrorism, which is not specifically connected to surveillance concerns.

Title II deals with all areas concerning the surveillance of alleged terrorists, those alleged to be involved in computer crimes, as well as agents of an overseas nation that are involved in covert behavior. Specifically, Title II permits governmental organizations to collect "foreign intelligence information" from both American and non-American citizens, which is described in section 203 Title II. Section 218 amended FISA to state that "[the] significant purpose of the surveillance is to obtain foreign intelligence information."[450]

The modification in language was engineered to eliminate the "wall" separating criminal investigations and surveillance with the primary intention to purpose to gather foreign intelligence, which hampered investigations when criminal and foreign surveillance intersected.[451] As shown in Chapter 1, the legal wall separating law enforcement agencies and intelligence gathering agencies was not as great as many have said; nonetheless the "wall" was a primary impetus for the Patriot Act. However, the Federal Surveillance Court of Review, after examining the problems surrounding the "wall," stated that the reason problems existed was not because of the law; rather, it was due to misinterpretations by the agencies in question.[452]

Although not linked to surveillance, Title II also mentions trade embar-

---

447. See Pub.L. 95–511, 92 Stat. 1783, enacted October 25, 1978, 50 U.S.C. ch. 36).

448. Title 18 of the US Code deals with Crimes and Criminal Proceedings in five parts: Part I–Crimes; Part II Criminal Procedure; Part III–Prisons and Prisoners; Part IV–Correction of Youthful Offenders; Part V–Immunity of Witnesses. However, Title 18, specifically Part 1–Chapter 113B–§ 2331 and § 2332a(a)), has been used to charge individuals, such as Zacarias Moussaoui, with terrorism.

449. ECPA Pub. L. 99–508, Oct. 21, 1986, 100 Stat. 1848, 18 U.S.C. § 2510).

450. See USA Patriot Act: Public Law Pub.L. 107–56.

451. See Andrew C. McCarthy, "Why Section 218 Should be Retained," *The Patriot Debates.* Retrieved on 2007–12–20.

452. United States Foreign Intelligence Surveillance Court of Review. On Motions for Review of Orders of the United States Foreign Intelligence Surveillance Court (Nos. 02–662 and 02–968). In re: Sealed Case No. 02–001, (2002–11–18).

goes in opposition to the Taliban–the leading junta in Afghanistan continually funded terrorist groups in order for them engage in terrorist acts–and the selling abroad of agricultural goods, medications, and/or any medical apparatus is now in accordance to one-year licenses produced and evaluated by the U.S. government. No agricultural goods, medications, or any medical apparatus could be exported to Syria or North Korea, due to their extensive history of funding terrorist groups.

Title II permits surveillance organizations to seize or catch verbal exchanges with pen register or trap and trace devices. It does not permit these surveillance procedures to be used in contravention of the First Amendment rights of American citizens. To aid in an investigation carried out to safeguard against international terrorist organizations or covert intelligence activities, the Title authorizes for the capture of communications reports (section 215) and any reports detailing the meeting times, the length of the electronic communication(s), along with any identifiable numbers or addresses of the apparatus that was being used (section 210). Such orders may be allowed *ex parte*, and once permission is given––in order to avoid hurting the investigation––the order may not reveal the causes regarding why the order was approved. Section 209 allowed law enforcement to secure access to voicemail, as applications for wiretaps are no longer needed; instead, all that is required is to request a normal search warrant.

Under section 211, the United States Code was altered to permit the government the right to gain access to the accounts of cable TV customers, with the noteworthy omission of access to accounts stating which videos and/or television shows the subscriber watched.

Any and all orders approved under section 215 must be divulged to the Permanent Select Committee on Intelligence of the House of Representatives and the Select Committee on Intelligence of the Senate. Every six months, the Attorney General has to present any details to the Committees on the Judiciary of the House of Representatives and the Senate, discussing the complete number of applications that were made for orders supporting the appeal for the production of material possessions, and the complete number of such orders that were approved, altered, or turned down.

Under section 211, the United States Code was altered to permit the government the right to gain access to the accounts of cable TV customers, with the noteworthy omission of access to accounts stating which videos and/or television shows the subscriber watched. Section 212 prevented a communications supplier from revealing the subject matter of communications with others. On the other hand, if the supplier "reasonably" feels that a major crisis might result that would include death and/or severe physical harm to any individual is impending, then the communications suppliers can reveal the data without worrying about possible lawsuits. The supplier may also reveal communications at the appeal of governmental organizations, if the consumer permits the disclosure, or in situations where they must do so in order to safeguard their rights or possessions. The Homeland Security Act of 2002 rescinded Section 212 and was substituted with a new and permanent emergency disclosure stipulation.[453]

For governmental agencies to engage in surveillance, the U.S. Attorney General or his/her assistants (specified under section 201) may allow a federal judge to permit a surveillance order to the FBI or any other federal organization. Each of the orders allowed must be evaluated by one of eleven District Court judges, of which at any one instant, three must reside within 20 miles of Washington, D.C., as mandated by section 208.

Title II changed the U.S. Code to permit a magistrate judge to distribute warrants outside of his/her jurisdiction for any orders regarding terrorism (section 219). Section 220 provided federal judges the authority to administer nationwide service of search warrants for electronic surveillance. Under FISA, any organization may need a common carrier, landowner, caretaker, or any other individual and have them provide any required information, facility, and/or technological support essential to achieve a current electronic surveillance. Moreover, they must safeguard the confidentiality of such assistance, and instigate as little commotion as possible concerning the current surveillance.

Section 206 made these rules even more stringent. Section 222 further reduced the type of aid an organization might need, and supplied for recompense of any individual who performed surveillance aid to the government agency. Section 225 permits legal immunity to anyone supplying a wire or electronic communication apparatus, property owner/landlord, caretaker, or anyone else who gives information, facilities, or technological aid in agreement with a court order or appeal for emergency aid. Section 223 permits anyone who feels his/her civil rights were violated due to the unlawful interception of communications to initiate civil proceedings against anyone who took part in the unlawful surveillance.

Section 201. Authority to Intercept Wire, Oral, and Electronic Communications Relating to Terrorism

Title III of the Omnibus Crime Control and Safe Streets Act of 1968[454] established a judicially administered practice under which federal, state, and

---

453. See Pub. L. No. 107–296, 116 Stat. 2135 (2002–11–25).
454. See 18 U.S.C. 2510 *et seq.*

local authorities may intercept wire, oral, or electronic communications. The practice, however, is only obtainable in association with the investigations of expressly selected felonies.

Section 201 added a number of terrorist crimes to Title III's list of chosen felonies: (1) chemical weapons offenses;[455] (2) the use of weapons of mass destruction;[456] (3) violent terrorist actions rising above America's borders;[457] (4) monetary transactions with countries supporting terrorist groups and/or terrorist acts;[458] (5) substantive funding of terrorists;[459] and 6) substantive funding of terrorist groups.[460]

Section 202. Authority to Intercept Wire, Oral, and Electronic Communications Relating to Computer Fraud and Abuse Offenses

Section 202 added the fraudulent use of computers and their abuse to the Title III felony list. This specific portion of the Patriot Act is accountable to the sunset conditions detailed in section 224.

Section 203. Authority to Share Criminal Investigative Information

Formerly, federal agents that discovered information regarding the behavior of terrorist organizations or of foreign operatives within American borders could not legally forward the data to their counterparts in federal intelligence organizations (CIA, DIA, NSA, etc.).[461] This section permits federal law enforcement agents the right to distribute a partial assortment of foreign intelligence data, in spite of previous restrictions.

> Proponents of the Patriot Act state that before its passage, federal law enforcement could not communicate with intelligence organizations (CIA, DIA, NSA, etc.).

Rule 6(e) of the Federal Rules of Criminal Procedure forbids speaking of issue that currently take place before a federal grand jury. The Rule distin-

---

455. See 18 U.S.C. 229.
456. See 18 U.S.C. 2332a.
457. See 18 U.S.C. 2332b.
458. See 18 U.S.C. 2332d.
459. See 18 U.S.C. 2339A.
460. See 18 U.S.C. 2339B.
461. See Cal Thomas & Bob Becker. "The Patriot Act's worth keeping (if we rein it in and scrutinize it)." *USA Today* (2005–06–22), Retrieved on 2008–10–10.

guishes exemptions for disclosing in other courtroom events, to avert exploitation of the grand jury procedure, for giving proof to other grand juries, and to state law enforcement agencies.[462] Section 203 created an exclusion for intelligence matter. It protects any data:

(1) Connected to the defense of the U.S. involving foreign aggression or any other foreign, aggressive act; against any subversive acts or international terrorism by an overseas country or its operatives, or against overseas intelligence operations;

(2) Regarding a foreign country or terrain associated to the national defense, safety, or any operations involving foreign affairs of the United States; or

(3) Representing overseas intelligence or counterintelligence as defined in section 3 of the National Security Act of 1947:[463]

(a) "information relating to the capabilities, intentions, or activities of foreign governments or elements thereof, foreign organizations, or foreign persons" or

(b) "information gathered and activities conducted to protect against espionage, other intelligence activities, sabotage, or assassinations conducted by or on behalf of foreign governments or elements thereof, foreign organizations, or foreign persons."[464]

In addition, when any such data becomes known during the sequence of a federal grand jury investigation, the information can be given to other federal law enforcement agencies, intelligence, protective, immigration, national defense, or national security officials, but only is used in an official context.[465] Within a sensible time period, U.S. Attorneys must alert the court of the disclosed information under seal. Prosecutors must abide by disclosure practices detailed by the Attorney General when distributing sensitive intelligence data that discloses the identity of an American citizen or a permanent resident alien.[466]

Section 204. Clarification of Intelligence Exceptions from Limitations on Interception and Disclosure of Wire, Oral and Electronic Communications

At one point, Title III indicated that the electronic capturing of wire or oral communications for clandestine intelligence should be presided over by

---

462. See Federal Rules of Criminal Procedure. Rule 6e: The Grand Jury: Recording and Disclosing the Proceedings.
463. See Pub. L. No. 235, 80 Cong., 61 Stat. 496.
464. See 50 U.S.C. 401a(2).
465. See Federal Rules of Criminal Procedure: Rule 6: The Grand Jury.
466. Ibid.

the various requirement of FISA instead of those concerning Title III, of chapter 121 of title 18 of the United States Code[467] or of the Federal Communications Act.[468] Section 204 alters this directive in 18 U.S.C. 2511(2)(f) to substantiate that in foreign intelligence operations, FISA guidelines rule the capturing of electronic communications and the utilization of pen registers and trap and trace devices, too. This segment is liable to the sunset provisions of section 224.

Section 205. Employment of Translators by the Federal Bureau of Investigation

Current statutes occasionally waive staff prerequisites and restrictions in order to fill certain jobs needed in foreign language ability, i.e., relates to hiring translators in regards to United States Information and Educational Exchange Programs;[469] and the hiring of competent linguists in regards to United States Foreign Service training.[470] Section 205 relinquishes otherwise appropriate staff prerequisites and restrictions to allow the FBI to employ translators quickly to sustain counterintelligence operations. The Director of the FBI will ensure that all compulsory safety prerequisites are met. The Attorney General will describe to the Committees on the Judiciary regarding how many translators work for the FBI and DOJ, on any obstacles concerning the use translators currently working for other government agencies, on the Bureau's requirements, and on his commendation, to fulfill the Bureau's needs for competent translators. This section was not subject to the sunset provisions of section 224.

Section 206. Roving Surveillance Authority under the Foreign Intelligence Surveillance Act of 1978

Concerning the same speech that was used in an earlier bill, the House Committee on the Judiciary explained: "Section 1805(c)(2)(B) of title 50, permits the FISA court to order third parties, like common carriers, custodians, landlords and others, who are specified in the order, (specified persons) to provide assistance and information to law enforcement authorities in the installation of a wiretap or the collection of information related to a foreign intelligence investigation."[471]

---

467. See Title 18, Chapter 121 USC: Stored Wire and Electronic Communications and Transactional Records Access.
468. See 47 U.S.C. 151.
469. See 22 U.S.C. 1474(1).
470. See 22 U.S.C. 4024(a)(4)(B).
471. See Section 1805(c)(2)(B) of title 50.

In essence, the change permits the FISA Court to force any additional individuals to aid in the setting up and to supply all data, property, or technological know-how needed, without naming such individuals.

Section 152 was altered to add words allowing the FISA Court to command the order to "other persons" if they (FISA Court) discover that the "actions of the target of the application may have the effect of thwarting the identification of a specified person," that must aid in the putting in place of any court-authorized intercept.[472] This specific alteration was designed to enlarge the authority in cases where the court realized that the behavior of a particular target could frustrate the detection of a specific individual in the order. Typically, this is achieved by the target relocating. The relocation requires the utilization of third parties supplementary to those specifically stated in the initial order to aid in the putting in place of the listening mechanism.

In essence, the change permits the FISA Court to force any additional individuals to aid in the setting up and to supply all data, property, or technological know-how needed, without naming such individuals. Nonetheless, the objective of the electronic surveillance is still required to be recognized or explained in the directive as detailed under existing statutes. "For example, international terrorists and foreign intelligence officers are trained to thwart surveillance by changing hotels, cell phones, Internet accounts, etc. just prior to important meetings or communications. Under present law, each time this happens, the government must return to the FISA Court for a new order just to change the name of the third party needed to assist in the new installation. The amendment permits the court to issue a generic order that can be presented to the new carrier, landlord or custodian directing their assistance to assure that the surveillance may be undertaken as soon as technically feasible."[473] This segment of the Patriot Act is covered under the sunset provisions of section 224.

Section 207. Duration of FISA Surveillance of Non-United States Persons Who Are Agents of a Foreign Power

Before the Patriot Act, save for a situation specifically aimed at a foreign nation, FISA surveillance directives and extensions ran out after 90 days, whereas FISA bodily search orders and extensions were operational for a

---

472. See Section 152 1805(c)(2)(B) of title 50.
473. See H.Rept. 107–256, at 59–60 (2001).

period of no more than 45 days.[474] Section 207 lengthened the term of bodily search orders to 90 days. Surveillance and bodily search orders are now operational for up to 120 days, with an extensions lasting for up 12 months.[475] This addition of time indicates a concession over the Department of Justice's initial pitch which had the mandatory cessation date for directives at 12 months, and not 120 days. This segment of the Act section is subject to the sunset provisions of section 224.

Section 208. Designation of Judges

FISA may be described as nothing but a sequence of measures designed to obtain court orders regarding specific foreign intelligence cases. It functions through a particular court that before section 208 was passed, contains seven judges, spread over the U.S., with two residing in the Washington, D.C. area. Section 208 sanctions the selection of four supplementary judges and mandates that three members of the court live within 20 miles of Washington, DC.[476] This segment of the Act is not covered under the sunset provisions of section 224.

Section 209. Seizure of Voice-Mail Messages Pursuant to Warrants

Section 209 regards voice mail as being like e-mail. Hence, federal agents are allowed to gain access with either a warrant or court order. They are no longer forced to follow the diktats of Title III and are applicable in the situation of live telephone exchanges.[477] This segment is covered under the sunset provisions of section 224.

The government can subpoena any and all electronic exchanges or a distant Internet service provider for the specific name, address and length of service of a possible terrorist, but the data is worthless if the individual in question has lied about his/her genuine identity.

---

474. See 50 U.S.C. 1805(e), 1824(d)(2000 ed.).
475. See ibid.
476. See 50 U.S.C. 1803(a).
477. See *United States v. Smith,* 155 F.3d 1050, 1055–56 (9th Cir. 1998).

Section 210. Scope of Subpoenas for Records of Electronic Communications

Terrorists and other wrongdoers often use assumed names in signing up for either Internet and/or telephone service. This causes a number of difficulties for law enforcement trying to make out the possible initiators of terrorist or any other illegal activity that frequently aids terrorists. The government can subpoena any and all electronic exchanges or a distant Internet service provider for the specific name, address and length of service of a possible terrorist, but the data is worthless if the individual in question has lied about his/her genuine identity. Allowing terrorist/criminal investigators to acquire credit card receipts and any other substantive information by a subpoena, coupled with subscriber information, will aid law enforcement in tracking a suspect and ascertain his/her true identity. This section altered 18 U.S.C. 2703(c) to allow a subpoena for documents dealing business transactions to incorporate data concerning how payment was made in order to aid law enforcement in ascertaining the user's name.[478] This section is not covered under the sunset provisions of section 224.

> Businesses proving telephone and electronic communications services may be obliged to make available to law enforcement a customer's identifying data without alerting their subscribers.

Section 211. Clarification of Scope

Businesses proving telephone and electronic communications services may be obliged to make available to law enforcement a customer's identifying data without alerting their subscribers.[479] In addition, cable companies were forbidden to disclose pertinent subscriber information without the subscriber's endorsement.[480] During the era when cable companies first offered communications services, doubt cropped up regarding whether law enforcement entry to their subscriber's information was to be presided over by the regulations relevant to the communications commerce or by previous cable regulations.[481]

---

478. See H.Rept. 107–236, at 56–7 (2001).
479. See 18 U.S.C. 2705(b).
480. See 47 U.S.C. 551 *et. seq.*
481. See In re *Application of U.S.A. for an Order Pursuant to 18 U.S.C. 2703(d),* 158 F.Supp.2d 644 (D.Md. 2001).

Section 211 settles this problem by altering the Communications Act,[482] making it clear that if a cable company proffers services, it is held to the standards established in Title III, and chapters 121 and 206 of title 18 of the United States Code (which centered on stored wire, electronic communications, documents pertaining to business transactions, and to pen registers and trap and trace mechanisms, respectively). However, any videos subscribed by the customer remain sheltered under the Communications Act protection. Section 211 is not covered under the sunset provisions of section 224.

Section 212. Emergency Disclosure of Electronic Communications to Protect Life and Limb

This section amended 18 U.S.C. 2702 to allow electronic communications service providers to divulge the communications (or documents involving such communications) of their customers or subscribers, if the supplier reasonably feels that a crisis linking immediate peril of death or severe physical harm to any individual necessitates disclosure of the data without holdup.

Likewise, this section altered federal statutes to permit communications providers to reveal noncontent data. Before the Act, the law stated that the communications provider was allowed to divulge content information, but not information that might be considered noncontent (i.e., how often the customer logs in). This change would erase that problem as the act permitted the service provider to give less-protected information.[483] This section was subject to the sunset provisions of section 224.

Section 213. Authority for Delaying Notice of the Execution of a Warrant

Rule 41 of the Federal Rules of Criminal Procedure appears to exclude belated notice regarding the implementation of "sneak and peek" warrants.[484] The Rule, as it was written, seemed to require that following the implementation of a federal search warrant, federal agents had to leave a duplicate of the warrant and a list of what they seized, as well as informing the issuing court what was done.[485]

Many of the subordinate federal courts were at odds regarding the degree to which the Rule mirrors the Fourth Amendment. The Ninth Circuit saw the Fourth Amendment in Rule 41, *United States v. Freitas,* 800 F.2d 1451, 1453 (9th Cir. 1986), whereas the Fourth Circuit did not, *United States v. Simons,*

---

482. See 47 U.S.C. 551.
483. See H.Rept. 107–236, at 58 (2001).
484. Rule 41 deals with Searches and Seizures.
485. See F.R.Crim.P. 41(d).

206 F.3d 392 (4th Cir. 2000). The Second Circuit, whose rationale the Congress felt swaying,[486] thought the soundness of sneak and peek warrants and of delayed notification worked better under Rule 41 standards.[487]

Section 213 was written with the conviction that the Fourth Amendment does not censure or ban sneak and peek warrants or delayed notice.

Section 213 was written with the conviction that the Fourth Amendment does not censure or ban sneak and peek warrants or delayed notice. For any investigations performed under a warrant in accordance with Rule 41, or performed under a warrant or any judicial court order in accordance with other rules of law, it assumes the position elaborated regarding delayed notification regulations in 18 U.S.C. 2705. There, the law stated that the government had the right to use electronic communications held in a storeroom or other facility for more than 180 days; thus, if a judicial order was delayed, it was allowed. A court has the right to demand a notification delay for a sensible time period, if a sensible reason exists regarding the fact that simultaneous notification may have any of following undesirable effects as detailed in section 2705. Section 2705 mentions:

(A) endangering the life or physical safety of an individual;
(B) flight from prosecution;
(C) destruction of or tampering with evidence;
(D) intimidation of potential witnesses; or
(E) otherwise seriously jeopardize an investigation or unduly delay a trial"

Any of these situations validate a notification of delay. Except for circumstances where the court reasons that seizure is rationally essential, this segment of the Patriot Act only allows delayed notification if the warrant disallows the seizure of any stored wire or electronic data (with the provision that it's authorized elsewhere) of any material goods, or of any wire or spoken communications. Section 213 was not covered under the sunset provisions of section 224.

Section 214. Pen Register and Trap and Trace Authority Under FISA

Trap and trace devices and pen registers are mechanisms that clandestinely identify the starting place and ending point of telephone calls made to

---

486. See 147 Cong.Rec. H7197 (daily ed. Oct. 23, 2001).
487. See United States v. Pangburn, 983 F.2d 449 (2d Cir. 1993).

and from a specific phone. Intelligence operatives have the right to them in accordance with a judicial order emanating from FISA. Section 214 allows the appeal from DOJ concerning the eradication of the prerequisites which restricted FISA pen register and trap and trace device guidelines to property used by foreign operatives or those involved in international terrorism or covert intelligence actions.[488] Even so, an agency and/or individual must guarantee that the mechanisms are pertinent as any data received by their use is vital to a foreign intelligence investigation.

Section 214 alters the lingo regarding FISA's pen register-trap and trace power in order to allow its utilization when capturing the starting place and ending point for electronic communications (e.g., e-mail), in addition to telephone communications.[489] Lastly, the section leaves no room for doubt that any applications for a FISA pen register-trap and trace order, akin to the applications for other FISA guidelines, that is to be aimed at gathering information from Americans and/or permanent resident aliens, can not be supported exclusively on any behavior safeguarded by the First Amendment.[490] Section 214 is covered under the sunset provisions of section 224.

Section 215. Access to Records and Other Items under the Foreign Intelligence Surveillance Act

Before the passage of the Patriot Act, FISA permitted high-ranking officers in the FBI to submit an application for a court order, in an investigation concerning foreign intelligence, to gain access to the documents of "common carriers, public accommodation providers, physical storage facility operators, and vehicle rental agencies."[491] Section 215 rewords the phrase, allowing for Assistant Special Agents in Charge within any Bureau field office to apply for the order.

Things wanted by the FBI no longer have to center around a recognized foreign operative or foreign nation, as was the scenario before the Patriot Act. Now, they may only be needed as an element in any investigation to safeguard the U.S. from international terrorists or covert intelligence actions; however, they are not allowed when linked with an American citizen and/or permanent resident based primarily on the First Amendment. Section 215 is covered under the sunset provisions of section 224.

---

488. See 50 U.S.C. 1842(c)(3)(2000 ed.).
489. See 50 U.S.C. 1842(d).
490. See 50 U.S.C. 1842, 1843.
491. See 50 U.S.C. 1861–1863 (2000 ed.).

Section 216. Modification of Authorities Relating to Use of Pen Registers and Trap and Trace Devices

With one crucial exception, Section 216 uses the same wording as found in a comparable section of the Patriot Act. Under 18 U.S.C. 3121(b), law enforcement acquired permission from a court by supplying documentation that the data to be gathered was germane to an imminent criminal investigation. At that point, law enforcement agents could set up and use a pen register and/or trap and trace device. However, court approval did not translate into securing or documenting the substance of any such message under the conditions of the court order. Under FISA, the government had to get court approval for a new pen/trap order in every area where the specific telephone to be targeted was situated. After 9/11, this situation was found untenable, especially when terrorists move from area to area to escape detection.

Section 216 did not alter the prerequisites listed under 18 U.S.C. 3121; rather, what changed was the law mandating that a U.S. attorney must confirm to the court that the data sought after was pertinent to a current criminal investigation. Moreover, the section did alter the present law stating the government had to attain the court order in the locale where the phone (or its equivalent) is sited. This section also authorized the court with jurisdiction regarding the crime to produce the order; hence, simplifying the investigation and removing the requirement to infringe upon the resources of courts and U.S. attorneys with no association to the investigation.

> Under the Patriot Act, 18 U.S.C. 3123(a) allows courts to issue one pen register/trap and trace order that could be used anywhere throughout the U.S.

Under the Patriot Act, 18 U.S.C. 3123(a) allows courts to issue one pen register/trap and trace order that could be used anywhere throughout the U.S. The bill separated 18 U.S.C. 3123(a) into two sections. Paragraph (a)(1) applied to federal investigations and stated that the directive may be used with any supplier of communication services throughout the U.S. whose aid was proper to the bringing about of the order. The second paragraph subsection (a)(2) dealt with state law enforcement and did not alter any of the power allowed state officials.

Specifically, this segment updated the law in order for everyone to know that this new authority pertains to twenty-first century technology. Before the Patriot Act, one found the law mentions a target "line"; now, the revision includes the words a "line or other facility." This entails various technologies, including a cellular number; a particular cellular phone recognized by its electronic serial number (ESN); an account set for Internet access and/or e-mail; or an Internet Protocol (IP) address, port number, or comparable computer network address or array of addresses. Moreover, since the law states such a broad range of such technologies, section 3123(b)(1)(C) gives candidates for a pen register or trap and trace orders to propose an accounting of the communications to be tracked using any of the aforementioned technologies.

Section 216 explains that judicial orders for the setting up of pen register and trap and trace devices may obtain any noncontent information–"dialing, routing, addressing, and signaling information"–utilized in the processing or transmitting of wire and electronic communications. For instance, a judicial order would not give law enforcement the authority to collect the heading of a message sent by e-mail, as that is considered to be "content." Moreover, agents would not be able to gather any data except that which was specified, and that includes an URL (Uniform Resource Locator). This idea, that any data correctly attained by using a pen register or trap and trace device is noncontent, pertains to each and every communications medium, and to authentic connections as well any which were attempted (i.e., busy signals).

Section [216](c) states that under 3127(2)(A), any court granting an order must have authority regarding the felony being investigated, and not just the communication connection upon which the mechanism will be placed. This section was altered to take into consideration the many technologies that pertain to "communication." Section [216](d) alters section 3124(d) to guarantee that service providers (i.e., Internet service, cellular telephone, etc.) are covered. Section 216 gives protection to any service providers that obey the terms of court orders, directing them to aid law enforcement in attaining any information considered noncontent. Section 216 was not covered under the sunset provisions of section 224.

Section 217. Interception of
Computer Trespasser Communications

Section 217 places emphasis on preventing any future "Cyberattacks" that might be leveled at the U.S. computer system. As the aggression could take any number of forms, the victims of such an assault should have the right to allow law enforcement the right to intercept and destroy the attacker's communications. Section 217 altered the statutes to make clear that law enforcement, if given the authority by the victims, can intercept any and all communications regarding the attackers–under restricted circumstances.

Specifically, Section [217](1) increases the definitions already listed under 18 U.S.C. 2510. For example, (1) "protected computer," at which point the Act states that the meaning is the same as that found in 1030 of title 18; and (2) the term "computer trespasser" is defined an any individual that accesses a protected computer lacking consent and hence, no rational anticipation of privacy exists in any message sent out or received, from the protected computer.

Section [217](2) of the Act altered the law so any individual that suffered due to the machination of a computer hacker could give the law the right to intercept the messages of the hacker, under restricted circumstances. This includes: (1) the possessor or user of the protected computer must allow for the capturing of the hacker's communications; (2) the individual intercepting the communication is required to be a part of an ongoing investigation; (3) the individual who intercepts the communication must feel that the information he/she gathers from the computer is germane to the investigation; and (4) information pertaining to the hacker is the only data the investigator can use.[492] This section was covered under the sunset provisions of section 224.

Section 218. Foreign Intelligence Information

One major impetus for the Patriot Act was to establish an effective liaison between criminal and intelligence investigators. FISA, as it was initially written, stated that a request for surveillance needed documentation that "the purpose for the surveillance is to obtain foreign intelligence information."[493] This often resulted in an individual questioning whether the order was obtained, so in order to ease FISA rules, the "purpose" of an investigation became "significant purpose," thus making it easier to collect counter intelligence information.

Section 219. Single-Jurisdiction Search Warrants for Terrorism

Rule 41(a) of the Federal Rules of Criminal Procedure states that in order to receive a search warrant, it must be within the area where the land, home, domicile, etc. is located; otherwise, the authorities would not receive the warrant.[494] The single exclusion from this rule is when either the property in question, or the individual, might leave the area before the authorities can serve their warrant. The result is added work for law enforcement since terrorists often move around in a peripatetic fashion. This could have serious repercussions regarding a terrorist investigation.[495] Section 219 bypasses this and gives a judge in his/her jurisdiction to issue a warrant that can be served

---

492. See H.Rept. 107–236, at 55–6 (2001).
493. See 50 U.S.C. 1804(a)(7)(B)(2000 ed.).
494. Op. cit. Federal Rules of Criminal Procedure.
495. See H.Rept. 107–236, at 72 (2001).

anywhere, either "within or outside the district."[496] The concern with this section centers on whether the U.S. has the right to use this power overseas.

Section 220. Nationwide Service of Search Warrants for Electronic Evidence

Title 18 U.S.C. 2703(a) mandates that a search warrant is necessary for compelling service providers to divulge information regarding unopened e-mails. This section is concerned primarily with the time impediments caused by the cross-jurisdictional character of the Internet. Federal Rules of Criminal Procedure 41 states specifically that the "warrant" be acquired "within the district" where the land, house, domicile, etc., is situated. An example would be a federal agent in Miami investigating a possible terrorist within his city. In order to gain access to the individual's e-mails, the agent, if the suspect's ISP account is located anywhere other than Florida, will have to work with other agents and judges in the state where the ISP is situated just to attain a search warrant. This was thought asinine, considering the nomadic lifestyle of terrorists.

Section 221. Trade Sanctions

The Trade Sanctions Reform and Export Enhancement Act of 2000, Title IX of Public Law 106–387, 114 Stat. 1549A–67, staunchly confines the Executive Branch's power to force independent agricultural and medical restrictions on other countries, subject to specific exceptions. One of the exceptions allows for all exports from a country trading with the U.S. in goods that could be "used to facilitate the development or production of a chemical or biological weapon or weapon of mass destruction "§904(2) (C), to be banned. Section 221 alters paragraph 904(2)(C) to expand the ban to include any goods or products that might aid in the design of weapons of mass destruction. Moreover, the section alters subsection 906(a) of the trade sanctions act to permit both agricultural and medical goods and services to be sold to Syria and North Korea, as well as Afghanistan.

Section 222. Assistance to Law Enforcement Agencies

FISA, Title III, and similar laws force communications service providers to aid authorities when executing various orders handed down by a court.[497] The House Committee on the Judiciary felt that "this Act is not intended to affect obligations under the Communications Assistance for Law Enforcement Act,[498] nor does the Act impose any additional technical obligation or

---

496. See F.R.Crim.P. 41(a)(3).
497. e.g., 50 U.S.C. 1805(c)(2)(B), 18 U.S.C. 2518(4).
498. e.g., 47 U.S.C. 1001 *et seq.*

requirement on a provider of wire or electronic communication service or other person to furnish facilities or technical assistance."[499] Section 222 makes sure that anyone involved in the execution of court orders will be reasonably reimbursed, in accordance with Section 216. This section was not covered under the sunset provisions of section 224.

Section 223. Civil Liability for Certain Unauthorized Disclosures

This permits any individual who states his/her rights were abridged because of the unlawful interception of any information the ability to sue the violator in court.

Section 224. Sunset

A number of the amendments allowing federal agents or intelligence officials greater ability to intercept messages expired regarding any intelligence investigations begun after 1–1–06 and to any criminal investigations concerning illegal conduct that occurred after 1–1–06. Title II and its various changes would have no longer had any impact, beginning 12–31–05, excluding the follow sections. Conversely, on 12–22–05, the termination date was lengthened to 2–3–06, but on 2–2–06, it was lengthened a second time to 3–10–06.

Title II Sections That Did Not Expire on March 10, 2006

Section	Section title
203(a)	Authority to share criminal investigation information : Authority to share Grand Jury information
203(c)	Authority to share criminal investigation information : Procedures
205	Employment of translators by the Federal Bureau of Investigation
208	Designation of judges
210	Scope of subpoenas for records of electronic communications
211	Clarification of scope
213	Authority for delaying notice of the execution of a warrant
216	Modification of authorities relating to use of pen registers and trap and trace devices
219	Single-jurisdiction search warrants for terrorism
221	Trade sanctions
222	Assistance to law enforcement agencies

---

499. See H.Rept. 107–236, at 62–3 (2001).

Section 225. Immunity for Compliance with FISA Wiretap

FISA commands may comprise directives needing communications service providers and others to assist officers in the execution of the order.[500] Section 225 prevents any organizations providing assistance to suffer from any civil lawsuits.[501] This section is subject to the sunset provisions of section 224.

TITLE III: INTERNATIONAL MONEY LAUNDERING ABATEMENT AND FINANCIAL ANTI-TERRORISM ACT OF 2001

This specific portion of the Patriot Act was one that Congress did on its own, with its primary purpose being to prevent, detect, and prosecute individuals involved in terrorism. Title III's sections mainly alter segments of the Money Laundering Control Act of 1986 and the Bank Secrecy Act of 1970.

Title III contains three subtitles. The first aims at increasing banking laws against money laundering, with an emphasis placed on the international offenders. The second is concerned chiefly with increasing the efficiency of contact between law enforcement authorities and banks, with an expansion regarding document keeping and reporting prerequisites. The third subtitle focuses on eliminating currency smuggling and counterfeiting, as well as making the sentence for someone counterfeiting foreign money four times stiffer than what it was before the act.

The U.S. Congress wrote that money laundering "provides the financial fuel that permits transnational criminal enterprises to conduct and expand their operations to the detriment of the safety and security of American citizens" and that it is critical to the financing of global terrorism and terrorist attacks.[502] Money laundering is used "as protective covering for the movement of criminal proceeds and the financing of crime and terrorism."[503] Findings (4) and (5) state that:

> certain jurisdictions outside of the United States that offer "offshore" banking and related facilities designed to provide anonymity, coupled with weak financial supervisory and enforcement regimes, provide essential tools to disguise ownership and movement of criminal funds, derived from, or used to commit, offenses ranging from narcotics trafficking, terrorism, arms smuggling, and traf-

---

500. See 50 U.S.C. 1805(c)(2)(B), 1824(c)(2)(B), 1842(c)(2)(B).
501. See 50 U.S.C. 1805(h).
502. See USA Patriot Act: Title III: International Money Laundering Abatement and Anti-Terrorist Financing Act of 2001. Section 301A(1).
503. Ibid. Section 302A(3).

ficking in human beings, to financial frauds that prey on law-abiding citizens.
. . . [T]ransactions involving such offshore jurisdictions make it difficult for law
enforcement officials and regulators to follow the trail of money earned by
criminals, organized international criminal enterprises, and global terrorist
organizations.[504]

Congress specifically stated that correspondent accounts are susceptible to
money launderers as it is much simpler to mask the IDs of individuals possessing the accounts when compared to other accounts, and that confidential
financial services are subject to exploitation by criminals.
Congress also found that:

United States anti-money laundering efforts are impeded by outmoded and
inadequate statutory provisions that make investigations, prosecutions, and for-
feitures more difficult, particularly in cases in which money laundering involves foreign persons, foreign banks, or foreign countries.[505]

and

the ability to mount effective counter-measures to international money launderers requires national, as well as bilateral and multilateral action, using tools
specially designed for that effort.[506]

The primary aims of the title are clearly delineated in section 302. It affirms that the purposes of this title are:

(1) to increase the strength of United States measures to prevent, detect, and
prosecute international money laundering and the financing of terrorism;
(2) to ensure that–
(A) banking transactions and financial relationships and the conduct of such
transactions and relationships, do not contravene the purposes of subchapter
II of chapter 53 of title 31, United States Code, section 21 of the Federal
Deposit Insurance Act, or chapter 2 of title I of Public Law 91-508 (84 Stat.
1116), or facilitate the evasion of any such provision; and
(B) the purposes of such provisions of law continue to be fulfilled, and such
provisions of law are effectively and efficiently administered;
(3) to strengthen the provisions put into place by the Money Laundering
Control Act of 1986 (18 U.S.C. 981 note), especially with respect to crimes by
non-United States nationals and foreign financial institutions;
(4) to provide a clear national mandate for subjecting to special scrutiny those

---

504. See USA Patriot Act, Title III, Section 302 (5) & (6).
505. See USA Patriot Act, Title III, Section 302 (8).
506. See USA Patriot Act, Title III, Section 302 (9).

foreign jurisdictions, financial institutions operating outside of the United States, and classes of international transactions or types of accounts that pose particular, identifiable opportunities for criminal abuse;

(5) to provide the Secretary of the Treasury (in this title referred to as the `Secretary') with broad discretion, subject to the safeguards provided by the Administrative Procedure Act under title 5, United States Code, to take measures tailored to the particular money laundering problems presented by specific foreign jurisdictions, financial institutions operating outside of the United States, and classes of international transactions or types of accounts;

(6) to ensure that the employment of such measures by the Secretary permits appropriate opportunity for comment by affected financial institutions;

(7) to provide guidance to domestic financial institutions on particular foreign jurisdictions, financial institutions operating outside of the United States, and classes of international transactions that are of primary money laundering concern to the United States Government;

(8) to ensure that the forfeiture of any assets in connection with the anti-terrorist efforts of the United States permits for adequate challenge consistent with providing due process rights;

(9) to clarify the terms of the safe harbor from civil liability for filing suspicious activity reports;

(10) to strengthen the authority of the Secretary to issue and administer geographic targeting orders, and to clarify that violations of such orders or any other requirement imposed under the authority contained in chapter 2 of title I of Public Law 91-508 and subchapters II and III of chapter 53 of title 31, United States Code, may result in criminal and civil penalties;

(11) to ensure that all appropriate elements of the financial services industry are subject to appropriate requirements to report potential money laundering transactions to proper authorities, and that jurisdictional disputes do not hinder examination of compliance by financial institutions with relevant reporting requirements;

(12) to strengthen the ability of financial institutions to maintain the integrity of their employee population; and

(13) to strengthen measures to prevent the use of the United States financial system for personal gain by corrupt foreign officials and to facilitate the repatriation of any stolen assets to the citizens of countries to whom such assets belong.[507]

Subtitle A: International Counter Money Laundering and Related Measures

International Counter Money Laundering and Related Measures is the name of Subtitle A and is the point where title III begins. Its primary pur-

---

507. See USA Patriot Act, Title III, Section 302(b).

pose was to install measures that contravene the international money laundering trade. This is achieved using different methods. It directs banks to assume innovative and unique methods to fight money laundering (special emphasis is placed on identifying criminals). It restricts and/or prohibits the utilization of specific kinds of bank accounts; it adds additional legislation oversees a bank's transactions with foreigners; it also adds strong consequences for dishonesty whereas new statutes were written to assist and promote open communication between banks and the federal government.

Section 311 necessitates the preservation of documents concerning the total number of all business transactions performed outside American borders in locales where money laundering is common. Moreover, that sensible measures be assumed by a bank to acquire and keep data on foreigners that benefit from owning an account that was initiated and kept in America, but does not actually possess ownership of the account. Finally, the bank must ID any foreign clientele that can use or direct business dealings through a payable account within American borders.

Section 314 affixes new rules that endeavor to promote joint efforts to prevent money laundering. This aim was primarily accomplished by commanding the U.S. Treasury and other organizations to generate rules that indicate how data should be allocated,[508] and by consenting to banks sharing the data with other banks, when permitted by the Secretary of Treasury. Section 327 make it more difficult for financial institutions to amalgamate or combine with other organizations if their reputation indicates a lack of effort at fighting money laundering; moreover, it makes it more difficult for insured banks to combine with noninsured banks, if the insured banks possesses a poor reputation in fighting money laundering.

Several segments (sections 312, 313, 319, and 325) are primarily concerned with the forfeiture of possessions if terrorism or money laundering is assumed. In order to work out the difficulties in spotting individuals engaged in money laundering, section 326 was created so it would be easier to ID people (individually or collectively) that performed money laundering and/or opened accounts in the U.S. The Secretary of the Treasury received the job of setting rules that establish the least principles that banks must assume to confirm the identity of those that open accounts.[509] These regulations took effect on June 9, 2003, though banks had until October 1, 2003 to comply.[510]

Section 313 forbids foreign shell banks that are not affiliated with a financial institution that has a substantive existence within America, or that does

---

508. See 31 CFR 100.
509. See 31 U.S.C. § 5318(l)(1).
510. See 31 U.S.C. § 5318(l)(6).

not receive direction from a financial supervisor in a non-U.S. country that regulates the allied depository, credit union, or foreign bank. The subtitle contains several segments that forbid or check particular accounts held at banks. Under section 312, banks must provide ways to recognize the proprietors of any non-U.S. financial institution that are not overtly registered and/or have a correspondent account with the bank, with the concerns of each individual owner in the bank made known to the U.S.

Section 319 states that deposits into banks outside the U.S. will be treated as if the funds were placed into any interbank account that the foreign financial institution has within American borders. Hence, any judicial orders or warrants may be brought against the money in the interbank account held at an American bank, up to the sum lying in the account at the foreign institution.

Section 325 forbids banks to allow their depositors to specifically regulate transactions that shift their money into, out of, or through in-house bank accounts. Banks are also not allowed to tell their depositors about the presence of such accounts, nor can they disclose any information that might alert the customer that such accounts subsist. This segment mandates that banks record and use methods for finding where the money is located; moreover, the banks must determine if commingling of funds with other depositors occurs. The restraints on concentration accounts were made because they seldom leave an effectual paper trail; thus, helping money launderers.

Several sections emphasizes illegal activity that occurs in countries outside the U.S. Section 315 contains clear-cut actions of illegal behavior regarding money laundering. This is comprised of:

1. Conducting an financial transaction in the United States with the intent to commit a violent felony;[511]
2. Bribing public officials and deceptive handling of public funds;
3. The illegal transport or unlawful sales to foreign countries regarding controlled munitions;[512]
4. Bringing in to the United States any gun or ammunition not expressly authorized by the United States Attorney General.[513]
5. The illegal transport of any article proscribed under the Export Administration Regulations.[514]
6. Any action where the United States would be compelled under an international treaty with a foreign country to hand over someone, or where

---

511. Amendment made to 18 U.S.C. § 1956(c)(7)(B)(ii).
512. Illegal export of controlled munitions is defined in the United States Munitions List, which is part of the Arms Export Control Act (22 U.S.C. § 2778).
513. See 18 U.S.C. § 922(l) and 18 U.S.C. § 925(d).
514. See Defined in 15 CFR 730–774.

America would be compelled to present a legal prosecution against someone due to the treaty;

7. the importing of incorrectly classified commodities;[515]
8. computer crime;[516]
9. Any criminal disobedience concerning the Foreign Agents Registration Act of 1938.

Section 320 permits the forfeiture of any property or item that was earned within the U.S. due to illegal acts against other nations that entail the construction, importing, trade, or delivery of a controlled substance.[517] Section 323 altered how a foreign country seeks a forfeiture order in American courts[518] by inserting a section that specifically details how the U.S. might submit an application for a restraining order[519] to safeguard the accessibility of material goods that are liable for a foreign forfeiture or a ruling orders confiscation.[520]

Great importance is stressed regarding the capability of a foreign judicial system to respect the procedures of due process when pondering an application for a forfeiture or confiscation judgment to be recorded and imposed within American borders.[521] Section 328 mandates that the Secretary of Treasury undertake all practical methods to persuade foreign countries to necessitate the insertion of the person's name that was the originator in wire transfer directions sent to the U.S. and other nations, with the data to stay with the transfer from where it began until it disburses. Section 330 states that the Secretary is also commanded to support global collaboration in criminal investigations involving money laundering, money crimes, and the finances of terrorist groups.

Section 329 initiated criminal fines and/or prison for dishonest public officials. Any individual working for the U.S. government that operates in an illegal manner—this includes the individual inducing the illegal action—while

> Section 329 initiated criminal fines for dishonest public officials. Anyone caught working illegally will receive a fine by a sum no more than tripled . . . could receive a prison sentence of 15 years.

---

515. See in 18 U.S.C. § 541.
516. See 18 U.S.C. § 1030.
517. See 18 U.S.C. § 981(A)(1)(B).
518. See 28 U.S.C. § 2467.
519. In accordance with 18 U.S.C. § 983(j).
520. See 28 U.S.C. § 2467(d)(3)(A).
521. See 28 U.S.C. § 2467(b)(1)(c) & 28 U.S.C. § 2467(d)(1)(D).

operating as an official of the U.S. government will receive a fine by a sum
no more than tripled regarding the bribe in question. On the other hand,
individuals convicted of public corruption could receive a prison sentence of
no more than 15 years, or they could face a fine and prison. Fines are also
valid for banks not complying with directives to cease any corresponding
accounts within 10 days, as dictated under Section 319. The bank can be
penalized up to $10,000 American dollars per day the account is open once
the original 10-day threshold has run out.[522]

Subtitle B–Bank Secrecy Act (BSA) Amendments and Related Improvements

Subtitle B amends the BSA in an effort to create difficulties for criminals,
specifically those classified as money launderers, while making it simpler for
legal authorities and various organizations to regulate money-laundering
businesses. The BSA was changed so a specified official or organization that
gains knowledge concerning suspicious behavior to inform U.S. intelligence
organizations (CIA, DIA, NSA, etc.). In addition, Subtitle B concentrates on
matters involving document recording and accounting by having the process
of documenting suspicious behavior easier; also, it becomes an obligation for
banks to document and give any and all information regarding suspicious
business operations; by creating plans emphasizing "anti-money laundering"
programs, as well as pin-pointing and specifying the anti-money laundering
approaches; and by requiring banks to file a report on anyone that conducts
business with them if the depositor has foreign receipts more than $10,000.
The subtitle enlarges the penalties for money laundering and creates new
consequences for disobedience of geographic targeting directives and specific document keeping prerequisites. Subtitle B legislated for the establishment
of a protected network, better defense regarding American financial institutions and directed United States Executive Directors of foreign banks to
assist any country that supported the America's drive to destroy terrorists.

Several steps were initiated to enhance document keeping and accounting.
An alteration was made by Section 351 that gave the banks protection from
legal responsibility regarding any revelations of suspicious business dealings
to suitable agencies, or for not alerting any individuals recognized in such a
discovery, while forbidding this information be made public.[523] Section 353
altered The Federal Deposit Insurance Act to permit written recommendations to include any beliefs that the employee in question is involved in

---

522. See 31 U.S.C. § 5318(k)(3)(C)(iii).
523. See 31 U.S.C. § 5318(g)(3).

unlawful endeavors. This data may be given if the bank is replying to an appeal from any other financial organization; however, the section states clearly no mandate exists concerning the discovery or protection from legal responsibility any individual making such a disclosure gave the information due to malice.[524]

Another change was made when Section 356 required the U.S. Department of Treasury to create new rules requiring financial advisors and dealers, listed with the Securities and Exchange Commission (SEC) under the Securities Exchange Act of 1934, to present Suspicious Activity Reports (SARs) when any dubious behavior is observed.[525] Furthermore, Section 355 stated that an account be conjointly written by the Secretary of Treasury, the Board of Governors of the Federal Reserve System, and the SEC Commission with suggestions for effectual rules for administering the various necessities of the Bank Secrecy Act concerning investment companies.

Subtitle B indicated that that there is no one definition of investment company since a number of "investment companies" exist. FinCEN stated that since so many already conduct business on a daily basis, the rules, regulations, and definitions should pertain to all investment companies; that is, all but commodity pools and other funds that chiefly invest in real estate. As the definition was expansive, it was restricted to investment companies allowing clients to cash in a piece of their investment within 24 months after the investment was made. Investment companies lacking $1,000,000 in assets at the conclusion of the quarter are barred from allowing this. In addition, it eliminates funds prepared within the United States, that are controlled and/or supported by an America, or that trades ownership to Americans.[526]

Section 359 stated that Money Services Businesses (MSBs) (organizations that conduct business using casual value transfer methods in a manner different from the conventional financial system) would be policed due to the section broadening the definition of "financial institution." By doing this, legal authorities could examine anti-money laundering practices in this section of the economy.

Section 365 altered the Bank Secrecy Act and made it mandatory that any individual with business transactions of over $10,000 in foreign money to file a document with FinCEN.[527] In addition, it is against the law to maneuver business dealings in a way that tries to avoid the BSA's reporting obligation.[528] Section 366 wanted to understand why there was an overabundance

---

524. See Section 18 of the Federal Deposit Insurance Act (12 U.S.C. § 1828)–section (w) was added.
525. See 31 CFR 103.11(ii), 31 CFR 103.19, and 31 CFR 103.19.
526. See *FinCEN,* "A report to congress in accordance with § 356(c) of the Uniting and Strengthening America by Providing Appropriate Tools Required to Intercept and Obstruct Terrorism Act of 2001 (USA Patriot Act)."
527. See 31 U.S.C. § 5331.
528. See 31 U.S.C. § 5324.

of Currency Transaction Reports (CTRs). During the 2002 fiscal year, more than 12,000,000 were filed and Congress worried that it harmed the efficiency of law enforcement.

They ordered a study that stated organizations were filing superfluous information for a number of reasons, and made a range of suggestions that could conceivably assuage the dilemma. For instance, the study suggested that FinCEN should strive to work with federal banking employees, as well as financial institutions in order to lessen the panic of unfavorable regulatory penalties, as well as avoiding erroneous exemption rulings, which includes giving an Advisory supporting the utilization of exemption procedures.[529]

A couple of sections in subtitle B focus on anti-money laundering programs and the overall plan to stop the illegal practice. Section 352 altered the Bank Secrecy Act[530] in order to have banks execute an anti-money laundering agenda. Organizations must apply the expansion of in-house rules, regulations, and controls; the title of compliance officer; a current worker training course; and an autonomous assessment task to analyze programs. The Secretary of the Treasury received the power to put into place the bare minimum benchmarks of these plans, but can excuse from the appliance of those benchmarks any bank or financial institution not contained in the regulations as detailed in title 31, of the Code of Federal Regulations.[531]

The section states that the Secretary of Treasury should devise rules "commensurate with the size, location, and activities of the financial institutions to which such regulations apply." These rules were created by a partnership between FinCEN and U.S. Treasury as 31 C.F.R. 103.137 on December 5, 2001. The primary goal was to spotlight and cajole insurance companies to create anti-money laundering agendas; however, this did not include depository banks since the BSA already mandated that they have in place anti-money laundering agendas.[532]

The BSA states that, "the President, acting through the Secretary and in consultation with the Attorney General, shall develop a national strategy for combating money laundering and related financial crimes."[533] In order to achieve these goals, a compendium of topics that is considered suitable is given.[534]

---

529. See Report to Congress: Use of Currency Transaction Reports" (October 2002). Submitted by FinCEN on behalf of the United States Department of Treasury.
530. See 31 U.S.C. § 5318(h).
531. See 31 CFR 103.
532. See 31 CFR 103.137 & Financial Crimes Enforcement Network; Amendment to the Bank Secrecy Act Regulations–Anti-Money Laundering Programs for Insurance Companies, *FinCEN* & United States Department of Treasury.
533. See 31 U.S.C. § 5341(a)(1).
534. 31 U.S.C. § 5341(b).

Section 353 enlarged civil and criminal punishment for the contravention of any instructions carried out under the BSA. In addition, punishment was increased for the civil and criminal contravention of rules given under section 21 of the Federal Deposit Insurance Act and section 123 of Public Law 91–508.[535] Section 123 of Public Law 91–508 states the rules presiding over document keeping for uninsured banks, or any other organization defined in 12 U.S.C. § 1953(b),[536] whereas section 21 of the Federal Deposit Insurance Act states the rules presiding over document keeping for insured banks.[537] The section increases the period of geographic targeting guidelines from two to six months.[538]

Section 362 gave the Secretary of Treasury the power to build a protected system that would allow financial documents necessary under the Banking Secrecy Act to be reported electronically. The secure system was needed in order for data to be sent detailing any potentially illegal behaviors to the financial organizations. Moreover, the system had to be completed within nine months of the ratification of the Patriot Act. Dennis Lormel, Head of the Terrorist Financing Operations Section (a subsection of the FBI's Counterterrorism Division), stated that the Patriot Act Communication System was built by FinCEN using prerequisites.[539]

Section 363 provides for the Secretary of Treasury to have the power to distribute punishment, involving money in a total that is equivalent to a sum no less than double the quantity of the business deal, but cannot exceed $1,000,000, on any bank or financial organization that carries out a civil[540] or criminal[541] infringement of various International anti-money laundering procedures.[542]

Section 364 gives the Board of Governors of the Federal Reserve System the power to sanction employees to perform as law enforcement officers to protect the building and employees of any U.S. Federal reserve bank, and any actions accomplished by or on behalf of the Board.

Section 364 gives the Board of Governors of the Federal Reserve System the power to sanction employees to perform as law enforcement officers to

---

535. See USA Patriot Act: Title III, Section 353(a) and (b).
536. See 12 U.S.C. § 1953.
537. See 12 U.S.C. § 1829b.
538. See USA Patriot Act: Title III, Section 353(d).
539. See http://www.fbi.gov/congress/congress02/lormel100902.htm.
540. See 31 U.S.C. § 5321(a).
541. See 31 U.S.C. § 5322.
542. See 31 U.S.C. § 5318(i) and 31 U.S.C. § 5318(j).

protect the building and employees of any U.S. Federal reserve bank, and any actions accomplished by or on behalf of the Board. The Board can, at its discretion, give this power to a U.S. Federal reserve institution; that is, as long as the institution follows the rules as dictated by the Board and which receive the imprimatur of the U.S. Attorney General. Law enforcement employees have the power to carry guns and to arrest anyone for illegal activity performed while on the property or inside the building(s) of the Board; likewise, if someone breaks the law in a reserve bank. Officers must have successfully finished law enforcement education and be approved to carry guns and make arrests.[543]

A number of other Bank Secrecy Act provisions were carefully evaluated and changed. Section 357 stated that an account be given regarding the viability and need of transferring the processing of data that the Department of the Treasury performs (due to the BSA) to organizations other than those supervised by the United States Internal Revenue Service (IRS). The report's conclusion was that, due to the nature and proficiency of the IRS, it should continue its job of data processing and assessment; moreover, it was felt that the IRS should continue to oversee processing due to its skill and expertise in running the Bank Secrecy Act since the 1970s.[544]

The BSA received several alterations from section 358. One such change mandated that a selected officer or organization that suspected illegal business dealings to tell American intelligence agencies. The confirmed rationale of the Bank Secrecy Act,[545] Section 123(a) of Public Law 91-508[546] and Section 21(a) of the Federal Deposit Insurance Act[547] were all changed to permit documents to be supplied to various organizations involved in either intelligence or counterintelligence endeavors, and that includes examining the data, in order to safeguard the country against terrorist acts. In addition, it was changed[548] so the Secretary of Treasury could make available reports and documents to various organizations, intelligence agencies, or self-regulatory organizations that are listed with the SEC or the Commodity Futures Trading Commission (CFTC) once the individual in charge asked for it. Exclusions for nondisclosure are provided if the conditions are covered under the Privacy Act of 1974.[549]

---

543. Section 11 of the Federal Reserve Act (12 U.S.C. § 248) was amended.
544. See U.S. Department of the Treasury: Report to Congress in Accordance with 357 of the Uniting and Strengthening America By Providing Appropriate Tools Required to Intercept and Obstruct Terrorism Act of 2001 (USA Patriot Act)."
545. See 31 U.S.C. § 5311.
546. See 12 U.S.C. § 1953(a).
547. See 12 U.S.C. § 1829b(a).
548. See 31 U.S.C. § 5319.
549. See 5 U.S.C. § 552.

A number of comparable changes were enacted as well. One such alteration was applied to the Right to Financial Privacy Act of 1978 in order to permit documents attained under the Act to be transmitted to an additional organization, if the documents are germane to intelligence or counterintelligence actions connected to international terrorism.[550] No particular methods detailed in the Financial Privacy Act under section 1114 pertain to governmental employees conducting inquiries or intelligence/counterintelligence actions, concerning domestic or international terrorism.

Any financial documents that are needed can now be attained by court order from a Federal grand jury.[551] Another change was made to the Fair Credit Reporting Act. Now, credit reporting agencies are required to supply reports of a consumer and every bit of data found in the consumer's file to any governmental organization that is allowed to carry out counterterrorism activities when given a written document by that organization requesting the information. The credit agency is forbidden to discuss with anyone that they supplied information to the governmental organization. The credit reporting agency, and any worker on its staff, will be protected by the U.S. government from any civil suits, if it can be shown everything was conducted with a modicum of good faith.[552]

FinCEN became an agency with the Department of Treasury.[553] The specific job responsibilities are discussed[554] while the Secretary of the Treasury received an extra duty of creating and sustaining operational processes, with deference to the government-wide information access provider and the financial crimes communications center run by FinCEN.[555]

Section 360 grants the President more power to direct any of the United States Executive Directors of the various international monetary organizations (i.e., the IMF) to wield their power to provide any loan or other use of the funds for nations showing that they support America and its War on Terrorism (also known as "voice and vote"). The Secretary of Treasury also receives the power to direct the Executive Directors to apply forcefully the "voice and vote" of the Executive Director to call for an assessment of payouts from their respective organizations to make sure that no money is given to any individual who commits, threatens to commit, or supports terrorism.[556]

---

550. See 12 U.S.C. § 3412(a).
551. See 12 U.S.C. § 3412(a).
552. See section 626 of theThe Fair Credit Reporting Act.
553. See 31 U.S.C. § 310(a).
554. See 31 U.S.C. § 310(b).
555. See 31 U.S.C. § 310(c).
556. See Presidential Executive Order 13224.

Subtitle C: Currency Crimes and Protection

Subtitle C centers on felonies relating to money. One of its major aims is to thwart bulk cash smuggling and permits property and/or material goods forfeiture in such instances. Moreover, it introduced several procedures dealing with counterfeiting while altering the Bank and Secrecy Act to elucidate international jurisdiction concerns.

Congress decided (in section 371 of the Patriot Act) that under the Bank and Secrecy Act, cash documenting was an important force in compelling criminals to steer clear of traditional banks to "clean" their money, causing them to utilize cash-based organizations and thus, evading conventional financial institutions. Because of this evasion, criminals transfer great sums of money in bulk form out of the United States and into various foreign banks or sold illegally. It should be noted that money launderers used bulk currency frequently as a method of evading the law; thus, an attempt to stop the laundering was initiated, mainly by emphasizing the elimination of illegal profits while increasing money launderers' possible punishment. Congress realized that statutes emphasizing the possible punishment of an individual or organization not documenting money transfers were ineffective. Hence, the law was rewritten to cover the act of smuggling bulk currency.

Consequently, a new segment[557] was added on to the BSA. It became a felony to elude currency documenting by hiding more than $10,000 on any individual or in any piece of luggage, goods, or other object that enters or exits the United States. The punishment for such an act is being sentenced to prison, up to five years, and the forfeiting of any land, real estate, or goods, up to the sum that was smuggled. Section 413 of the Controlled Substances Act specifically deals with the apprehension and forfeiture of such items.[558] If the defendant has insufficient assets to allow the court to seize enough substitute property to cover the amount being smuggled, then the court is authorized to make a personal money judgment up to the amount to be forfeited.

In addition, section 372 altered the BSA by having the punishment of not properly documenting currency[559] include the defendant losing his/her land, material possessions, real estate, etc., that was implicated in the crime, as well as any property leading back to the defendant.[560]

Section 373 altered Section 1960 of title 18 of the United States Code.[561] Prior to this, the code proscribed and punished unlawful money transmitting

---

557. See 21 U.S.C. § 5332.
558. See Section 413 of the Controlled Substances Act.
559. See 31 U.S.C. § 5313, 31 U.S.C. § 5316 and 31 U.S.C. § 5324.
560. See 31 U.S.C. § 5317(c).
561. See 18 U.S.C. § 1960.

organizations, but due to the Patriot Act, it now also forbids any unlicensed money transmitting organizations, with comparable consequences if caught. This section prosecuted Yehuda Abraham when he arranged money transfers for Hemant Lakhani (a very well-known and wealthy British arms merchant) who was then apprehended in August 2003 by governmental authorities. Lakhani was caught attempting to pawn a missile to an undercover FBI special agent pretending to be a Somali radical.[562]

The Patriot Act's Section 374 changed the definition for domestic counterfeiting. Now, it includes analog, digital, or electronic picture imitations, with the resulting punishment for such acts detailed in various parts of the U.S. Code.[563] If someone is caught counterfeiting, the outcome could be 20 years incarceration for the act itself[564] as well as for distributing the counterfeit money.[565] In addition, it is a felony to possess an analog, digital, or electronic likeness of any debt or additional security of the U.S.[566] Likewise, making an impression of the devices used to construct such a debt,[567] or have in one's possession or attempt to market the impressions of devices utilized for debts and/or securities.[568] The penalties for such violations of the law are severe: offenders will be imprisoned for up to 25 years.

Government statutes consider linking elements of dissimilar currency to be a counterfeiting crime, and the Patriot Act amplified the possible prison sentence from five years 10 years.[569] It also increased prison time from five years to 10 years for counterfeiting governmental securities and debts of several American lending institutions.[570]

Comparable alterations were completed under section 375 emphasizing foreign debt and currency. Prior to this, the possible sentence for counterfeiting government securities, documents, and debts of a foreign nation was five years in prison; however, this was amended and criminal counterfeiting foreign items could receive up to 20 years incarceration.[571] An individual uttering false international debts or securities could receive a prison sentence of 20 years, up from five as it originally was.[572] 18 U.S.C. § 481 received an addendum stating that anyone caught manufacturing or owning any devices

---

562. See "The Patriot Act: Justice Department Claims Success" (2005-07-20), Retrieved from npr.org on 2008-06-04.
563. See 18 U.S.C. § 470.
564. See 18 U.S.C. § 471.
565. See 18 U.S.C. § 472.
566. See 18 U.S.C. § 473(a).
567. See 18 U.S.C. § 476.
568. See 18 U.S.C. § 476.
569. See 18 U.S.C. § 484.
570. See 18 U.S.C. § 493.
571. See 18 U.S.C. § 478.
572. See 18 U.S.C. § 479.

used for counterfeiting could receive up 20 years incarceration. An individual who manufactures or utters foreign financial institution notes could be sentenced up to 20 years in prison.[573]

Section 376 altered18 U.S.C. § 1956, which made illegal owning or possessing any devices used in money laundering to also include substantive support or capital to overseas terrorists (as defined by the U.S. government) in its meaning of "unlawful activity."[574]

Section 377 altered the U.S. Code. Now, anyone undertaking an illegal act, and anyone conspiring with that individual, beyond the authority of the U.S. which would be characterized as a crime within American borders, will be put on trial under the authority of 18 U.S.C. § 1029. This section emphasizes fraudulent and related endeavors with regards to access mechanisms. This is only pertinent when:

- the crimes include an access mechanism distributed, possessed, administered, or directed by a financial organization, account distributor, credit card network constituent, or other article lying within the purview of the U.S.;
- and the individual moves, distributes, reassigns to or through, or otherwise puts in storage, hides, or holds within the legal purview of the U.S., anything used to aid in the commission of the crime or the profits of such crime and/or land, real estate, material goods, resulting from the crime.

TITLE IV: PROTECTING THE BORDER

Title IV changes much of the Immigration and Nationality Act. The U.S. Attorney General (AG) received more authority in terms of law enforcement and the ability to investigate, as did the Immigration and Naturalization Service (INS). Disparagement of Title IV focused on its not mentioning judicial review for groups listed as terrorist.

Subtitle A: Protecting the Northern Border

The AG received the authority to ignore the limit concerning the quantity of full time employees (FTEs) allocated to the INS for duty along America's northern border, Canada.[575] Money was apportioned so the total number

---

573. See 18 U.S.C. § 482, 18 U.S.C. § 483.
574. See 18 U.S.C. § 1956(c)(7)(D).
575. See USA Patriot Act: Section 401.

of federal agents (U.S. Border Patrol) could triple. In addition, Customs Service employees and INS examiners, alongside an extra $50,000,000 for the INS and the U.S. Customs Service, was set aside so our Northern border would have state of the art equipment for monitoring individuals entering and exiting the U.S.[576] The INS received the power to approve overtime compensation up to $30,000 per year to its workers.[577]

The State Department and the INS received access to specific data in the criminal history documents of individuals applying for visas and/or entry into the United States.[578] The data contains any criminal acts as detailed in the National Crime Information Center's (NCIC) Interstate Identification Index (III) and (2) the Wanted Persons File and any additional data kept by the NCIC. Such data is supplied as an extraction from a computerized visa network or any additional apt network system, and is free. On the other hand, if the State Department wishes to acquire the complete criminal history of an applicant, it must provide the applicant's biometric data to the Criminal Justice Information Services (CJIS) Division of the Federal Bureau of Investigation.

It was essential that the State Department understand the rules governing the process for obtaining biometric data and the circumstances under which they could use the data.[579] Furthermore, it was required that a technology criterion, to be used by various federal agencies, be constructed by the National Institute of Standards and Technology (NIST) to authenticate the ID of individuals attempting to secure a visa to come to the U.S. In essence, the criterion would perform in depth background investigations, substantiate ID, and guarantee that the individual was not granted another visa under a different name. This account was made public on November 13, 2002,[580] but the NIST subsequently stated that the system was no better than the one used in 1998.[581] Section 303(a) of the Enhanced Border Security and Visa Entry Reform Act of 2002 outdated this section.

Subtitle B: Enhanced Immigration Provisions

The Immigration and Nationality Act (INA) altered[582] its wording to forbid foreigners that were affiliated with any organization or group that sup-

---

576. See Ibid 402.
577. See Ibid Section 404. This section altered The Department of Justice Appropriations Act, 2001.
578. See Ibid Section 403. This altered 8 U.S.C. § 1105 or Section 105 of the Immigration and Nationality Act.
579. Final regulations are detailed in 22 CFR 40.5.
580. See "Use of Technology Standards and Interoperable Databases With Machine-Readable, Tamper-Resistant Travel Documents." (2002-11-13). *National Institute of Standards and Technology.*
581. See NIST Image Group's Fingerprint Research, see the section "NIST Patriot Act Work."
582. See 8 U.S.C. § 1182–(a)(3).

ports terrorism from entering the U.S.[583] This incorporated any foreigners that use their reputation or eminence to influence others to aid terrorism. This ban also includes the family of such a foreigner, at least for a five-year period after the individual's last terrorist act; however, this is not applicable in situations where family members lacked knowledge regarding the terrorist acts. Likewise, the rule does not apply in situations where a consulate officer or the Attorney General has knowledge indicating the individual has forsaken all terrorist acts. The Secretary of State, after speaking to the Attorney General, can make the determination that an individual involved in past terrorist acts could endanger the lives of American citizens if he/she gains entrance; thus, the individual will not be admitted into the U.S.

"Terrorist activity" was changed to embrace acts utilizing any potentially hazardous mechanism—not just bombs and guns.

Several words were redefined in the INA. "Terrorist activity" was changed to embrace acts utilizing any potentially hazardous mechanism—not just bombs and guns. Terrorist activity now includes the act of collecting intelligence data on likely terrorist objectives, the request of money for a terrorist organization or requesting others to perform terrorist acts. Any individual providing aid to someone preparing to carry out terrorist acts is defined as committing terrorist acts; that is, if the person providing aid realizes that the person being helped is about to engage in terrorist activities. Aid includes giving substantive assistance, such as a safe place to stay, a means to move around, access to a phone or computer, money, anything that provides monetary assistance, bogus documents or ID, weapons (and this includes weapons of mass destructions) bombs, or instruction in how to execute the terrorist act.[584]

The INA standards for deciding who is or is not a terrorist organization was altered so the meaning of terrorist act, as detailed in section 140(d)(2) of the Foreign Relations Authorization Act, Fiscal Years 1988 and 1989[585] was included. Seven days before an organization is to be labeled as terrorist, the Secretary of State is mandated to make a top secret notice of the impending ruling, and in writing, must detail the reasons behind the resolution. This notification is to be given to the Speaker and Minority Leader of the House of Representatives, the President *pro tempore* of the U.S. Senate, the Majority,

---

583. See op. cit. 139 section 411.
584. Ibid.
585. See 22 U.S.C. § 2656f(d)(2)j. It states, "terrorism" as "premeditated, politically motivated violence, perpetrated against noncombatant targets by subnational groups or clandestine agents."

and Minority Leaders of the United States Senate, and any members of the pertinent committees of the House of Representatives and the Senate.[586]

The Secretary is required to print the information in the *Federal Register* seven days after supplying the announcement. The Secretary of State can, at any time, choose to relabel any group at the completion of a 24-month relabeling interlude for an extra 24 months, if the circumstances that originally instigated the original label has not altered. The amendment is retroactive, but it cannot be used against individuals who became members of a group, but then departed, before it was labeled as a terrorist organization in accordance with 8 U.S.C. § 1189.[587]

A new section (section 236A) was inserted into the INA[588] that calls for the Attorney General, or a designated officer, to obtain and hold any foreigner engaged in terrorist acts, or that is engaged in an action that potentially threatens the U.S., or who cannot enter the country or is liable for deportation if they attempt to enter for the following reasons: (1) if they try to spy; (2) if they try to sell abroad any possessions, technological equipment, or classified data; and (3) attempt to have power over the government or attempt to bring it down the government. In addition, if the individual has, or will have, been involved in terrorist acts.[589]

> The Attorney General or deputy may continue holding the foreigner(s) until they are moved out of the U.S.; that is, unless the government thinks they should not be moved, at which point they are set free.

The Attorney General or deputy may continue holding the foreigner(s) until they are moved out of the U.S.; that is, unless the government thinks they should not be moved, at which point they are set free. A foreigner can be held up to three months[590] but could be detained up to a period of 180 days if the individual(s) is seen as a grave security menace. The alien either must undergo removal procedures or be arrested no later than seven days after his/her incarceration; otherwise, he/she must be released.

The foreigner's certification must be evaluated every 180 days by the Attorney General, who has the option of revoking it, unless it is forbidden by the law. Every 180 days, the foreigner may request, in writing, that the certification be reassessed. Any type of judicial review concerning section 412 can occur under a writ of habeas corpus. This process can commence if a request

---

586. See 8 U.S.C. § 1189.
587. See Op Cit. No 145 411(c)(3)(A).
588. See 8 U.S.C. § 1226a.
589. See Op. Cit No. 148 section 412.
590. See 8 U.S.C. § 1232(a)(1)(A).

is made with the United States Supreme Court, by any Justice sitting on the Supreme Court, by any circuit judge of the United States Court of Appeals for the District of Columbia, or by any district court possessing the authority to hear the request. The final order can be appealed to the United States Court of Appeals for the District of Columbia.

A report must be given to Attorney General every 180 days detailing the following: (1) the specific number of people certified by the INA, (2) the reasons for certification, (3) the home country of the individual who received certification, (4) the amount of time each certified alien was in jail, and (5) the exact number of foreigners receiving certification that were not removed, or a motion made by the AG that the individuals were no longer aliens and should be released from jail.

Whether or not an individual is allowed to enter the U.S. remains confidential, unless such documents are required by a court in order for justice to be served.[591] Section 413 changed this so the Secretary of State could offer another government data about foreigners listed in the State Department's computer system. This database, along with other pertinent documents, permits the Department to avert, examine, or punish activities that would represent a felony within the U.S.

Due to section 414, Congress felt that the Secretary of State should accelerate the completion of the integrated entry and exit data network system for use around the country at any point of entry, as detailed in the Illegal Immigration Reform and Immigrant Responsibility Act of 1996 (IIRIRA).[592] In addition, it was felt that the Attorney General should commence using the Integrated Entry and Exit Data System Task Force, as detailed in the third section of the Immigration and Naturalization Service Data Management Improvement Act of 2000. This task force is comprised of 16 individuals, each representing a number of governmental organizations, and assesses how the AG can commence carrying out the execution of the integrated entry and exit data system.

Serious thought was given to how America could advance the flow of individuals at these entry points by improving the networks for data compilation and its sharing, augmenting collaboration between John Q. Public and private agencies, as well as augmenting the collaboration between various federal agencies, and increasing collaboration between the federal and state governmental agencies. In addition, emphasis was placed regarding how to modify information technology systems while accounting for myriad information networks, infrastructure, and the processing measures found at different points of entry, including airports, seaports, and land borders. The sec-

591. See 8 U.S.C. § 1202.
592. See Section 10, Illegal Immigration Reform and Immigrant Responsibility Act of 1996.

tion makes certain that funds are available for the implementation of the integrated entry and exit data system.

The section detailed specifically that the key emphasis of development was to be placed on the deployment of biometric equipment and the expansion of tamper-resistant credentials comprehensible at ports of entry. Likewise, the network was to interface with law enforcement databases around the country. After one year, the Office of Homeland Security was required to give a report to Congress on the types of data required by governmental organizations to check successfully all visa candidates and applicants for entry into the country.

Section 416 mandates that the AG execute and increase the foreign student monitoring program initially created under section 641(a) of the IIRIRA[593] while documenting the specific date and port of entry for each foreign student. The program expanded in order to comprise of other sanctioned educational institutions, such as pilot training, language training, or professional schools accepted by the A.G., in discussion with the Secretary of Education and the Secretary of State. Under section 416, the Department of Justice received $36,800,000 to put into action section 641(a) of the IIRIRA.

The INA permitted the AG and Secretary of State to ignore the visa requirements for aliens meeting specific conditions.[594] Section 417 required the Secretary of State to review the visa waiver system, and state to Congress the review's results, each year until September 30, 2007. Moreover, a check was to be made regarding a system of deterrent measures to avert the counterfeiting and stealing of passports, as well as establishing that nations labeled under the visa waiver program have initiated a system to acquire tamper-resistant passports. In order to meet the criteria for the waiver, the INA stated that the foreigner must have offered a legitimate machine-readable passport. From October 1, 2003 to September 30, 2007 this prerequisite was waived, if the Secretary of State found that the foreigner's home country made advancements toward guaranteeing that machine readable passports were usually obtainable to its citizens, or was taking sensible steps to defend against the misuse of nonmachine readable passports.[595]

Section 418 required the Secretary of State to decide whether "consulate shopping" presented a problem. Consulate shopping is submitting an application for a visa at various consulate posts, hoping to find someone compassionate enough to endorse the applicant's desire for a visa. Thus far, no report has ever been filed by the Secretary of State.

---

593. See 8 U.S.C. § 1372(a).
594. See 8 U.S.C. § 1187.
595. See 8 U.S.C. § 1187(a)(3).

Subtitle C: Preservation of Immigration
Benefits for Victims of Terrorism

The House of Representatives John Conyers (D-MI) and Senator Patrick Leahy (D-VT) introduced Subtitle C, as they acknowledged that some families would be unable for permanent residence in the U.S. as they could not meet specific deadlines due to 9/11, or were disqualified for special immigration status since family members died in the attacks.[596]

The legislation classifies an "age-out" defense for children who are part of an appeal for residency, as it permits individuals who reached their twenty-first birthday in September, 2001, with parents who applied for residency before September 11, 2001, to be described as a child for three months after reaching age 21. Individuals who reached age 21 after 9/11, would be considered children for an addition 45 days after their birthday.[597] Allowances were made so the AG could offer momentary administrative reprieve for humanitarian reasons and/or to make sure family unity still existed to individuals who lost a close family member as a direct result of the attacks.[598]

In order to carry this out, the AG received the power to create suitable standards for proof indicating that death, disability, or the loss of a job because of physical impairment or damage to a business transpired due to the hijackers attacks. The AG did not need to disseminate the rules before applying the subtitle.[599] This did not apply to individuals thought to be terrorists or family members of terrorists.[600]

Section 421 permitted special immigrant status to be given to family members of individuals killed or maimed due to the hijackers attacks, thus nullifying their petition for residency. If a family member wished to receive this consideration, he/she had to abide by the procedures detailed in section 204 of the INA.[601]

Under section 422, anyone who came to the United States as a spouse or child of the primary alien who was killed or maimed due to the 9/11 attacks was allowed one year extra time on their nonimmigrant status after the attacks took place. They had the opportunity to receive an "employment authorization" endorsement no more than 30 days after making their application for it. If the individual could not file a timely application for a modification or extension of nonimmigrant standing due to 9/11, they received a 60-day extension.

---

596. See Office of Patrick Leahy, USA Patriot Act Section–by-section analysis. Retrieved 2008–02–03.
597. See USA Patriot Act Section 424.
598. See Ibid. Section 425.
599. See Ibid Section 426.
600. See Ibid Section 427.
601. See 8 U.S.C. § 1154.

On the other hand, if a nonimmigrant was legally in the United States on September 10, 2001 but could not leave due to the attacks, he/she was not regarded as being unlawfully in the country from September 11 to November 11, 2001. If the nonimmigrant was out of the country and could not return to the U.S. to file a request for an extension of their status, they were given an additional 60 days to file, while their standing continued to the date their status would normally end, or 60 days afterwards, whichever came later.

The circumstances under which delays in filing were to be considered were: (1) offices closed, (2), United States Postal Service or other courier service ceasing work or long delays, (3) other businesses closing, thus causing impediments to travel essential to fulfill legal necessities.

The situations considered legitimate departure and return setbacks were: (1) offices closing; (2) airlines closing or flight delays; and (3) any other businesses closing, thus causing impediments to travel essential to fulfill legal necessities.

If an immigrant received a Diversity Immigrant Visa (also known as the "Green Card Lottery") but could not use it due to 9/11, he/she could use it in from October 1, 2001, to April 1, 2002. The situations considered legitimate reasons why immigrants were delayed were: (1) offices closed; (2) United States Postal Service or other courier service ceasing work or long delays; (3) airlines closing or flight delays; and (4) any other businesses closing, thus causing impediments to travel essential to fulfill legal necessities.

If the primary nonimmigrant that received a Diversity Immigrant Visa died due to 911, then family members were permitted the same status until June 30, 2002.

If a nonimmigrant could not enter the country due to 9/11 and their visa was to run out before December 31, 2001, then a time extension was granted until December 31, 2001. Likewise, any nonimmigrant given parole by the AG[602] but could not enter the country due to 9/11, received a parole extension of 60 days. In both cases, the circumstances that were to be considered were: (1) offices closing; (2) airlines closing or flight delays; and (3) any other businesses closing, thus causing impediments to travel essential to fulfill legal necessities.

According to the INA, American citizens needed to be married for a total of two years before the non-American spouse could receive citizen status.[603] Section 423 ignored the two-year standard for someone married to or children of an American citizen killed by the hijackers' attacks on 9/11. The spouse or children had to have submitted a petition to the AG within 24 months of the attacks.

---

602. See 8 U.S.C. § 1182(d).

TITLE V: REMOVING OBSTACLES
TO INVESTIGATING TERRORISM

Section 501 gives the AG the authority to shell out reward money in accordance with various ads asking for help in order to extinguish terrorism and avert future terrorist acts. Recompense over $250,000 cannot be issued unless the AG or President approves, and once the sum is accepted, the AG is required to tell, in writing, the Chair and ranking minority members sitting on the Committee on Appropriations and the Judiciary of the Senate and of the House of Representatives. Any American Executive agency,[604] as well as the Army, Navy, and Air Force, may supply the money.[605]

Section 502 changes the State Department Basic Authorities Act of 1956.[606] Now, the State Department has the authority to proffer rewards, with the agreement of the AG, if a terrorist group is significantly taken apart (it does not have to completely obliterated, just so long as it is noteworthy)[607] as well as helping authorities recognize any of the primary principals of terrorist groups.[608] In addition, the Secretary of State was authorized to offer more than $5,000,000, if he/she feels it would stave off terrorist acts against the U.S.[609]

The DNA (deoxyribonucleic acid) Analysis Backlog Elimination Act of 2000 chiefly permits any of the 50 states to run DNA tests in the Federal Bureau of Investigation's Combined DNA Index System, and to gather and analyze DNA evidence of vicious and sexual criminals. Section 3 requires the gathering of DNA specimens of federal inmates that were found guilty of murder, sexually abusing others, the sexual abuse of a child, taking part in sex trafficking, peonage and/or slavery, abduction of others, and theft;[610] or for military transgressions in opposition to the Uniform Code of Military Justice, for which the offender could be incarcerated for more than 12 months.[611] Section 503 changed the DNA Analysis Backlog Elimination Act to take in terrorist acts,[612] and/or violent offenses[613] in the compendium of eligible federal crimes.

---

603. See 8 U.S.C. § 1151(b)(2)(A)(i).
604. See 5 U.S.C. § 105.
605. See 5 U.S.C. § 102.
606. See Public Law 885, August 1, 1956; 22 U.S.C. 2708.
607. See 22 U.S.C. § 2708(b)(5).
608. See 22 U.S.C. § 2708(b)(6).
609. See 22 U.S.C. § 2708(e)(1).
610. See 42 U.S.C. § 14135a(d)(2).
611. See 10 U.S.C. § 1565(d).
612. See 18 U.S.C. § 2332 b(g)(5)(B).
613. See 18 U.S.C. § 16.

Section 106 of FISA stated specifically how the gathering of foreign intelligence by duly licensed officers might take place using electronic surveillance.[614] Section 305 of FISA stated how duly licensed operatives might obtain evidence by using physical searches and how it could be used.[615] Section 504 of the Patriot Act adapted FISA to permit federal operatives that obtain information using electronic surveillance or physical searches to check with federal law enforcement personnel to organize all efforts at investigating or defending against likely or actual attacks, sabotage, or foreign terrorist acts and/or covert intelligence actions by an intelligence agency of a foreign nation.

Before the Patriot Act, FISA allowed counterintelligence operatives to access telephone fees and transactional documents using National Security Letters (NSLs).[616] Electronic service suppliers had to obey an appeal for information regarding subscriber billing data, or electronic communication transactional documents when requested by the FBI. The admission by any individual receiving an NSL was proscribed, because under § 2709(c) they were not allowed to discuss with anyone that the FBI wanted or had attained access to confidential documents. The Right to Financial Privacy Act of 1978 gave the Bureau power to call for banks and other financial organizations to make available data regarding a customer's or entity's financial dealings.[617] The Fair Credit Reporting Act mandated that credit reporting agencies give the Bureau the names and addresses of all financial organizations where the specific individual maintained, or currently maintains, an account.[618]

Section 505 allows NSLs to be used by FBI Special Agents in charge at local field offices, unlike before where the authority to ask for NSLs was highly restricted. Under FISA, a counterintelligence operative could request access to telephone charges and transactional documents containing personal information like name and long distance charges to the customer;[619] likewise, authorities could find the same information for a worker of the access source.[620] The Patriot Act changed this. Now, authorities can attain the needed data only if written documentation is given that the data is "relevant to an authorized investigation to protect against international terrorism or clandestine intelligence activities, provided that such an investigation of a United States person is not conducted solely on the basis of activities protected by

614. See 50 U.S.C. § 1806.
615. See 50 U.S.C. § 1825.
616. See 18 U.S.C. § 2709.
617. See Section 1114(a)(5)(A) of the Right to Financial Privacy Act of 1978.
618. See Section 624 of the Fair Credit Reporting Act.
619. See 18 U.S.C. § 2709(b)(1).
620. See 18 U.S.C. § 2709(b)(2).

the First Amendment to the Constitution of the United States."[621]

In 2004, the American Civil Liberties Union (ACLU) sued the United States government for an unnamed access provider in *American Civil Liberties Union v. Ashcroft* (2004)[622] arguing that 18 U.S.C. § 2709, the statute that gave the FBI its legal authority to use NSLs, infringed upon the freedoms as detailed by the First and Fourth Amendments. According to the ACLU:

- Section 2709 did not state any legal procedures where a telephone or Internet access organization could contest an NSL subpoena, and
- Section 2709 did not allow an organization receiving an NSL to reveal that he/she had received such a plea from the Federal Bureau of Investigation, and overshadows the Bureau's requirement for confidentiality in counterterrorism investigations.

The court agreed, stating that "NSLs contravened the Fourth Amendment since they did not allow for a judicial dispute regarding an NSL request." In addition, the court ruled that the proscription regarding disclosure in 18 U.S.C. § 2709(c) was unconstitutional as it breached the right of free speech as found in the First Amendment.

Title 18, Section 1030 of the U.S. Code detailed the penalties available concerning a number of computer crimes. This comprised illegal access, by means of a computer to:

- classified information alluding to the creation, producing, or use of atomic bombs; the assembly of nuclear matter; or the utilization of nuclear matter in the making of energy[623]
- data enclosed in the financial documents of a financial organization, branch, or agency of the U.S., or data from any shielded computer
- any private computer located in a United States governmental department or organization.

This includes committing illegal acts with a computer in a variety of situations.

Section 506 gave the U.S. Secret Service the authority to investigate crimes, although the Bureau retained the principal power in investigating crimes pertaining to the illegal access of secret information dealing with nuclear power,[624] unless the President, Vice President, President-elect, Vice

---

621. See USA Patriot Act, Section 505.
622. See American Civil Liberties Union v. Ashcroft (2004).
623. See Section 11, paragraph of the Atomic Energy Act.
624. Ibid.

President-elect, and/or their families or other associated individuals.[625] The Secret Service retained the power to apprehend anyone committing bank fraud.[626]

Section 444 of the General Education Provisions Act[627] confines giving money to educational institutions limiting parental access to the scholastic records of their children, or allows data to be given to individuals or agencies of the general public regarding students lacking the written permission of that student's parents. Section 507 added more to the General Education Provisions Act. Paragraph j permits the AG or his/her assistant to gather and keep scholastic records pertinent to an investigation or prosecution of a crime that is classified as a federal terrorist crime[628] which the educational organization or institution has in its possession. The AG or his/her assistant must guarantee that the records in question contain data stating that a terrorist act could occur.[629] Any educational institution giving the documents to the legal authorities will be shielded from any legal responsibility that could occur due to their giving the records to the government.

The National Education Statistics Act of 1994 was changed to permit the AG and his/her assistant to tender a written request to a court for an ex parte directive to gather all data from the National Center for Education Statistics (NCES) connecting to investigations and criminal actions regarding a terrorist act[630] or an operation involving either domestic or international terrorism.[631] However, the National Education Statistics Act of 1994 was repealed on June 2, 2006.[632]

TITLE VI: PROVIDING FOR VICTIMS OF TERRORISM, PUBLIC SAFETY OFFICERS AND THEIR FAMILIES

The Patriot Act's sixth title was an anti-terrorism bill approved by Congress after 9/11. Its primary purpose was to supply assistance to the families of Public Safety Officers who were hurt or slain in the attacks, while altering the Victims of Crime Act of 1984.

---

625. See 18 U.S.C. § 3056–(a).
626. See 18 U.S.C. § 3056(b)(3).
627. See 20 U.S.C. § 1232g.
628. See 18 U.S.C. § 2332b(g)(5)(B).
629. See 20 U.S.C. § 1232g(j)(2).
630. See 18 U.S.C. § 2332b(g)(5)(B).
631. See 18 U.S.C. § 2331.
632. See H.R.3801 (Pub. L. 103–382).

Subtitle A: Aid to Families of Public Safety Officers

Title I of the Omnibus Crime Control and Safe Streets Act of 1968 contained riders allowing for the compensation of public safety officers or the relatives of officers that are slain or have received a shattering wound in the line of duty. Section 611 accelerated the doling out of such payments, and the individual, or their family members, will receive the money no more than 30 days after the injury was sustained, if the wound occurred while investigating terrorist acts, or while the individual was involved in a rescue mission due to such acts. Section 612 altered Public Law 107–37,[633] which makes available funds for any public safety officers who was badly injured on 9/11. The alteration incorporated "permanent and total disability" in the permissible grounds regarding how an officer could receive remuneration, which increased from $100,000 to $250,000.[634]

The Assistant AG received greater power under section 214, and could make grants[635] to any agency administering Office of Justice Programs, which were created in 1968.[636]

Subtitle B: Amendments to the Victims of Crime Act of 1984

The Crime Victim Fund (controlled by the Victims of Crime Act of 1984), permits privately owned organizations or private individuals to donate into the Fund.[637] Section 621 changed the way money is distributed from the Fund. The Director must dole out no less than 90 percent, and no more than 110 percent of the sum dispersed from the Fund from the year before. This provision is not applicable if the sum of cash in the Fund is double what was handed out in the prior fiscal year; if this is the scenario, the director can dole out up to 120 percent of the sum disseminated in the prior fiscal year. The director should allocate sums to take care of the judicial branch's organizational expenses in conjunction with money to grant programs.[638]

Any money remaining after the distribution was set aside in the Fund for future financial years, without a financial year constraint. Section 111 of the Departments of Commerce, Justice, and State, the Judiciary, and Related

---

633. This has been called "an Act to provide for the expedited payment of certain benefits for a public safety officer who was killed or suffered a catastrophic injury as a direct and proximate result of a personal injury sustained in the line of duty in connection with the terrorist attacks of September 11, 2001."

634. See USA Patriot Act: Section 612. It altered Section 1201(a) of the Omnibus Crime Control and Safe Streets Act of 1968 (42 U.S.C. § 3796).

635. See Pub. L. 105–277 and P.L. 106–113.

636. See Omnibus Crime Control and Safe Streets Act of 1968 (Pub.L. 90–351, June 19, 1968, 82 Stat. 197. 42 U.S.C. § 3711.

637. See 42 U.S.C. § 10601(b).

638. See 42 U.S.C. § 10601(d).

Agencies Appropriations Act, 2002 (H.R. 2500) altered this system. Moreover, the Patriot Act altered the allocation percentages of the residual sum left in the Fund from a specific fiscal year. Crime victim compensation[639] and crime victim assistance[640] were lowered from 48.5 percent to 47.5 percent, whereas money for display projects, program assessment, compliance endeavors, education and technological aid assistance to qualified crime victim aid programs and for the monetary backing of assistance to victims of federal crime by qualified crime victim aid programs increased from 3 percent to 5 percent.[641]

Another change concerned the emergency funds clause regarding money to be used against terrorism in the Victims of Crime Act.[642] Prior to the Patriot Act, the Director had the option of keeping any fraction of the Fund that was paid in during a fiscal year that exceeded 110% of the entire sum paid into the Fund during the previous fiscal year as an emergency reserve; that is, as long the total sum did not go over $100,000,000.[643] Now, the director has the option of reserving up to $50,000,000 from the quantities of money moved into the Fund as a response to 9/11. Moreover, the methods of replenishing the funds are discussed.

The Air Transportation Safety and System Stabilization Act[644] established the September 11th Victim Compensation Fund, becoming a federal remuneration that should used as a main payer to the 50 States.[645]

Grants from the Crime Victim Fund may be made to various crime victim recompense programs if the program is suitable. Section 622(a) and (b) of the PA enlarged the sum obtainable to such programs from 40 percent to 60 percent of the entire quantity within the Fund's coffers. Whether or not a program is suitable may be found in 42 U.S.C. § 10602(b). The limitations on funding programs where the injured party was an American citizen in the U.S. is not a factor; now, a program can offer recompense to American citizens that were treated badly abroad. Anyone can make an application for the compensation, regardless of his/her wealth as means testing was abolished.[646]

Under the Victims of Crime Act, the Director had the option of making an annual endowment from the Crime Victims Fund to sustain crime victim aid programs. Section 623 gives the director more leeway when offering aid to crime victims. Now he/she can offer funds to individuals living in District

---

639. See 42 U.S.C. § 10602.
640. See 42 U.S.C. § 10603(a).
641. See 42 U.S.C. § 10603(c).
642. See 42 U.S.C. § 10601.
643. Ibid.
644. See Public Law 107–42.
645. See USA Patriot Act, § 621(e).
646. See 42 U.S.C. § 10602(c).

of Columbia, Puerto Rico, the Virgin Islands, and/or any other region or possession of the United States.[647] The Victims of Crime Act was modified to purposely avert prejudice against victims because of any difference of opinion they might have with the methods a state is using in prosecuting a criminal case.[648] Grants may be available for program assessment and compliance endeavors of crime victim aid programs; likewise, funding may be available for education and technical aid services.[649] The director also has the authority to utilize the funds for fellowships and clinical internships, as well as offering various programs of training and workshops for the production and distribution of data arising from demonstrations, polls, and special projects.[650]

The Victims of Crime Act offers recompense and aid to victims of terrorism or mass violence.[651] Section 624 of the PA permits the director to create secondary grants for states with suitable crime victim reparation and aid programs, and to agencies emphasizing victim services, including federal, state, or local administration. In addition, NGOs (nongovernmental organizations) offering aid to crime victims are also eligible. The money could be used in a number of ways, i.e., crisis relief, which includes crisis response attempts, aid, recompense, and educational and technological aid for for investigations and prosecutions of terrorists.[652]

It eliminated the constraints on offering such grants to individuals considered ineligible for recompense under title VIII of the Omnibus Diplomatic Security and Antiterrorism Act of 1986 (better known as the Victims of Terrorism Compensation Act).[653] However, the utilization of the emergency reserve situated for use in responding to terrorist[654] is to be decreased by any sum awarded to the victim under the Victims of Terrorism Compensation Act.[655]

TITLE VII: INCREASED INFORMATION SHARING FOR CRITICAL INFRASTRUCTURE PROTECTION

This title, unlike the other eight, consists of one, lone section. The intent of the title is to boost the aptitude of U.S. law enforcement to counteract terrorist acts that traverse jurisdictional borders. The Patriot Act accomplished

---

647. See 42 U.S.C. § 10603(b)(1).
648. See 42 U.S.C. § 10603(c)(1)(A).
649. See 42 U.S.C. § 10603(c)(2).
650. See 42 U.S.C. § 10603(c)(3).
651. See 42 U.S.C. § 10603b.
652. See 42 U.S.C. § 10603b(b).
653. See 42 U.S.C. § 10603b(a)(1).
654. See 42 U.S.C. § 10601–(b).
655. See 42 U.S.C. § 10603c(b).

this by altering the Omnibus Crime Control and Safe Streets Act of 1968.

Title VII permits the Director of the Bureau of Justice Assistance to offer grants as well as having the authority to enter into contracts with other agencies[656] dealing with terrorist groups crossing jurisdictional borders. In addition, it gave the Bureau resources in order to perform this function.

Section 701 is Section VII's only title and is called *Expansion of Regional Information Sharing System to Facilitate Federal-State-Local Law Enforcement Response Related to Terrorist Attacks.* It alters 42 U.S.C. § 3796h: *Regional information sharing systems grants,* an element to be found in the Omnibus Crime Control and Safe Streets Act of 1968. This specific code, established before the Patriot Act was written, permitted the Director of the Bureau of Justice Assistance to "make grants and enter into contracts" with state and local law enforcement, as well as nonprofit agencies to bring to an end criminal actions crossing jurisdictional borders.[657]

Section 701 added information about terrorist acts and conspiracies to the definition of criminal activities.[658] Moreover, grants of money and services may be made for groups and/or individuals working on how to ensure that classified information remains secure. Money may be doled out for organizations that emphasize solutions to the problem of multiple jurisdictions concerning terrorist acts. The Bureau of Justice Assistance had their budge significantly increased in order to carry out the functions just mentioned.[659]

TITLE VIII: STRENGETHENING THE CRIMINAL LAWS AGAINST TERRORISM

Seventeen sections comprise Title VIII and great emphasis is placed on creating new meanings for terrorism; moreover, the Title established rules with which to deal with terrorist acts.

The U.S. Code contains a variety of rules regarding railroads.[660] Section 801 received a new segment punishing individuals that commit a bevy of crimes.[661]

(1) wrecks, derails, sets fire to, or disables a mass transportation vehicle or ferry;

(2) places or causes to be placed any biological agent or toxin for use as a weapon, destructive substance, or destructive device in, upon, or near a mass

---

656. See USA Patriot Act: Section 701 amended 42 U.S.C. § 3796h.
657. Ibid.
658. Ibid.
659. Ibid.
660. See title 18, chapter 97.
661. See 18 U.S.C. § 1993.

transportation vehicle or ferry, without previously obtaining the permission of the mass transportation provider, and with intent to endanger the safety of any passenger or employee of the mass transportation provider, or with a reckless disregard for the safety of human life;

(3) sets fire to, or places any biological agent or toxin for use as a weapon, destructive substance, or destructive device in, upon, or near any garage, terminal, structure, supply, or facility used in the operation of, or in support of the operation of, a mass transportation vehicle or ferry, without previously obtaining the permission of the mass transportation provider, and knowing or having reason to know such activity would likely derail, disable, or wreck a mass transportation vehicle or ferry used, operated, or employed by the mass transportation provider;

(4) removes appurtenances from, damages, or otherwise impairs the operation of a mass transportation signal system, including a train control system, centralized dispatching system, or rail grade crossing warning signal without authorization from the mass transportation provider;

(5) interferes with, disables, or incapacitates any dispatcher, driver, captain, or person while they are employed in dispatching, operating, or maintaining a mass transportation vehicle or ferry, with intent to endanger the safety of any passenger or employee of the mass transportation provider, or with a reckless disregard for the safety of human life;

(6) commits an act, including the use of a dangerous weapon, with the intent to cause death or serious bodily injury to an employee or passenger of a mass transportation provider or any other person while any of the foregoing are on the property of a mass transportation provider;

(7) conveys or causes to be conveyed false information, knowing the information to be false, concerning an attempt or alleged attempt being made or to be made, to do any act which would be a crime prohibited by this subsection; or

(8) attempts, threatens, or conspires to do any of the aforesaid acts, shall be fined under this title or imprisoned not more than twenty years, or both, if such act is committed, or in the case of a threat or conspiracy such act would be committed, on, against, or affecting a mass transportation provider engaged in or affecting interstate or foreign commerce, or if in the course of committing such act, that person travels or communicates across a State line in order to commit such act, or transports materials across a State line in aid of the commission of such act.[662]

Section 802 redefines domestic terrorism:

(a) DOMESTIC TERRORISM DEFINED–Section 2331 of title 18, United States Code, is amended–

---

662. See USA Patriot Act: Section 801, Section 1993.

(1) in paragraph (1)(B)(iii), by striking 'by assassination or kidnapping' and inserting 'by mass destruction, assassination, or kidnapping';
(2) in paragraph (3), by striking 'and';
(3) in paragraph (4), by striking the period at the end and inserting '; and'; and
(4) by adding at the end the following:
(5) the term `domestic terrorism' means activities that–
(A) involve acts dangerous to human life that are a violation of the criminal laws of the United States or of any State;
(B) appear to be intended–
(i) to intimidate or coerce a civilian population;
(ii) to influence the policy of a government by intimidation or coercion; or
(iii) to affect the conduct of a government by mass destruction, assassination, or kidnapping; and
(C) occur primarily within the territorial jurisdiction of the United States.'[663]

In a terrorist investigation, the AG can look into:

- the manufacturing of flawed national-defense goods or substances, national-defense property, or national-defense services,[664]
- the demolition or tampering with a submarine mine, torpedo, building or harbor-defense network, or the defying of any Presidential Executive Order governing individuals and/or craft inside the restrictions of defensive ocean locales, 18 U.S.C. § 2152,
- an attack on the President, the President-elect, the Vice President or the individuals in line to be President in an emergency,[665]
- an attack on any member of the U.S. Congress or a member-of-congress-elect,[666]
- destroying any building designed to produce power,[667]
- the assault of any U.S. property or possessions,[668]
- a plot to harm or demolish explicit property inside a foreign nation that belongs to a foreign nation that is at peace with the Untied States,[669]
- the demolition of any structure, motor vehicle, or other private or valid property that is chartered or held by the U.S. government through the utilization of conflagration or a bomb,[670]
- intimidation designed to destroy or harm another individual.[671]

---

663. See Ibid, Section 801.
664. See 18 U.S.C. § 2156.
665. See 18 U.S.C. § 1751(e).
666. See 18 U.S.C. § 351(e).
667. This is in reference to the meaning of an energy facility, as stated in 18 U.S.C. § 1366, which is 18 U.S.C. § 1366(c); also alludes to the act itself, which is 18 U.S.C. § 1366(b).
668. See 18 U.S.C. § 1361.
669. See 18 U.S.C. § 956(b).
670. Ibid.
671. See 18 U.S.C. § 844(e).

Other changes led to the subsequent acts being placed within the definition of "International terrorism":[672]

- the obliteration of aircraft or aircraft hangars,[673]
- hostility and/or aggressive acts at international airports,[674]
- setting fires inside specific maritime and protective jurisdictions,[675]
- the utilization of biological weaponry,[676]
- the utilization of the Variola Virus,[677]
- the utilization of chemical warfare,[678]
- the abduction or murder of members of congress, the Executive Cabinet, and Supreme Court justices,[679]
- the utilization of nuclear weapons in a terrorist act,[680]
- involvement in nuclear and/or weapons of mass destruction intimidation to the United States,[681]
- the utilization of synthetic explosives,[682]
- the burning and bombing of any governmental possessions that could cause death, or actually does so,[683]
- the burning and bombing of goods and/or possession utilized in interstate trade,[684]
- the murder or attempted murder during an assault on a Federal building with any type of dangerous weapon,[685]
- the plan to kill, abduct, or disfigure individuals outside the U.S.,[686]
- illegal entry to secure computers,[687]
- the murder or attempted murder of officials and workers of the United States,[688]
- the intentional slaying or manslaughter of foreign officers, authorized visitors, or internationally protected individuals,[689]

---

672. 18 U.S.C. § 2332b was changed.
673. See 18 U.S.C. § 32.
674. See 18 U.S.C. § 37.
675. See 18 U.S.C. § 81.
676. See 18 U.S.C. § 175 and 18 U.S.C. § 175b.
677. See 18 U.S.C. § 175c. The Variola Virus is more commonly referred to as Smallpox.
678. See 18 U.S.C. § 229.
679. See 18 U.S.C. § 351(a), (b), (c) and (d).
680. See 18 U.S.C. § 831.
681. See 18 U.S.C. § 832.
682. See 18 U.S.C. § 842(m) or (n).
683. See 18 U.S.C. § 844(f)(2) or (3).
684. See 18 U.S.C. § 844(i).
685. See 18 U.S.C. § 930(c).
686. See 18 U.S.C. § 956(a)(1).
687. see 18 U.S.C. § 956(a)(1), 18 U.S.C. § 1030(a)(1), 18 U.S.C. § 1030(a)(5)(A)(i), and 18 U.S.C. § 1030(a)(5)(B)(ii) through (v).
688. See 18 U.S.C. § 1114.
689. See 18 U.S.C. § 1116.

- the criminal taking of individuals and holding them hostage,[690]
- the destruction of governmental assets or contracts,[691]
- destroying communication cables, posts, or networks,[692]
- damage to structures or property inside exclusive maritime and/or protective jurisdiction of the United States,[693]
- destroying a facility that produces energy,[694]
- Presidential and Presidential staff murder and/or abduction,[695]
- the destruction of trains,[696]
- terrorist assaults and additional acts of aggression against mass transportation organizations,[697]
- destroying national defense items, buildings, or utilities,[698]
- charges concerning national defense items, buildings, or utilities,[699]
- aggression against maritime navigation,[700]
- aggression against maritime set policies,[701]
- murders and other assaults against Americans outside the Untied States,[702]
- the utilization of weapons of mass destruction,[703]
- terrorist acts rising above national borders,[704]
- terrorist violence against public locales and facilities,[705]
- the utilization of anti-aircraft missile systems,[706]
- the utilization of radiological distribution systems,[707]
- protecting terrorists,[708]
- breathing,[709]
- supplying substantive aid to individual terrorists,[710]

---

690. See 18 U.S.C. § 1203.
691. See 18 U.S.C. § 1361.
692. See 18 U.S.C. § 1362.
693. See 18 U.S.C. § 1363.
694. See 18 U.S.C. § 1366–(a).
695. See 18 U.S.C. § 1751(a), (b), (c), or (d).
696. See 18 U.S.C. § 1992.
697. See 18 U.S.C. § 1993.
698. See 18 U.S.C. § 2155.
699. See 18 U.S.C. § 2156.
700. See 18 U.S.C. § 2280.
701. See 18 U.S.C. § 2281.
702. See 18 U.S.C. § 2332.
703. See 18 U.S.C. § 2332a.
704. See 18 U.S.C. § 2332b.
705. See 18 U.S.C. § 2332f.
706. See 18 U.S.C. § 2332g.
707. See 18 U.S.C. § 2332h.
708. See 18 U.S.C. § 2339.
709. See 18 U.S.C. § 2339S.
710. See 18 U.S.C. § 2339A.

- supplying substantive aid to terrorist groups,[711]
- sponsoring terrorism,[712] or
- torture,[713]
- incapacitating of nuclear reactors or fuel,[714]
- airline hijacking,[715] attacking a flight personnel with a dangerous weapon,[716] imperiling others by utilizing bombs or highly combustible mechanisms on aircraft,[717] murder or attempted murder on an aircraft,[718]
- destroying an interstate gas or dangerous liquid pipeline building.[719]

A variety of procedures was carried out with the hope of preventing and penalizing behavior that indicates terrorist support. Section 803 alters the law regarding terrorism[720] to take in a new section that prevents the protecting and hiding of terrorists.[721] In essence, any individual caught helping a person they know has committed a crime, as labeled under any one of 11 Federal codes[722] is liable for a fine, incarceration up to 10 years, or both.[723] Any of these breaches of the law can be tried in any federal judicial district where the crime occurred, or in any other region as dictated by law.[724]

Section 804 changed 18 U.S.C. § 7: *Special maritime and territorial jurisdiction of the United States defined.*[725] It was changed so whenever an illegal act is perpetrated upon a citizen or against a U.S. national, the American consulate, military, and/or over U.S. missions residing within foreign countries are thought to be part of American jurisdiction; thus, an attack against a citizen is the same as an attack against America.[726] It ends by adding a clause saying that this paragraph does not trump any international agreement that it comes into conflict with, and that it does not apply to members of the Armed forces who commit an offense outside the U.S. that would have

---

711. See 18 U.S.C. § 2339B.
712. See 18 U.S.C. § 2339C.
713. See 18 U.S.C. § 2340A.
714. See Section 236 of the Atomic Energy Act of 1954 (42 U.S.C. § 2284).
715. See 49 U.S.C. § 46502.
716. See 49 U.S.C. § 46504.
717. See 49 U.S.C. § 46505(b)(3) or (c).
718. See 49 U.S.C. § 46506.
719. See 49 U.S.C. § 60123(b).
720. See Title 18, chapter 113B.
721. See 18 U.S.C. § 2339.
722. See These codes are, in turn, 18 U.S.C. § 32; 18 U.S.C. § 175; 18 U.S.C. § 229; 18 U.S.C. § 831; 18 U.S.C. § 844(f)(2) and (3); 18 U.S.C. § 1366(a); 18 U.S.C. § 2280; 18 U.S.C. § 2332a; 18 U.S.C. § 2332b; section 236(a) of the Atomic Energy Act of 1954 (42 U.S.C. § 2284); and 49 U.S.C. § 46502 (source: 18 U.S.C. § 2339).
723. See 18 U.S.C. § 2339(a).
724. See 18 U.S.C. § 2339(b).
725. See 18 U.S.C. § 7.
726. See Title VIII, Sec. 804.

resulted in a year or longer imprisonment had it been committed within the U.S.[96].

Section 805 alters the law on giving substantive provisions to terrorists;[727] thus, an individual being tried could face prosecution in any federal judicial district where the crime occurred, or in any other region as dictated by law.[728] The section added four codes under the title.[729] Section 805 states that a person offering any professional advice and/or money is considered have given substantive support to terrorists.[730]

Section 806 changed American forfeiture law[731] to permit the legal authorities to confiscate all overseas and domestic property from any group or person that is thought to be organizing or already committing terrorist acts against the United States or its citizens. Possessions may also be confiscated if they were attained or preserved by any person or organization for the rationale of aiding terrorists.

Section 807 stated that nothing in the Trade Sanctions Reform and Export Enhancement Act of 2000 curbed criminal bans concerning the providing of substantive aid to terrorists. There is no longer a statute of limitations for terrorists due to Section 809. Now, regardless of how much time has passed since the act occurred, a terrorist can be prosecuted in court and receive the death penalty regarding the demise or harm of any individual.[732] Section 819 added to the maximum punishment for wiping out an energy facility, supplying substantive aid to terrorists, and/or their organizations. In addition, obliterating important national defense resources, incapacitating nuclear plants or fuel, and seriously damaging or the ruination of an interstate gas or dangerous liquid pipeline operation could lead to 20 years incarceration.[733]

Section 811 added terrorist plots (referred to as conspiracy provision in the act) to the U.S. Code that covers setting fires anywhere in the U.S.;[734] murdering anyone within federal buildings;[735] the devastation of communications links, bases, or networks;[736] the devastation of property anywhere with the United States;[737] smashing trains;[738] significant aid to terrorists;[739] torture;[740] the

---

727. See 18 U.S.C. § 2339A.
728. Ibid.
729. See 18 U.S.C. § 229, 18 U.S.C. § 1993, 42 U.S.C. § 2284, and 49 U.S.C. § 60123(b) (source: USA Patriot Act (U.S. H.R. 3162, Public Law 107–56), Title VIII, Sec. 805, (a)(1).
730. See 18 U.S.C. § 2339A (a)(1)(A)–(B).
731. See 18 U.S.C. § 981.
732. 18 U.S.C. § 3286 was the code that was amended.
733. 18 U.S.C. § 81 was the code that was amended.
734. Ibid.
735. See 18 U.S.C. § 930(c).
736. See 18 U.S.C. § 1362.
737. See 18 U.S.C. § 1363.
738. See 18 U.S.C. § 1992.
739. See 18 U.S.C. § 2339A.
740. See 18 U.S.C. § 2340A.

disruption of nuclear plants or fuel;[741] hindering airline personnel;[742] entering an aircraft with weapons or bombs;[743] and the ruination of interstate fuel or dangerous liquid pipeline plant.[744] Section 812 states that terrorists, upon release from prison, will receive supervision for the remainder of their lives; that is, if they performed a terrorist act that caused death, or a reasonable anticipation of, death or severe physical damage to any individual.[745]

A number of characteristics regarding cyberterrorism are detailed in title VIII. Section 814 made clear that punishments pertain to anyone who harms or acquires illegal access to a secure computer, thus causing an individual to lose more than $5,000; unfavorably affecting an individual's medical check-up, diagnosis, or treatment; leads an individual to be wounded; produces a danger to community health or security; or brings about harm to a governmental computer that is utilized in administering justice, and/or the defense and security of the United States.[746] Only with these explicit acts can a civil suit be brought against a lawbreaker.[747] In addition, section 814 forbids any illegal activity using a secure computer, as well as any illegal activities aimed at a "firm, association, educational institution, financial institution, government entity, or other legal entity."[748]

Section 814 changed a variety of words concerning cyberterrorism. For instance "protected computer" now comprises a "computer located outside the United States that is used in a manner that affects interstate or foreign commerce or communication of the United States." Another redefinition includes "damage," which includes harm to the reliability or accessibility of information, a computer program, a network, or data. Other terms include "loss," "person," and "conviction."[749]

Anyone caught attempting to hack a secure computer can expect to spend more time in prison. The sentence for attempting to damage a protected computer by using viruses, Trojans, worms, etc, as well as any other software mechanism could receive up to 10 years imprisonment, while the term for illegal access and subsequent damage to a projected computer is five or more years imprisonment. If the offense occurs a second time, the likely prison term is increased to 20 years. Federal sentencing rules were amended to

---

741. See 42 U.S.C. § 2284.
742. See 49 U.S.C. § 46504.
743. See 49 U.S.C. § 46505.
744. See 49 U.S.C. § 60123.
745. 18 U.S.C. § 3583 was the code altered.
746. See 18 U.S.C. § 1030(a)(5).
747. See 18 U.S.C. § 1030(g). It was made clear that "No action may be brought under this subsection for the negligent design or manufacture of computer hardware, computer software, or firmware."
748. See 18 U.S.C. § 1030(a)(7).
749. See USA Patriot Act: Section 814.

allow any individual convicted of computer fraud and/or exploitation to get an appropriate sentence, with no deliberation regarding a mandatory period of imprisonment.

Section 815 added another defense against lawsuits where it is asserted that illegal access occurred regarding accumulated communications and the capturing of such communications.[750] It permits an Internet Service Provider to demonstrate confidence on the appeal from a governmental organization ordering them to safeguard documents and other proof in its control, awaiting the issuance of a judicial command or other procedure.[751]

Section 816 details the growth and backing for cyber security forensic capacities. It commands the AG to create local computer forensic labs that are capable of carrying out forensic analyses of captured computer data involving illegal acts and cyberterrorism, and that can train and educate law enforcement personnel in computer offenses. Likewise, a primary goal is to endorse the distribution of federal law enforcement know-how regarding the investigation and trial of computer-based offenses with state and local law enforcement and district attorneys. Fifty million American dollars was set aside for the development of such laboratories.

Section 817 increased the biological weapons law.[752] 18 U.S.C. § 175 was altered to give a new meaning regarding the utilization of biological agents, poison, or delivery system as a weapon, except when employed in a peaceful manner. The Patriot Act established a punishment whereby a person would receive more than 10 years incarceration, as well as paying a penalty for any individual who cannot confirm rationally that he/she is using a biological agent, poison, or delivery system for these reasons, or both in conjunction with each other.[753]

In addition, section 817 proscribes specific individuals from sending, carrying, or receiving a "select" biological agent.[754] A restricted individual is anyone accused by the law, or was found guilty of a felony punishable with an incarceration of one year or longer, is running from the law, convicted narcotics addicts, illegal aliens, an alien from a country supports terrorism, and/or anyone considered mentally ill that was sentenced to an institution for the mental illness. If a person transports or receives selected agents, he/she is subject to criminal fines and/or incarceration for 10 years.

---

750. See 18 U.S.C. §121.
751. See 18 U.S.C. § 2703(f).
752. See title 18, chapter 10.
753. See 18 U.S.C. § 175(b).
754. For a definition of "select" see subsection (j) of section 72.6 of title 42, Code of Federal Regulations.

TITLE IX: IMPROVED INTELLIGENCE

Title IX alters the National Security Act of 1947. Under section 901, the Director of Central Intelligence (DCI) must create rules and the main concerns for any foreign intelligence data gathered under FISA, as well as assisting the AG to guarantee that electronic and physical search data is distributed for proficient and successful foreign intelligence use. Conversely, the Patriot Act restricted the director. He/she lacks the power to order, administer, or commence FISA-based electronic surveillance or physical search operations, except for the fact that it was sanctioned by law or executive order.[755]

Section 902 stated that international terrorist activities fell within the purview of foreign intelligence, as detailed in the National Security Act of 1947.[756] Several alterations were made regarding other intelligence matters. Section 903 centered on the fact that Congressional leaders should support individuals within the intelligence community, as they (intelligence personnel) attempted to continue intelligence dealings with any people and/or groups as they conducted legal intelligence interests. Section 904 sanctioned the rearrangement of submitting news to Congress about intelligence matters until either February 1, 2002, or at some point after February 1, 2002. These dates were given if the officer in charge stated that submitting the report on February 1, 2002 would hinder the efforts of individuals engaged in counterterrorism. Any such delay had to be approved by Congress before it was endorsed.

The Patriot Act mandated that this translation service should be made available by February 1, 2002; however, this was not what transpired, and the report[757] was handed in over 60 days late. Section 907 commanded an account be written by February 1, 2002 on the viability and benefits of completely changing the configuration of the Foreign Terrorist Asset Tracking Center and the Office of Foreign Assets Control of the Department of the Treasury. The requested report was never written and a complaint was made stating that by not providing a report was contravening the Patriot Act.[758]

Section 905 emphasizes topics involving the admission of foreign intelligence data. Except for information that could put at risk any current law enforcement investigation, the AG, or the leader of any other division or

---

755. The change was made to Section 103(c) of the National Security Act of 1947 (50 U.S.C. § 403–3(c).

756. Section 3 of the National Security Act of 1947 (50 U.S.C. § 401a) was amended.

757. Entitled "Director of Central Intelligence Report on the National Virtual Translation Center: A Concept Plan to Enhance the Intelligence Community's Foreign Language Capabilities, April 29, 2002."

758. The complaint was made by The Senate Select Committee on Intelligence.

organization within the federal government possessing law enforcement duties, must disclose to the DCI any foreign intelligence attained by the DOJ. The AG and DCI were instructed to develop measures for the AG so he/she could notify the director, in a judicious style, of any intent of investigating the illegal actions of a foreign intelligence informant or probable foreign intelligence informant founded on the intelligence warning of an element in the intelligence community.[759]

Title IX requested accounts be made regarding dissimilar intelligence-related governmental organizations. Section 906 requested an account be given into the most efficacious manner of creating the National Virtual Translation Center, with the primary aim being the development of automatic translation centers to aid with the judicious and correct translation of data received from foreign intelligence sources.

Section 908 gave the AG power to train officers in how to identify and utilize foreign intelligence data correctly within the scope of their specific job. This includes individuals employed by the U.S. that do not generally come across or distribute foreign intelligence in the day to day work of their job.

TITLE X: MISCELLANEOUS

Title 10 is the last title comprising the Patriot Act. It is short with each section specifying a particular duty.

Section 1001: Review of the Department of Justice

The Inspector General of the Department of Justice will assign one individual who will take care of all civil rights and/or civil liberties abuse allegations. How to reach this individual will be disseminated through the media.

Section 1002: Sense of Congress

Both houses of Congress stated that all Americans condemned 9/11. In addition, Sikh-Americans should not receive any prejudicial treatment from other Americans.

---

759. See section 105B of the National Security Act of 1947 (50 U.S.C. § 403–5b).

Section 1003: Definition of "Electronic Intelligence"

FISA had one of its four definitions regarding electronic snooping altered.[760]

Section 1004: Venue in Money Laudering Cases

The authority and venue for prosecuting money launderers was extended to permit the apprehension and trial in any location where money laundering occurs or where such business dealings are made.

Section 1005: First Responders Assistance Act

From the years of 2003 to 2007, up to $25,000,000 was permitted for appropriation each 12-month period from 2003 to 2007 for anti-terrorism efforts at the state-level.

Section 1006: Inadmissibility of Aliens Engaged in Money Laundering

Foreigners participating in money laundering or attempting to enter United States so they can participate, may not be admitted.

Section 1007: Authorization of Funds for DEA Police Training in South and Central America

President Bush had the duty of supplying, at the minimum, $5,000,000 to Turkey for drug enforcement, while South and East Asia will receive money for chemical controls.

Section 1008

A study regarding the viability of using a biometric system, with access to FBI files at consular points all over the world (including America) will be conducted. It will be linked to the Bureau's database to identify alleged lawbreakers.

Section 1009: Study of Access

The Bureau will have access to funds up to $250,000 so it can supply a computer-based register of alleged terrorists' names to the airlines.

---

760. The new definition reads: "Electronic surveillance is the acquisition by an electronic, mechanical, or other surveillance device of the contents of any wire communication to or from a person in the United States, without the consent of any party thereto, if such acquisition occurs in the United States, but does not include the acquisition of those communications of computer trespassers that would be permissible under section 2511 (2)(i) of title 18." There are 3 other definitions of electronic surveillance in FISA.

Section 1010

Provisional power to deal with local and state governments for the functioning of defensive measures at U.S. armed forces installations. The Department of Defense's financial support may be utilized for confidential dealing for security reasons.

Section 1011: Crimes Against Charitable Americans

Charity scams were altered. Solicitors must quickly tell an individual that they want money or anything else of potential significance.

Section 1012: Limitation on Issuance of Hazmat Licenses

In order to secure a license to convey dangerous materials, the driver must undergo a thorough background investigation and display that he/she is prepared to manage the materials.

Section 1013: Expressing the Sense of the Senate Concerning the Provision of Funding for Bioterrorism Preparedness and Response

The Senate felt that the U.S. was not ready to guard against terrorist depredations and thus, an effort had to be made to prepare all individuals involved in the safeguarding process—this included local and state personnel, as well as federal.

Section 1014: Grant Program for State and Local State and Local Domestic Preparedness Support

Each individual state can obtain funds to purchase equipment and instruction for first responders (law enforcement, fire fighters, and emergency medical technicians).

Section 1015: Expansion and Reauthorization of the Crime Identification Technology Act for Antiterrorism Grants to States and Localities

Section 1016: Critical Infrastructures Protection

Chapter 5

GRUMBLINGS ACROSS THE LAND

After Congress passed the Patriot Act (PA), civil liberties groups across the U.S. condemned it, declaring that it gave law enforcement the power to overrun each individual's privacy. Moreover, judicial review disappeared and thus, federal law enforcement and the CIA could engage in spying activities without having to worry about censure from a judge. The Bush Administration stated that the tragedy of September 11 was the primary impetus to commence a top-secret National Security Agency operation, "to eavesdrop on telephone and e-mail communications between the United States and people overseas without a warrant."[761]

> From the beginning, civil liberties groups have criticized the Patriot Act, saying that it allowed law enforcement to invade the privacy of citizens.

After 9/11, several lawmakers came up with a bevy of suggestions, as a rejoinder to the attacks, less than seven days after the attacks transpired. President Bush affixed his signature to the USA PATRIOT Act on October 26, 2001, thus it became law. The PA enacted several noteworthy alterations to over 15 key laws, but because it was passed into law at such a quick pace, there was little debate in either the House or Senate regarding the effects of the new law.

The PA was a negotiated adaptation of the Anti-Terrorism Act of 2001 (ATA), a highly influential legislative package whose primary purpose was to reinforce America's security against terrorist acts. The ATA had a number of provisos that greatly expanded the power of law enforcement and intelligence organizations. Before 9/11, it was difficult to gain access to private

---

761. See "The USA PATRIOT Act: Preserving Life and Liberty" United States Department of Justice.

communications and/or personal data, but the PA amended that. The final bill contained several favorable add-ons as compared to the original proposal. Most noteworthy were "sunset provisions" (which stated that several segments of the PA would terminate after a specific period had passed, unless Congress renewed them) pertaining to electronic surveillance, as well as an alteration allowing for judicial supervision of the FBI's Carnivore system.

As mentioned, there was little discussion in Congress regarding the possible pitfalls concerning the Patriot Act. A number of the provisions concerning electronic surveillance were discussed before 9/11, but received scathing criticism. John Podesta, Chief of Staff for Bill Clinton from 1998–2001, said:

> The events of September 11 convinced . . . overwhelming majorities in Congress that law enforcement and national security officials need new legal tools to fight terrorism. But we should not forget what gave rise to the original opposition—many aspects of the bill increase the opportunity for law enforcement and the intelligence community to return to an era where they monitored and sometimes harassed individuals who were merely exercising their First Amendment rights. Nothing that occurred on September 11 mandates that we return to such an era.[762]

Once the proposals were made, John Ashcroft, the AG in Bush's first administration, gave legislators one week to ratify the bill, without changes. Patrick Leahy (D-VT) chair of the Senate Judiciary Committee convinced Ashcroft to acquiesce to a few changes, while House representatives made noteworthy enhancements.

Wide-ranging and rushed compromises in the Senate produced a bipartisan bill, primarily due to the hard work of Leahy. Thomas Daschle (D-SD), Senate majority leader, wanted agreement to authorize the proposal with no debate or change; Senator Russ Feingold (D-WI) was the sole individual to complain. Inconsequential alterations were made by House representatives, which approved the proposal 357 to 66. In a short time, the House and Senate differences were ironed out, and the PA became law on October 26, 2001.

Many Acts and statutes were changed, including

- Wiretap Statute (Title III)
- Electronic Communications Privacy Act
- Computer Fraud and Abuse Act
- Foreign Intelligence Surveillance Act
- Family Education Rights and Privacy Act

---

762. See John Podesta, American Bar Association. ABAnet.org (Winter, 2002).

- Pen Register and Trap and Trace Statute
- Money Laundering Act
- Immigration and Nationality Act
- Money Laundering Control Act
- Bank Secrecy Act
- Right to Financial Privacy Act
- Fair Credit Reporting Act

At the time, Russ Feingold stated that the PA might deleteriously affect the civil liberties of immigrants. He worried that law enforcement received too much power and that immigrants would suffer because of it. Specifically, he said:

Now here is where my caution in the aftermath of the terrorist attacks and my concerns over the reach of the anti-terrorism bill come together. To the extent that the expansive new immigration powers that the bill grants to the Attorney General are subject to abuse, who do we think that is most likely to bear the brunt of the abuse? It won't be immigrants from Ireland. It won't be immigrants from El Salvador or Nicaragua. It won't even be immigrants from Haiti or Africa. It will be immigrants from Arab, Muslim and South Asian countries. In the wake of these terrible events out government has been given vast new powers and they may fall most heavily on a minority of our population who already feel particularly acutely the pain of this disaster.[763]

One area touched by the PA includes online privacy with the Internet. The Act gives law enforcement the power to approve setting up pen registers and trap and trace devices, as well as being able to install such mechanisms to document all computer traffic. The PA gives the* government greater authority to access the personal business data and student information, even though the individual being watched is not suspected of any illegal acts; rather, he/she might receive important information that is considered germane to a current criminal investigation.

The PA, although accepted by huge majorities in both Houses of Congress, was from the beginning, divisive, and various elements in it were

> The PA gives the government greater authority to access the personal business data and student information, even though the individual being watched is not suspected of any illegal acts; rather, he/she might receive important information that is considered germane to a current criminal investigation.

---

763. Address given October 12, 2001, to the Associated Press Managing Editors Conference at the Milwaukee Art Museum, Milwaukee, Wisconsin.

quickly nullified or altered by triumphant legal confrontations over constitutional violations to civil liberties. The PA had a number of "sunset" provisions, with the majority being recertified by the *USA PATRIOT Improvement and Reauthorization Act of 2005 and the USA PATRIOT Act Additional Reauthorizing Amendments Act.* Each act reauthorized included alteration to the first PA, as well as other federal statutes.

One statute amended was the Electronic Control Privacy Act (ECPA) which was an amendment to Title III of the *Omnibus Crime Control and Safe Streets Act of 1968,* often called the "Wiretap Statute." This came about primarily due to two Supreme Court cases: *Katz v. United States*[764] and *Berger v. New York,* as well as from disapproval from the American public regarding the FBI's Counter Intelligence Program, better known from its acronym as COINTELPRO. The Supreme Court ruled in both cases that the Fourth Amendment's protections concerning search and seizure disallowed warrantless wiretaps. COINTELPRO was used by the FBI to investigate and disrupt dissenting political groups operating within the U.S. COINTELPRO's operations from 1956 to 1971 centered primarily on groups containing political radicals.[765]

> COINTELPRO was used by the FBI to investigate and disrupt dissenting political groups operating within the U.S. COINTELPRO's operations from 1956 to 1971 centered primarily on groups containing political radicals.

This included any organization whose central aim was violently bringing down the United States government, civil rights groups that abhorred violence such as Southern Christian Leadership Conference (Martin Luther King's organization), as well as other fringe groups like the Ku Klux Klan and the American Nazi Party.[766] The Church Committee[767] stated that the majority of surveillance operations used by COINTELPRO was unlawful.[768] Accordingly, Title III of the *Omnibus Crime Control and Safe Streets Act,* while acknowledging the fact that wiretaps are an integral part of law enforcement, stated that much of the wiretapping conducted by COINTELPRO was ille-

---

764. See Chapter 2.
765. See Nelson Blackstock (1975). *COINTELPRO: The FBI's Secret War on Political Freedom.* Pathfinder, New York.
766. See Paul Wolf, COINTELPRO: The Untold American Story (2001–09–01). Retrieved on 2008–12–29.
767. See Chapter 1.
768. See Ward Churchill & Jim Vander Wall (1990). *The COINTELPRO Papers: Documents from the FBI's Secret Wars Against Domestic Dissent.* Boston: South End Press.

gal and was used to listen in to the confidential discussions of American citizens without their permission.[769]

These private dialogues were, in turn, used in court; thus, to safeguard the reliability of the court system while making certain the confidentiality of American citizens was not infringed, the Act supplied a legal system within allowing for wiretaps and the interception of communications could be utilized. The Act mandated that a judicial order allowing for the utilization of such procedures against Americans be duly authorized, with consequences for someone not receiving such authorization. The noteworthy exclusion to this occurs in section 18 U.S.C. § 2511(3), which states that in situations where the President must safeguard the country from specific and/or likely aggressive actions from another country.

When Title III was established, telecommunications was in its infancy and since that time many advances in communications technology have been made. This made it necessary to update the law to take into account these new developments. Thus the ECPA was passed, and extended Title III to also protect wire, oral, and electronic communications while in transit, as well as protecting stored electronic communications. The ECPA also extended the prohibition of the use of pen register and/or trap and trace devices to record dialing information used in the process of transmitting wire or electronic communications without a search warrant.

Before the PA, the *Immigration and Nationality Act of 1952* (INA), often referred to as the *McCarran-Walter Act*,[770] was the means by which the entry of foreigners into the U.S. was restricted. It gave Uncle Sam the power to expel immigrants or naturalized citizens occupied in seditious behavior, as well as preventing individuals thought to be subversive from setting foot inside U.S. territory. The Act was listed under Title 8 (which governed immigration and citizenship) of the U. S. Code. Before the INA, a number of laws managed immigration but were scattered across a variety of different statutes. The INA was amended by the *Immigration and Nationality Act of 1965*, and then again with the *Immigration Reform and Control Act of 1986*. Since the inception of the PA, a range of different legal Acts, consisting of the Real ID Act of 2005, has altered Title 8.

Naturally, the mechanism that brought the PA into existence was 9/11. Soon after, President George W. Bush proclaimed a War on Terror and Senators from both sides of the aisle began work on legislation that allows legal authorities more leeway when fighting terrorism within the U.S.

The Washington Post wrote that Viet Dinh, then Assistant Attorney General, began working to enlarge the power of federal agencies, allegedly supported

---

769. See Pub.L. 90–351, 42 U.S.C. § 3711.
770. See Public Law No. 82–414.

by the belief that John Ashcroft wanted to provide for law enforcement any means necessary to defeat the terrorists.[771] At the same time, Jim Dempsey of the Center for Democracy and Technology (CDT) was worried that civil liberties might be trodden under during the sprint to legislate against possible terrorists.[772]

EARLIEST BILLS INITIATED

Only a few weeks after 9/11, a variety of bills altering anti-terrorism statutes were brought before Congress. The first was the *Combating Terrorism Act of 2001,* presented by Senators Orrin Hatch (R-UT) and Jon Kyl (R-AZ), with backing from Senators Dianne Feinstein (D-CA) and Chuck Schumer (D-NY) on September 13.[773] One of its measures indicated that a report be written regarding the ability of the National Guard to preemptively prevent any domestic terrorists from using weapons of mass destruction, and suggested that the military should begin studying how to prevent terrorism. In addition, various federal organizations were called upon to measure their ability to deal with terrorism, and called for the CIA to have the right to enlist terrorist informers and planned for law enforcement to divulge any foreign intelligence that was exposed while wiretaps (and any other operations allowing for eavesdropping) were used. This modification also suggested that too little was being done to obstruct and examine terrorist money making, and wanted to amplify actions to avert the "cleaning" of money gathered by terrorism.[774]

One bill, the *Public Safety and Cyber Security Enhancement Act* was brought up on 09-20-2001 within the House of Representatives by Senator Lamar Smith (R-TX).[775] The bill's primary goal centered on the illegal access of safeguarded computers and suggested making changes to the statutes involving cable customers' confidentiality; likewise, it asked for a number of alterations concerning pen register and trap and trace laws. The bill was to make an exemption regarding the collecting of foreign intelligence in the statutes mandating that a court order was needed for pen register and trap and trace surveillance. It would have taken away any constraints regarding the government's right to access cable customer documents and only proscribed law enforce-

---

771. See O'Harrow, Jr., Robert (2002–10–27). "Six Weeks in Autumn," *The Washington Post,* pp. W06. Retrieved on 2007–12–29.

772. Ibid.

773. See Center for Democracy and Technology. United States Congress, Senate Amendment 1562, September 13, 2001.

774. Ibid.

775. See H.R. 2915.

ment of disclosing the viewing habits of cable service customers.[776]

Senators Bob Graham (D-FL) and Jay Rockefeller (D-WV) brought to the Senate floor the *Intelligence to Prevent Terrorism Act* on September 28. The bill called for a bevy of alterations concerning the Director of Central Intelligence (DCI). The most noteworthy modification recommended was to necessitate the Attorney General or the leader of any agency or organization to reveal to the DCI any foreign intelligence attained during a criminal investigation.

In addition, it would have been obligatory that both the DCI and Secretary of the Treasury give an account to Congress about whether it would be a good idea to revitalize the Office of Foreign Assets Control and its Foreign Terrorist Asset Tracking Center. There was some question as to whether it could supply the scrutiny and distribution of foreign intelligence as it related to the monetary capacity and capital of international terrorist groups. The DCI would have had to create and sustain a National Virtual Translation Center for judicious and precise records of foreign intelligence for the intelligence community. The Attorney General would have presented an agenda of instruction to American executives concerning the discovery and utilization of foreign intelligence.[777]

Senators Orrin Hatch (R-UT) and Arlen Specter (R-PA), in conjunction with Senator Patrick Leahy (D-VT) had worked with the Attorney General with on a plan entitled the *Anti-Terrorism Act of 2001*. A number of the most notorious facets of the Patriot Act were originally an element of this draft and was later launched as the PATRIOT Act/USA Act, which was the foundation for the final version of the Patriot Act. Some of the issues discussed included expanding roving wiretaps from the exclusive province of national agencies into the sphere of influence for foreign intelligence surveillance; likewise, an increase of wiretaps from phones to Internet equipment was also discussed.

Different law enforcement organizations would have been able to distribute wiretap data and would have increased the capacity of surveillance subpoenas to permit greater access to private documents, which included a number of different items including books and papers.[778] The individual bills initiated by Senator Graham and the suggested Anti-Terrorism Act bill were submitted to the Select Committee on Intelligence. *The Washington Post* wrote that several civil liberties organizations were invited to join in on discussion

---

776. Public Safety and Cyber Security Enhancement Act (2001). *Center for Democracy and Technology.* Retrieved 2008–02–02.
777. See *Intelligence to Prevent Terrorism Act of 2001* (2001). Congressional Research Service. Retrieved on 2008–01–23.
778. See *Anti-Terrorism Act of 2001*.

regarding the proposed bill, but Justice officials grew angry that they had been invited. Thus began the breakdown on communication between the Democrats and Republicans.[779]

In the House of Representatives, the *Financial Anti-Terrorism Act* was discussed. The bill, which became part of the Patriot Act, was launched during mid-October by House Representative Mike Oxley (R-OH), was approved, and then submitted to the Committee on Banking, Housing, and Urban Affairs.[780] It recommended intensifying financial law enforcement using a variety of procedures, which embraced creating FinCEN as an agency with the Treasury Department, boosting forfeiture statutes and averting the formation of business dealing to sidestep antimoney laundering laws.[781] It also suggested the creation of procedures that would enhance the collaboration between the public and private segments, especially the telling and thwarting financial wrongdoing, i.e., money laundering[782] and any other procedures that could aid in the fight against international money laundering.[783]

THE PATRIOT ACT COMES TO LIFE

The Patriot Act's first introduction to the House of Representatives occurred on October 2, 2001 and was called *Provide Appropriate Tools Required to Intercept and Obstruct Terrorism (PATRIOT) Act of 2001,* though it passed the House as the *Uniting and Strengthening America (USA) Act* (H.R. 2975) on 10–12–01.[784] The basis for the passage was the *Anti-Terrorism Act,* which had been altered after talks between Attorney General John Ashcroft and Senators Patrick Leahy (D-VT), Paul Sarbanes (D-MD), Bob Graham (D-FL), Trent Lott (R-MS) and Orrin Hatch (R-UT). Its introduction into the Senate was as the *USA Act of 2001* by Tom Daschle (D-SD, at which point Senator Russ Feingold (D-WI) suggested several alterations be made before it was passed (and the Senate agreed). Feingold altered the section concerning the capture of computer hacker communications,[785] restricted the roving wiretap power granted under the auspices of FISA,[786] and changed the sections con-

---

779. Op. cit. O'Harrow.
780. See H.R. 3004.
781. See "Title I: Strengthening Law Enforcement." October 17, 2001. *Congressional Research Service,* CRS Summary of H.R. 3004.
782. See "Title II: Public-Private Cooperation." October 17, 2001 *Congressional Research Service,* CRS Summary of H.R. 3004.
783. See "Title III: Combatting International Money Laundering." October 17, 2001. *Congressional Research Service,* CRS Summary of H.R. 3004.
784. See H.R. 2975.
785. See Senate Amendment 1899.
786. See Senate Amendment 1900.

cerned with access to business documents under FISA.[21] The USA Act was placed in indefinite stasis as the Senate and House proposals could not be resolved in time.[787]

On 10-23-01, the *USA PATRIOT Act,* H.R. 3162, received its introduction into the House. It integrated H.R. 2975 and S. 1510, along with many components of H.R. 3004 (the *Financial Anti-Terrorism Act).*[788] While several political leaders voiced their anxieties,[789] a motion was made to shelve normal protocol and thus, the bill was passed.[790]

Only one individual voted against the Act, Russ Feingold,[791] who thought several provisions were disagreeable. Feingold did not like the manner in which the bill was whisked speedily through Congress.[792] In addition, sections involving wiretapping, the alterations to the search and seizure statutes,[793] the enlarged authority under FISA that permitted the police to put their hands on business documents[794] and the various changes made to arrest and expulsion statutes for immigrants.[795] The Act had a number of "sunset" clauses, primarily due to the dogged persistence of Representative Richard "Dick" Armey (R-TX).[796] However, the Act took into consideration any current foreign intelligence investigations and permitted them to carry on once the sunset sections had concluded.

On October 31, 2001, Attorney General John Ashcroft announced at a Department of Justice speech the new authority found within the Patriot Act

> The Department of Justice is also moving forcefully to implement new authorities in our antiterrorism law. Today, the Immigration and Naturalization Service has issued guidance to immigration personnel informing them about the new power that the USA Patriot Act provides for them in terms of the detention, arrest, and removal of terrorist aliens.
>
> The act broadens the grounds of inadmissibility, that is grounds for which admission to the United States can be denied, to include representatives of groups that publicly endorse terrorist activity in the United States. It also makes aliens inadmissible if they provide material support to a designated terrorist organization; even if they don't specifically intend to support this terror-

---

787. See S11247 (2001). U.S. Congressional Record. *U.S. Government Printing Office.* Retrieved on 2007–12–20.
788. See H.R. 3162.
789. See S10990 (October 25, 2001). U.S. Congressional Record. *U.S. Government Printing Office.* Retrieved on 2007–12–20.
790. See Passed 357–66; Roll number 398 (October 23 2001).
791. See Record vote number 313 for H.R. 3192. Passed 98–1.
792. See S11020 (October 25th, 2001). Congressional Record. *U.S. Government Printing Office.*
793. See S11021 (October 25th, 2001). Congressional Record. *U.S. Government Printing Office.*
794. See S11022 (October 25th, 2001). Congressional Record. *U.S. Government Printing Office.*
795. Ibid.
796. Op. cit. O'Harrow.

ist activity, they are giving support to the organization which conducts terrorist activities, they can be denied admission to the United States. In most cases, aliens will be inadmissible under these new provisions for past support they had given to terrorist organizations.

In addition, the USA Patriot Act requires the detention of aliens whom the attorney general certifies to be a threat to national security, or who are determined to have engaged–to have been engaged–let me start that over again. One, the attorney general, if he certifies that they are a threat to national security, they must be detained by a requirement of the USA Patriot Act; or two, if they are determined to have been engaged in terrorist activities. Once arrested, aliens must be charged with a criminal or immigration offense within seven days, under the act.

If the charges are dismissed, the aliens will be released. Otherwise, charged aliens must be detained until they are removed from the United States, according to the act, or until they are determined no longer to pose a threat to national security. This measure, which is the equivalent of denying bail to violent offenders, will prevent dangerous aliens from being released to mingle among the American citizens that they would harm.

Finally, I am today asking the secretary of State to designate 46 groups as terrorists organizations under the USA Patriot Act. All these groups have committed or planned violent terrorist acts, or serve as fronts for terrorist organizations.

The groups to be designated as terrorist organizations include those linked to the al-Qaeda network, whose assets the president has frozen, pursuant to an executive order. The remainder of the groups to be designated have been found by the Department of State, in its 'Patterns of Global Terrorism' report, to have engaged–to have been engaged in terrorist activity. Designating these groups as terrorist organizations will enable us to prevent aliens who are affiliated with them from entering the United States.

In addition, any aliens who are inadmissible because of their affiliation with these groups at the time they manage to enter our country would also be subject to removal.

Now these restrictions apply to the groups' representatives and members. Also inadmissible are aliens who use their positions of prominence to endorse terrorist activity. As the president has emphasized, America's new war against terrorism has two fronts. Our armed forces will fight abroad against terrorism and the states that support terrorists abroad. It falls to all Americans to fight terrorism at home. Our borders divide these two fronts.

The U.S.A. Patriot Act authorized vital new weapons for us to fight the war at the borders and here at home, and the Justice Department is committed to ensuring that these weapons are deployed quickly, that they're deployed efficiently, and that they're deployed effectively.[797]

---

797. Attorney General Press Briefing, October 31, 2001. *CNN.com transcripts.* Retrieved on 2008-02-02.

PROBLEMS

Almost immediately after its birth, the Patriot Act was questioned by various politicians in Congress. On June 13, 2002, the House Judiciary committee penned a missive to the Attorney General in which he was asked 50 questions regarding the Patriot Act's utilization and usefulness. Basically, the letter wanted specific answers regarding the investigation of terrorists and/or terrorist attacks.[798] Of the 50 questions, 28 were answered openly, with seven being answered privately.[799] At the same time, civil liberties groups such as the American Civil Liberties Union and the Electronic Privacy Information Center (EPIC) was forging full steam ahead opposing the most contentious elements of the Act.

Ninety days following the official rejoinder to the House Judiciary Committee, EPIC filed a Freedom of Information (FOI) request in search of the data that the DOJ did not release to the public.[800] Although the DOJ did let go of a number of documents in reply to the appeal, not all of the information was released, stating that specific responsive reports were free from from disclosure. As the DOJ would not release them, the ACLU and EPIC sued them.[801] Finally, Ellen Segal Huvelle, District Judge for the District of Columbia, commanded DOJ to finish its handling of the FOI request by January 15, 2003.[802]

During this time, Senators Lisa Murkowski (R-AK) and Ron Wyden (D-OR), introduced to their Senate colleagues *Protecting the Rights of Individuals Act*,[803] one of the first in a long line of efforts to amend Patriot Act. Some of the alterations included those pertaining to FISA, especially regarding the restraints of "sneak and peek" warrants and "roving wiretaps," the tightening of the classification of what is and is not construed as terrorism, and the restoration of judicial review when organizations wanted to gain entrance into library and/or business documents. In addition, FISA's central aim would be re-established; that is, surveillance would be used for foreign intelligence reasons, whereas the Patriot Act had amended FISA to be used for anything "significant." The bill suggested a temporary cessation of data gathering by various organizations, with the exception of circumstances permit-

798. See Frank James Sensenbrenner & John Conyers Jr. (June 13, 2002). Letter to Attorney General John Ashcroft.
799. See Daniel J. Bryant (July 26, 2002). Response to 50 questions. *United States Department of Justice.*
800. See *Electronic Privacy Information Center* (October 25, 2002) FOI complaint.
801. See ACLU and EPIC v. Department of Justice, Civil Action No. 02–2077. March 21, 2003.
802. See ACLU and EPIC v. Department of Justice, Civil Action No. 03–2522. (D.D.C. ESH), PATRIOT Act. FOIA. EPIC website, retrieved 2008–02–02.
803. See S.1552.

ted by statutes and would have prohibited governmental access to educational documents, unless detailed facts could be produced explaining why the records were needed in the course of an investigation.[804]

Other bills were introduced to rein in the power of the Patriot Act. In the House, on 9–24–2003, Dennis Kucinich (D-OH) and Ron Paul (R-TX) initiated debate on their plan, the *Benjamin Franklin True Patriot Act,*[805] the name which was based on Benjamin Franklin's well known dictum: "those who would give up Essential Liberty, to purchase a little temporary Safety, deserve neither Liberty nor Safety." It recommended a 90-day evaluation, during which time 11 segments of the Act would have died away. Specific sections of the Act, such as those pertaining to "sneak and peek" warrants, pen register and trap and trace authorities, detention and expulsion of noncitizens, with the FBI gaining the power to access any and all records under FISA would have lapsed. Moreover, the use of National Security Letters and the expanded meaning of domestic terrorism, would have been taken off the books; thus, several of the most contentious passages in the Patriot Act would have been removed. The Benjamin Franklin Act languished in Congress and in order to be reconsidered, needs to be reintroduced.

In late January 2003, a draft copy of the *Domestic Security Enhancement Act of 2003* was released to the public.[806] Within days, it became known as "Patriot II" or "Son of Patriot." "Patriot II" called for more changes so the Patriot Act could be extended.[807] It called for amendments to FISA, incorporating the meaning of a foreign influence with regard to FISA, while permitting the utilization of wiretaps 15 days after Congress sanctioned the use of the military (at present, federal statutes permit this only after war has been declared). "Patriot II" would have permitted various Federal organizations to attain a foreign nation's verbal communications and would have increased the number of pen registers under FISA to pertain to American citizens.

It suggested that the FISA Court of Review be permitted to utilize an attorney vetted so he/she possessed a security authorization to bolster the verdict of the FISC, and would have enlarged the utilization of various techniques used by law enforcement under FISA. Patriot II would have prevented terrorist detainee information from being disclosed and would have restricted what individuals in a Grand Jury terrorism case could reveal. In addition, some measures would have likely improved the country's ability to fight ter-

---

804. See Analysis of the Protecting the Rights of Individuals Act (2003). *Electronic Frontiers Foundation.*

805. See H.R. 3171.

806. See Now with Bill Moyers (February 7th, 2007). PBS.

807. See Ryan Singel (2003–03–12). "A Chilly Response to 'Patriot II,'" *Politics: Law,* Wired News. Retrieved on 2007–12–29.

rorism, i.e., the creation of a terrorism ID database. Other suggested alterations were to characterize terrorism as a crime, as well as detailing the legal
structure needed with which to put on trial anyone suspected of terrorist acts.

The DOJ announced that Patriot II was only an outline,[808] but it still
caused great political storm, with both sides of the aisle condemning it for
intruding upon privacy and civil liberties.[809] Senator Leahy protested, stating
that, "If there is going to be a sequel to the USA PATRIOT Act, the process
of writing it should be open and accountable. It should not be shrouded in
secrecy, steeped in unilateralism or tinged with partisanship. The early signals from the Administration about its intentions for this bill are ominous,
and I hope Justice Department officials will change the way they are handling this."[810]

A Gallup poll taken in 2005 asked this question: "Based on what you have
read or heard, do you think the Patriot Act goes too far, is about right, or
does not go far enough in restricting people's civil liberties in order to fight
terrorism?" The results indicated that between 2003 and 2004, approximately 25 percent of all American citizens felt that the Act went to far in its
pursuit of safety; however, most Americans felt the Act did nothing wrong,
and was acceptable in its pursuit of American safety regarding terrorism.[811] In
order to assuage the 25 percent of Americans that did not like the Patriot Act,
DOJ created a website called "www.lifeandliberty.gov" that guarded the Act
from civil liberties organizations like the ACLU and EPIC.[812]

During this period, John Ashcroft traveled to 16 cities, orating only to individuals who agreed with the Patriot Act and acknowledged its significance
for American safety.[813] The speeches alluded to a number of important acts
in American history, the Revolutionary War, The Civil War, and World War
II. Ashcroft stated that the Patriot Act's sections doing away with the "wall"
that kept foreign intelligence organizations from distributing important data
with domestic law enforcement, roving wiretaps, and the enlarged competence of the U.S. Joint Terrorism Task Force would help protect American

---

808. See Statement of Barbara Comstock (February 7th, 2007). *United States Department of Justice*
(Director of Public Affairs).
809. See Lawrence Morahan, (2003–02–13). "Patriot 2 Raises Concerns for Civil Liberties Groups,"
The Nation, CNS News. Retrieved on 2007–12–20.
810. See Patrick Leahy (February 10, 2003), Comments of Senator Patrick Leahy Ranking
Democratic Member, Senate Judiciary Committee, on the Justice Department's Secrecy in Drafting
a Sequel to the USA PATRIOT Act. Office of Patrick Leahy, Senator for Vermont.
811. See *"USA Today*/CNN/Gallup Poll results" (2005–05–20). *USA Today.* Retrieved on
2007–12–20.
812. See Henry Owen III, (January 2007). "The Life and Liberty.gov Web site review." *Government
Information Quarterly* 24 (1): 229–229. Retrieved on 2008–02–02.
813. See Eric Lichtblau (2003–09–08). "Ashcroft's Tour Rallies Supporters and Detractors." *The New
York Times.* Retrieved on 2008 2007–12–26.

lives from terrorist depredations.

Ashcroft stated that 132 people had either been convicted for their crimes or pled guilty, in order to avoid court. In addition, more than 3,000 individuals, all thought to be likely terrorists, had been apprehended in countries around the world. Of those apprehended, one was Sami Amin Al-Arian who, along with seven of his colleagues, were arrested on 50 charges, including utilizing an Islamic think tank to get money to the terrorist group, the Palestinian Islamic Jihad.[814]

Ashcroft's motive in giving this information was to show people that the Patriot Act was working in the manner it was envisioned; that is, the "wall" between intelligence and law enforcement had disappeared. The speeches were, for the most part, successful, but drew criticism in some states.[815] In other places, the Patriot Act drew controversy and faced conflict from several State and local governments. For example, in February 2003, one city in California, Arcata, passed a decree barring city workers (and that included both law enforcement and librarians) from aiding or collaborating with any federal investigators using the Patriot Act, as it would breach civil liberties– in essence, nullifying federal law.[816]

In time, eight states (Alaska, California, Colorado, Hawaii, Idaho, Maine, Montana, and Vermont), along with 396 cities and counties (which includes some of the largest cities in the U.S. (New York City; Los Angeles; Dallas; Chicago; Eugene, Oregon; Philadelphia; and Cambridge, Massachusetts) approved decrees censuring the Patriot Act for its attack on civil liberties. While these resolutions show the lengths a sovereign state will go through to fight the U.S. government, in reality, the acts were only symbolic, as federal law supersedes state and local law.

The *Security and Freedom Ensured Act* (SAFE)[817] was launched on October 2, 2003 by Senators Larry Craig (R-ID), John E. Sununu (R-NH), and Richard Durbin (D-IL) and would have restricted the extent of roving wiretaps.[818] In addition, it amended the "sneak and peek" waiting period from "within a reasonable period" to a date lasting no longer than seven days after the warrant was implemented,[819] reinstated the condition for apprehension of business documents that give undeniable evidence that the documents are those of a

---

814. See "FBI charges Florida professor with terrorist activities," (2003–02–20). *CNN.* Retrieved on 2007–12–20.

815. See Jane Ann Morrison, & Glenn Puit Puit (2003–08–27). "Ashcroft touts Patriot Act's virtues," *Las Vegas Review-Journal.* Retrieved on 2008–02–02.

816. See Evelyn Nieves (2003–04–21). "Local Officials Rise Up to Defy The Patriot Act", *Washington Post,* p. A01. Retrieved on 2008–01–03.

817. See S.1709.

818. See Security and Freedom Ensured Act of 2003, S.1709 Section 2.

819. See Security and Freedom Ensured Act of 2003, S.1709 Section 3.

foreign spy and/or a foreign government,[820] and thwarted the utilization of National Security Letters to get access to someone's library records.[821] Several of the sunset provisions would have been extended: (1) section 213 (Authority for delaying notice of the execution of a warrant, (2) section 216 (Modification of authorities relating to use of pen registers and trap and trace devices, (3) section 219 (Single-jurisdiction search warrants for terrorism) and section 505 (Miscellaneous national security authorities).[822] The Electronic Frontier Foundation (EFF) supported the bill,[823] as did Senator Feingold.[824]

The SAFE Act took away some of the Patriot Act's power regarding more grievous sections. "Sneak and Peek" warrants, reinstate the condition that the apprehension of business documents must give undeniable evidence of a foreign spy and/or a foreign government, and thwarted the utilization of National Security Letters to get access to someone's library records. Unfortunately, due to the partisan approach of many senators, the bill never went any further.

In response, Attorney General Ashcroft penned a four-page dispatch to Congress advising them not to make great changes in the Act, warning that President Bush would veto the bill if they approved it.[825] In reply, Senator Durbin stated that it was possible to keep civil liberties while fighting terrorism.[826] SAFE was submitted to the Senate Judiciary Committee on April 7, 2004 and civil liberties organizations across the country held their breath in anticipation. Unfortunately, due to the partisan approach of many senators, the bill never went any further.[827]

THE EFF

The Electronic Frontier Foundation, of the various civil liberties organizations in America, has been the vanguard in its condemnation of the Patriot Act and the Bush Administration. In their opinion, only part of the Patriot

---

820. See Security and Freedom Ensured Act of 2003, S.1709 Section 4.
821. See Security and Freedom Ensured Act of 2003, S.1709 Section 5.
822. See Security and Freedom Ensured Act of 2003, S.1709 Section 6.
823. See EFF: Analysis of the SAFE Act, Electronic Frontiers Foundation website. Retrieved 2008-01-22.
824. See S12377 (October 2nd, 2003) Congressional Record. *U.S. Government Printing Office.*
825. See "Ashcroft: Bush would veto bill scaling back Patriot Act" (2004-01-29). Washington/ Politics, *USA Today.*
826. See "Ashcroft warns of Bush veto on scaled-back Patriot bill" (2004-01-29). CNN. Retrieved on 2007-11-29.
827. See John E. Sununu (2005-11-16). "SAFE Act Co-Sponsors Say Patriot Act Conference Report Unacceptable." Retrieved on 2008-01-08.

Act is good for America, i.e., providing financial support to the victims in 9/11 and/or creating new services for translation; for the most part, the Patriot Act is harmful.[828] Moreover, they lambasted the Bush Administration's addition of several computer misdeeds to the already long compendium of deeds felt to be terrorist connected.[829] They have written extensively about Title II and the various problems it causes.

Sections 202 and 217 are both concerned with the sanction of intercept commands for the investigation of computer felonies. The EFF feels that since no citations exist showing that computer crimes are linked to terrorism, both sections should be stricken from the law.[830] Section 204 changed FISA to permit the gaining of foreign intelligence data from non-American informants by means of a wide variety of measures, was heavily censured as taking away protections preventing unchecked surveillance. The EFF felt that Congressional leaders did not elucidate that the United States could, if it chose, to disregard pen-trap statutes if the data is attained outside American borders. In their opinion, Section 204 illustrates how inept and dangerous the Patriot Act is.

Section 204 modified 18 U.S.C. § 2511(2)(f) to include chapter 206 of the U.S. Code (which deals with the regulation of pen registers and trap and trace devices) and includes electronic devices in the list of mechanisms that agencies can intercept communications. The section in contention states that. In the EFF's opinion, the Patriot Act should be taken off the books and fixed.[831]

Section 206, one of the more contentious areas in the Patriot Act, permits roving surveillance; likewise, it permits governmental organizations to necessitate full aid in order to engage in such surveillance. The EFF disagreed strenuously as they thought it gave the FBI free rein to do whatever it wanted in terms of surveilling Americans who had not broken any laws. Since the legal standards for surveillance have all but been gutted (in their opinion), it is likely that American citizens will have their Fourth Amendment rights infringed upon.[832]

Section 207 is yet another contentious area for the EFF. They state that it

---

828. See EFF, "EFF analysis of the provisions of the USA Patriot Act that relate to online activities," "Were our Freedoms the Problem?" Retrieved 2008-01-20.
829. See EFF, "EFF analysis of the provisions of the USA PATRIOT Act that relate to online activities," "B. Computer Crimes under CFAA Defined as 'Terrorist Offenses,'" retrieved 2008-01-20.
830. See EFF, "Let the Sun Set on PATRIOT–Section 202: Section 202, 'Authority to Intercept Wire, Oral, And Electronic Communications Relating to Computer Fraud and Abuse Offenses,'" and Section 217, "Interception of Computer Trespasser Communications." Retrieved on 2008-01-20.
831. See EFF, "Section 204: Clarification of Intelligence Exceptions From Limitations on Interception and Disclosure of Wire, Oral, and Electronic Communications." Retrieved on 2008-01-20.
832. See EFF, "Let the Sun Set on Patriot: Section 206." Retrieved on 2008-01-20.

permits an extra 12 months of surveillance regarding foreign agents. More-over, 207 lengthened the period of surveillance of foreign operatives from 45 days to 90 days; likewise, physical search directives were extended up to 120 days, with judicial increases up to 12 months. The EFF felt the law govern-ing wiretaps did not need adjusting, as they were already efficient. They feel that the lower standards of probable cause regarding FISA surveillance take away legal protections preventing the misuse of such standards. In fact, the EFF feels that the one group that will primarily profit from Section 207 is the FBI, as they would not have to complete as much paperwork to spy on peo-ple.[833]

Before the Patriot Act (and Section 209), governmental agents needed to request a Title III wiretap order[834] to open voicemail. Their primary reason for complaining is that if law enforcement wants to obtain the information contained in voicemail, all they need do is apply for an order that will be established upon the Electronic Communications Privacy Act (ECPA), which offers much less safety from governmental snooping in private matters.[835]

> Before the Patriot Act, gaining access to voicemail was much tougher under a Title III Wiretap; After the Patriot Act, there are less protections against gov-ernmental snooping in private matters.

Furthermore, the FBI could get access to an individual's voice mail only if the Bureau could show a judge that "probable cause" existed indicating that the individual in question was guilty of engaging in criminal behavior. Now, all it need to do is show "reasonable grounds" for the search; likewise, if a subpoena is used, all that needs to be shown is "relevance" to the inves-tigation. Before, federal law enforcement, at some point, had to inform the individual that the government had listened to private voicemail messages. Now, if a search warrant is used, the only way an American citizen will find that his/her privacy has been violated is by the government telling him/her when they are in court.[836]

Before the Patriot Act, the only way for federal law enforcement to listen

---

833. See EFF, "Let the Sun Set on PATRIOT–Section 207: 'Duration of FISA Surveillance of Non-United States Persons Who Are Agents of a Foreign Power.'" Retrieved on 2008-01-20.
834. A Title III wiretap is a wiretap acquired through Title III of the Omnibus Crime Control and Safe Streets Act of 1968, which was written to deal with wiretaps. This law established Title 18, chapter 19 of the United States Code (entitled "Wire Interception and Interception of Oral Communications," it includes 18 U.S.C. § 2510–18 U.S.C. § 2520).
835. See EFF, "Let the Sun Set on PATRIOT–Section 209: 'Seizure of VoiceMail Messages Pursuant to Warrants.'" Retrieved on 2008-01-20.
836. Ibid.

to private voicemail was if a person was a suspect of a serious crime; even so, the number of crimes giving the government the power to listen was small. With the passage of the PA, everything changed as it allowed law enforcement to listen to messages for practically any type of criminal investigation. Moreover, before the PA, if the legal authorities listened to your voicemail, the information could not be used against you in a trial, which was commonly referred to as the exclusionary rule. The ECPA lacked this maxim, giving the power to the government to not only listen to private messages, but agents were allowed to use any such evidence gained from listening in against the defendant in court. It was felt that this violated the Fourth Amendment.[837]

The EFF was up in arms regarding section 212, which permits the emergency disclosure of electronic communications to safeguard life, because in their opinion, an Internet Service Provider or phone service company should not have the authority to hand over a subscriber's private documents and messages without that subscriber's approval. The EFF disagrees with this, though the only time it should be used is when law enforcement believes that to not do so would cause the death or severe injury to someone else. In addition, the group disagrees with section 225 of the Homeland Security Act of 2002 (also known as the Cyber Security Enhancement Act of 2002, which rescinded and took the place of section 212), as they felt it increases the authority of the PA.[838]

Section 214, which altered different segments of FISA concerned with pen registers and trap and trace devices, is also disliked, as the EFF thinks that under the law, FISA was preferable to that under the PA. Under FISA, any court orders signed by a judge were restricted to the investigation of foreign dangers to American safety. The EFF feels that now, American citizens can be spied upon just like enemy agents. They also condemn Section 214 for being too fuzzy in stating which information can be legally trapped.[839]

Section 215, another hotly contested, contentious issue increases the capability of a governmental organization to gain access to documents and other things collected under FISA—although the government is forbidden to place surveillance on American citizens who are engaging in actions guarded by the First Amendment. The EFF felt that for Section 215 to work, the government must infringe upon an American's Fourth Amendment rights to pri-

---

837. "Let the Sun Set on PATRIOT—Section 209: 'Seizure of VoiceMail Messages Pursuant to Warrants,'" *EFF*. Retrieved 2007–12–20.

838. See EFF, "Let the Sun Set on PATRIOT—Section 212 and Homeland Security Act Section 225: 'Emergency Disclosure of Electronic Communications to Protect Life and Limb.'" Retrieved 2008–01–20.

839. See EFF, "Let the Sun Set on PATRIOT—Section 214: 'Pen Register and Trap and Trace Authority Under FISA.'" Retrieved on 2008–01–20.

vacy, without having to produce evidence that the documents are sorely required in an ongoing investigation.[840]

According to the EFF: ". . . under Section 215 the FBI can investigate United States persons (citizens and legal residents) based at least in part on their exercise of First Amendment rights, and can investigate non-U.S. persons based solely on their free speech activities or religious practices. You could be investigated based on the political or religious meetings you attend, the websites you visit, or even the books that you read. As a result, Americans may be chilled from exercising these Constitutional rights. Already, attendance at and donations to mosques have dropped significantly, as many Muslims reasonably fear that they will be targeted for investigation based solely on their religious beliefs.[841] The EFF feels that American civil liberties are being trod upon, especially as an American citizen cannot go to court to challenge the legitimacy of a FISA directive. FISA surveillance directive leaves a U.S. citizen with no means to go to court and challenge its legality.[842]

Section 220 grants authority to federal courts to produce electronic surveillance search warrants that are not limited to any one area within the United States. The EFF thinks that this section should have been excised as it is primarily concerned with criminal investigations and not terrorism. Section 220 allows various law enforcement groups to look for judges who have evidenced prejudice toward law enforcement. In essence, the FBI would have the ability to look around and choose a judge least likely to say no to a suspicious search warrant, even if the warrant skips the prerequisites of the Fourth Amendment. Moreover, 221 diminishes the probability that smaller Internet Service Providers or phone companies will attempt to safeguard the constitutional rights of their subscribers due to the logistics involved; that is, it would be difficult for a person in Starkville, Mississippi to fly to Los Angeles to argue the merits of constitutional law to a judge inclined to think there are too many civil liberties in the U.S. The EFF is afraid that most of the search warrants issued will be *ex parte,* meaning that the individual named on the search warrant need not be there when the order is executed.[843]

In the beginning, the EFF felt that Section 223 (it permits individuals to sue those who made illegal disclosures of communication) was salutary. However, they now feel that the section is more akin to a "Trojan Horse."[844]

---

840. See EFF, "Let the Sun Set on PATRIOT–Section 215: 'Access to Records and Other Items Under the Foreign Intelligence Surveillance Act.'" Retrieved on 2008–01–20.
841. Ibid.
842. See EFF, "Let the Sun Set on PATRIOT–Section 215: 'Access to Records and Other Items Under the Foreign Intelligence Surveillance Act.'" Retrieved on 2007–12–20.
843. See EFF, "Let the Sun Set on PATRIOT–Section 220: 'Nationwide Service of Search Warrants for Electronic Evidence.'" Retrieved on 2008–01–20.

The EFF feels that:

1. An interested party cannot sue the federal government for deliberately violating the law, as is an American citizen's right with everyone else. Here, the infringement must be willful, a tougher standard.
2. Before the PA, each citizen had the right to have a jury trial if he/she sued the government. No longer. Now, a judge will hear all civil suits brought against the federal government.
3. Unlike a situation when any other person or group is the defendant, if you choose to sue Uncle Sam for unlawful wiretapping, the plaintiff must first initiate an administrative process with the group that conducted the wiretapping. Basically, the plaintiff must tell the individual(s) engaged that they are about to be sued, and then the plaintiff must wait to see what the defendant has to say. In other words, the defendant has the right to decide about the lawsuit.
4. Before the PA, not only could the plaintiff sue for a monetary award, he/she had the right to sue for declaratory relief from a judge. For instance, an ISP could petition the court to state that a specific kind of wiretapping wanted by Uncle Sam to use is illegal. A plaintiff could then sue for the court to command that any unlawful wiretapping cease.

Section 223 considerably lessened a judge's capacity to deal with illegal surveillance, in that the plaintiff can only sue the government for damages. What this means is that no plaintiff can sue the government to put a stop to an unlawful wiretap; at the most, the plaintiff might sue for damages while the unlawful wiretap is being used.[845]

Section 225 gives legal immunity to any individual or group that aids the government in its quest for surveillance that is pursuant to a judicial command or appeal for emergency aid. In the EFF's opinion, a never-ending succession of gag orders will prevent a person's case from being heard in the "secret courts."[846]

---

844. See EFF, "Let the Sun Set on PATRIOT–Section 223: 'Civil Liability for Certain Unauthorized Disclosures.'" Retrieved on 2008–01–20.

845. See EFF, "Let the Sun Set on PATRIOT–Section 223: 'Civil Liability for Certain Unauthorized Disclosures.'" Retrieved on 2008–01–20.

846. EFF, "Let the Sun Set on PATRIOT–Section 225: Immunity for Compliance With FISA Wiretap. Retrieved on 2008–01–20.

THE PATRIOT ACT IS CHALLENGED

The Courts repealed a number of the Patriot Act's sections. In Section 805, the federal government could bar American citizens from supplying material aid for groups considered terrorist organizations, with support including any type of expert advice. Two such groups were the Kurdistan Workers Party (PDK) and the Liberation Tigers of Tamil Eelam (LTTE). The Humanitarian Law Project felt this was an outrage, and sued the federal government saying that the Patriot Act was unconstitutional.[847] The federal court agreed in December, 2004; section 805(a)(2)(B) was found unconstitutional because it infringed upon the First and Fifth Amendments and whose language was unclear; thus, it was possible, according to judicial reasoning, to make any speech whatsoever protected by the First Amendment.[848]

The judge felt that due to the vagueness of the statute, a normal person with average IQ would not be sure whether he/she was breaking the law and could be charged with a crime of which he/she was unconscious. This use of imprecise language could allow capricious and inequitable enforcement of the law, with the result that a citizen could lose his/her First Amendment rights.[849] Soon thereafter, DOJ announced the law was intended to deal with individuals who gave material aid in the form of expert advice, and that American citizens are just as unsafe with them as they were the people who taught terrorists how to "build a bomb."[850]

In June, 2004, a jury in Idaho acquitted Sami Al-Hussayen, a graduate student accused of providing "expert assistance" to terrorists through a website. The jury reached its verdict after seven days of deliberation. "The message is that the First Amendment is important and meaningful in this country," said David Nevin, lead attorney for Al-Hussayen. "The system worked."[851]

Title V changed the Electronic Communications Privacy Act's National Security Letter (NSL) provisos.[852] In November, 2005, the magazine *Business-Week* stated that the FBI had distributed many thousands of NSLs and had attained over 1,000,000 personal documents, including monetary, credit, employment, and medical records from the patrons of specific Las Vegas businesses. A Justice officer, speaking anonymously, said such appeals were

---

847. See *Humanitarian Law Project v. John Ashcroft.*
848. Ibid.
849. Ibid.
850. See Mark Corallo, spokesman for the United States Department of Justice. Cited in: Frieden, Terry (2004–01–27). "Federal judge rules part of Patriot Act unconstitutional," *Law Center,* CNN. Retrieved on 2007–11–23.
851. See Bob Fick. Jury acquits Saudi graduate student of charges he used computer skills to promote terrorism (2004–06–11). *Associated Press.* Retrieved on 2008–02–02.
852. See 18 U.S.C. § 2709.

allowed under section 505 of the Patriot Act and in spite of the huge number of requests maintained that, "We are not inclined to ask courts to endorse fishing expeditions."[853]

The ACLU disputed the use of NSLs and on April 9, 2004 filed a civil suit for an anonymous individual against the United States.[854] The details of the suit, brought to trial by the ACLU, are unknown, other than the fact that the party represented by the ACLU was an ISP, and that the central issue involved either the use of wiretaps or clandestinely subpoenaed customer documents from telephone and internet companies, supposedly in the interest of investigating terrorist behavior. Due to the NSL provisos, Uncle Sam prevented the ACLU from disclosing that they had filed a case for nearly a month, after which the group was allowed to make public a heavily edited description of the grievance.[855]

The ACLU stated that using NSLs infringed upon each citizen's First and Fourth Amendment rights, since section 2709 did not detail specifically any legal procedure that would permit a telephone or ISP to resist an NSL subpoena in court. In addition, they argued that section 2709 barred the receiver of an NSL subpoena from revealing that he/she had obtained such an order from the FBI, and thus, civil liberties prevailed over the Bureau's necessity for concealment in counterterrorism investigations.[856]

Consequently, the court ruled that the NSL stipulations of the ECPA were unconstitutional. It stated that nowhere in the provision could they find any implied entitlement for the individual getting the subpoena to legally challenge it in judicial proceedings as is necessitated by the U.S. Constitution. The court found the ACLU's argument persuasive, and ruled the section unconstitutional.[857] This ruling basically dismissed any asserted presumptive legal requirement for total secrecy regarding terrorism cases. It should be noted, however, that the PA is influenced only if the restraints on NSLs in terrorist cases also pertain to nonterrorism cases, i.e., similar to ones sanctioned by the Act, and even if the NSL is done away with, the individual continued under a gag order. Later, Congress attempted to fix this problem in a reauthorization Act, but when they failed to eradicate the nondisclosure stipulation, a federal court, again, found NSLs unconstitutional as they thwarted courts from employing judicial review.[858]

---

853. Richard. H. Dunham. "The Patriot Act: Business Balks" (2005–11–10). *Business Week.* Retrieved on 2008–01–20.

854. See Doe v. Ashcroft, 334 F.Supp.2d 471 (S.D.N.Y. 2004).

855. See "Part of Patriot Act Struck Down," *Politics: Law* (2004–09–29). *Wired.* Retrieved on 2007–12–20.

856. Op. cit. 92.

857. Op. cit 93.

858. See American Civil Liberties Union (2007–09–06). "Federal Court Strikes Down National Security Letter Provision of Patriot Act. Retrieved on 2008–02–02.

In 2004, in *Doe v. Gonzales,* it was held that the NSL provisos of 18 U.S.C. § 2709 contravened both the First and Fourth Amendments of the Constitution; shortly thereafter, the DOJ appealed. The reauthorization Act altered the statute making judicial review a condition of NSLs, but the section involving a permanent gag order was not eliminated. On September 6, 2007, U.S. District Judge Victor Marrero found that the utilization of NSLs to obtain e-mail and telephone information from private companies for use in counterterrorist cases was "the legislative equivalent of breaking and entering, with an ominous free pass to the hijacking of constitutional values."[859]

The court ruled that NSLs were unconstitutional because its stipulations regarding gag orders were unconstitutional while preventing judicial review.[860]

Another provision struck down was the so-called "sneak and peek" provisions of the Patriot Act. As the Patriot Act permitted law enforcement personnel to engage in "sneak and peek searches," there were many critics, including the ACLU and EPIC, who excoriated the Act because, in their opinion, it infringed upon an American citizen's Fourth Amendment rights.[861] Supporters believed that utilizing sneak and peek searches were justified, since the momentary gap in notice of a search order prevents terrorists from alerting any other individuals being investigated.[862]

In 2004, the FBI utilized this stipulation to investigate and clandestinely observe the dwelling of Brandon Mayfield, who was mistakenly incarcerated for two weeks due to the belief that he was involved in the Madrid train bombings. The cause for this snafu? Agents had incorrectly deduced his involvement as they thought they had his fingerprint on a parcel of detonators located at the area where the bombing occurred.[863] FBI special agents confiscated three hard drives of data and ten DNA samples saved on Q-Tips, and took 335 photographs of Mayfield's private things.

Afterwards, he sued the United States, arguing that his civil rights were contravened by his capture and by the investigation carried out by the FBI against him. Moreover, he stressed that the sneak and peek searches were unconstitutional.[864]

---

859. Adam Liptak. "Judge voids F.B.I. Tool Granted by Patriot Act" (2007–09–07). *The New York Times.* Retrieved on 2008–05–06.

860. See Dan Eggen. "Judge Invalidates Patriot Act Provisions" (September 7, 2007). *The Washington Post.* Retrieved on 2007–12–29.

861. See Heather Mac Donald. "Sneak-and-Peek in the Full Light of Day." *American Bar Association.* Retrieved on 2007–12–20.

862. Ibid.

863. *See Special Report: A Review of the FBI's Handling of the Brandon Mayfield Case* (March 2006), United States Department of Justice. Retrieved on 2007–11–07.

864. Ibid.

The government offered a publicly apology,[865] but Mayfield was not appeased and continued his fight in courts. On September 26, 2007, Judge Ann Aiken, a United States Judge for the District of Oregon, ruled that the law was unconstitutional as the FBI's search was unreasonable and contravened Mayfield's Fourth Amendment rights.[866]

Representatives Bernie Sanders (I-VT), Jerrold Nadler (D-NY), John Conyers Jr., Clement Leroy Otter (R-ID), and Ron Paul (R-TX) hoped to amend the *Commerce, Justice, State Appropriations Bill of 2005* which would sever funding to the Justice Department for any searches performed using section 215 as the legal basis.[867] During the first vote, the proposal was defeated, with a split vote of 210–210.[868] While the initial vote was unfavorable to the proposal, it remained open and a number of Representatives were won over and changed their votes.[869] On June 15, 2005, another effort at limiting section 215 searches was undertaken, and this time it was successful, as it was attached to a House appropriations bill.[870] The tally was 238 for and 187 against the Sanders proposal.[871]

While much of the proposed legislation was in opposition to the Patriot Act, some were for it. In July, 2004, Republican Senator Jon Kyl of Arizona announced the *Tools to Fight Terrorism Act*.[872] On September 13, Kyl told the Senate Judiciary Committee that he was worried since no legislation regarding anti-terrorism had occurred since the Patriot Act had become law in 2001.[873] Kyl's proposal would have granted the power to FBI special agents to request warrants for the investigation of "lone wolf terrorists," permitted a greater exchange of intelligence data between federal government and personnel at the state and local levels, penalized anyone making a joke of terrorism by pulling hoaxes on unsuspecting people, and enforced 30-year mandatory-minimum penalty for anyone having within his/her possession shoulder-fired, anti-aircraft missiles, nuclear bombs, and/or the variola virus.[874] However, the Senate never considered the proposal.

---

865. See "Apology Note from the United States Government" (2006–11–29). *The Washington Post.* Retrieved on 2008–01–03.

866. See Susan Jo Keller. "Judge Rules Provisions in Patriot Act to Be Illegal," (September 27, 2007). *The New York Times.* Retrieved on 2008–01–03.

867. See H.R. 4754, THOMAS.

868. See Roll number 339, July 8th, 2004.

869. See "House GOP Defends Patriot Act Powers," *Politics, In Congress* (July 9, 2004). *The Washington Post.* Retrieved on 2008–01–05.

870. See H.R. 2862, THOMAS.

871. See Roll number 258, June 15th, 2005. Retrieved on 2007–12–29.

872. See S. 2679.

873. See A Review of the Tools to Fight Terrorism Act (Senate Hearing). Statement of Chairman Kyl (September 13th, 2004). United States Senate Committee on the Judiciary, Subcommittee on Terrorism, Technology, and Homeland Security. Retrieved on 2008–02–22.

874. See Jon Kyl. "Giving Law Enforcement Some Overdue Tools In the Fight Against Terrorism" (September 20, 2004). *Truth News.* Retrieved on 2008–02–02.

As more time elapsed from the Patriot Act becoming law, many of the sunset clauses started expiring. President Bush pushed for a renewal of the Act, and in his State of the Union Address for 2004, he stated:

> Inside the United States, where the [War on Terror] began, we must continue to give our homeland security and law enforcement personnel every tool they need to defend us. And one of those essential tools is the Patriot Act, which allows federal law enforcement to better share information, to track terrorists, to disrupt their cells, and to seize their assets. For years, we have used similar provisions to catch embezzlers and drug traffickers. If these methods are good for hunting criminals, they are even more important for hunting terrorists. Key provisions of the Patriot Act are set to expire next year. The terrorist threat will not expire on that schedule. Our law enforcement needs this vital legislation to protect our citizens. You need to renew the Patriot Act.[875]

In addition, when Alberto Gonzales began his tenure as Attorney General, President Bush mentioned that many of the key components of the Patriot Act were going to expire at the end of the year (2004), and that it would be a blow in the effort to stop terrorism.[876]

During April, 2005, Gonzales, at a Senate Judiciary meeting, told the various members that the Patriot Act not only worked, it worked well. In addition, while a few changes were needed, each of 16 sections facing its "sunset," should be reauthorized. He specifically mentioned sections 215 (the section permitting the government the right to gain a judicial order with the FISA court so the authorities could see someone's personal information) and 216 (the section allowing law enforcement the ability to gain a roving wiretap). He stated that Section 215 had not been used by the federal government . . .

> to order to obtain library or bookstore records, medical records or gun sale records. Rather, the provision to date has been used only to obtain driver's license records, public accommodation records, apartment leasing records, credit card records and subscriber information, such as names and addresses for telephone numbers captured through court-authorized pen register devices.[877]

---

875. See The White House-Press Release. State of the Union Address (2004–01–20). Retrieved on 2007–12–20.
876. See United States Department of Justice "President Thanks Attorney General Gonzales at Swearing-In Ceremony" (February 14th, 2004). Press release. Retrieved on 2007–12–28.
877. See "Transcript: Senate Judiciary Hearing on the Patriot Act" (2005–04–05). *Washingtonpost.com.* Retrieved on 2007–12–20.

Section 217 (the section detailing how "sneak and peek" warrants could be used) caused some members of the Committee to indicate concern, but the DOJ defended their use, saying they were vital for the war on terror.[878]

The President campaigned tirelessly for the Patriot Act's reauthorization. During June, 2005, he spoke to the Ohio State Highway Patrol Academy where he stated that the Patriot Act needed to be reauthorized as it had already protected Americans from terrorists, and that not authorizing it would, in essence, be a catastrophe for the country. Moreover, he said that the American citizens could not allow Congress to erect a "wall" between law enforcement and the intelligence community, as had been the case before 9/11.[879]

Politics make strange bedfellows and the usual divergent political groups pulled together in their ire regarding the Patriot Act. The EFF, the ACLU, the CDT (Center for Democracy and Technology), and EPIC joined forces with normally quiescent groups such as the American Library Association (ALA) and the American Booksellers Foundation for Freedom of Expression. Each group vented its spleen with section 215.[880] In addition, normal conservative stalwarts like the American Conservative Union, Gun Owners of America, and the United States Libertarian Party wrote about why the Patriot Act was not good for the United States.[881]

An anxious period of time occurred as believers and critics of the PA disputed with one another regarding their political stance. The stress finally caused a rupture on June 10. Testimony was proceeding in the House regarding the Patriot Act's reauthorization when the Chairman of the House Judiciary Committee, James Sensenbrenner, suddenly closed the hearings after House Democrats started into a monologue concerning why the prisoners at Guantanamo Bay were being deprived of their civil liberties. Sensenbrenner would have none of it and stated that the PA had nothing to do with the Cuban base.[882] While the Chair left in a huff, the testimony did not stop. Jerrold Nadler, a leading Democrat from New York, along with other Democratic representatives and their witnesses, spoke at length, though the microphones were silenced.

Pat Roberts, Republican Senator from Kansas, in a closed meeting of the Senate Select Committee on Intelligence, put forth proposal which would

---

878. Ibid.

879. See Andrew Zajac. "Debate on USA Patriot Act" (2005–04–06). *Chicago Tribune.* Retrieved on 2007–12–28.

880. See Jane Gordon. "In Patriot's Cradle, the Patriot Act Faces Scrutiny" (2005–04–24). *New York Times.* Retrieved on 2007–09–08.

881. See Anita Ramasastry, (2004–04–20). "Reform the Patriot Act to Ensure Civil Liberties," *Law Center,* CNN. Retrieved on 2008–01–03.

882. See Mike Allen, "Panel Chairman Leaves Hearing," Politics (2005–06–11). *The Washington Post.* Retrieved on 2007–09–08.

change the principal rationale of FISA warrants from foreign intelligence to almost anything, even that which had nothing to do with foreign intelligence. Almost immediately, the ACLU criticized the move[883] stating that the Republicans wanted to shape the debate about the PA into discussions they controlled. In addition, the ACLU felt that instead of bringing the PA into line with its purported purpose of catching terrorists, the Republicans wanted to spy on American citizens.[884]

The proposal was unveiled in the House on July 21, and was entitled the USA Patriot and Terrorism Prevention Reauthorization Act of 2005. One of its primary goals was to do away with the sunset dates for the surveillance provisos; that is, it would have turned certain sections of the PA into permanent fixtures for the United States. Various changes to the PA were discussed and passed, with several alterations including making the list of terrorist crimes larger,[885] made it mandatory that before any surveillance could be conducted regarding any libraries or bookstores, the Director of the FBI had to personally sign off (this centers on Section 215),[886] in order to receive a roving wiretap, law enforcement personnel had to make an account to the court issuing the order within 15 days of it being used,[887] while the range for using "sneak-and-peek" warrants was narrowed.[888]

The use and practice of NSLs was also changed—now, individuals receiving an NSL had the right to contact an attorney of his/her choice and confront the letter in court.[889] By allowing this, many problems would be averted, especially concerning the punishment of individuals receiving NSLs that are mentally compromised, experiencing great anxiety, are scared of being hurt, or are afraid they will lose their job if they to receive an NSL.[890] Other changes center on normalizing punishment for terrorist violence and other aggressive acts perpetrated against railroads and mass transit organizations[891] and expounding upon the meaning of terrorism in forfeiture statutes.[892]

Congressman Howard Berman (D-CA) suggested a modification that mandated an account to Congress on the growth and utilization of data mining technology by various groups and organizations within the federal gov-

---

883. See Dorothy M. Ehrlich. "Patriotism vs. the USA Patriot Act," *Open forum* (2005–07–04). *San Francisco Herald.* Retrieved on 2007–12–29.

884. See "Panel to weigh beefed-up Patriot Act," *Nation, Washington* (2005–06–05). *The Boston Globe.* Retrieved on 2007–12–29.

885. See H. AMDT 498 (21st June, 2005). Proposed by Daniel E. Lungren (R-CA).

886. See H. AMDT 489 (21st June, 2005). Proposed by Jeff Flake (R-AZ).

887. See H. AMDT 490 (21st June, 2005). Proposed by Darrell E. Issa (R-CA).

888. See H. AMDT 495 (21st June, 2005). Proposed by Jeff Flake (R-AZ).

889. See H. AMDT 492 (21st June, 2005). Proposed by Jeff Flake (R-AZ).

890. See H. AMDT 493 (21st June, 2005). Proposed by Maxine Waters (D-CA).

891. See H. AMDT 491 (21st June, 2005). Proposed by Shelley Moore Capito (R-WV).

892. See Roll call 414 for H.R. 3199. July 21st, 2005.

ernment.[893] Other changes were suggested for additional sections not enclosed by the PA; for example, a new term, fresh for the twenty-first century, was called "narcoterrorism." The proposal passed with a vote of 257–171;[894] however, upon its introduction into the Senate, another proposal written by Arlen Specter (R-PA) took its place,[895] at which point a meeting between the two bodies of the legislative branch was called for.

On September 11, the House of Representatives stated that each member, regardless of his/her party loyalty, disagreed with Specter's proposal. They agreed to a confab and then tried to initiate a number of alterations to the proposal, but several Senators, including Larry Craig (R-ID), John Sununu (R-NH), Lisa Murkowski (R-AK), Richard Durbin (D-IL), Russ Feingold (D-WI), and Ken Salazar (D-CO), stated they would obstruct the proposal unless additional alterations were made.[896] The House wrote a report, which was given to the Senate for consideration, but the Senate threw it out. On December 16, the Senate rejected it and would not cease discussion concerning legislation to renew the PA.[897]

At that point, a closure motion was commanded, but it did not succeed, being short a mere seven votes shy of the tally needed; thus, the PA's prospects dimmed somewhat, especially as the various sections facing sunsets threatened to run out. Finally, on December 21, the Senate agreed[898] to lengthen by 180 days the terminating sections of the PA.[899] In the House, Judiciary Committee Chair James Sensenbrenner had the constitutional right to obstruct ratification of the 180-day expansion. On the very next day, the House turned down the 180-day time addition and voted for a mere 30-day extension,[900] a modification the Senate agreed with.[901]

Later, on February 1, the House decided to add more time to the sunsets raising the date to March 10.[902] On March 2, the Senate passed the PA's reauthorization with a tally of 95–4, although Senator Feingold tried unsuccessfully to keep the sunsets extended.[903] Likewise, the House agreed to author-

---

893. See H. AMDT 497 (21st June, 2005). Proposed by Howard L. Berman (D-CA).

894. See Roll call 414 for H.R. 3199. July 21st, 2005.

895. See S.1389.

896. See Jesse J. Holland, "Bipartisan group of senators threatens to hold up Patriot Act reauthorization" (2005–11–27). *The America's Intelligence Wire*. Retrieved on 2008–02–02.

897. See Senate Roll Call 358 for H.R. 3199, (2005–12–16).

898. See (S.2167).

899. See U.S. Government Printing Office. S14424 (2005–12–22) Congressional Record.

900. See "U.S. House Approves Patriot Act Extension; Senate to Vote Soon" (2006–02–01). *Top Worldwide,* Bloomberg. Retrieved on 2007–12–29.

901. See Laurie Kellman, "Congress Closer to Extending Patriot Act" (2006–02–02). *San Francisco Herald.* Retrieved on 2008–03–03.

902. See John Diamond. "Senate passes Patriot Act changes," Washington/Politics, *USA Today.* Retrieved on 2008–02–03.

903. Ibid.

ize the PA with a tally of 280–138.[904] On March 8, President Bush endorsed the reauthorization.[905]

After the reauthorization was signed, the President stated that,

> The executive branch shall construe the provisions of H.R. 3199 that call for furnishing information to entities outside the executive branch, such as sections 106A and 119, in a manner consistent with the President's constitutional authority to supervise the unitary executive branch and to withhold information the disclosure of which could impair foreign relations, national security, the deliberative processes of the Executive, or the performance of the Executive's constitutional duties.[906]

To many people, this sounded like the President did not consider himself constrained by the rule of law. When he affixed his signature, President Bush added a small addendum, claiming that he did not feel it obligatory to tell Congress how the FBI utilized its increased investigative powers.[907]

Patrick Leahy was incensed by the President's attitude, stating that the Chief Executive's comments were, ". . . nothing short of a radical effort to re-shape the constitutional separation of powers and evade accountability and responsibility for following the law. . . . The President's signing statements are not the law, and we should not allow them to be the last word. The President's constitutional duty is to faithfully execute the laws as written by the Congress. It is our duty to ensure, by means of congressional oversight, that he does so."[908]

A primary reason that the Patriot Act was decried in the press (and still is) centered on the fact that many new definitions regarding who and what a "terrorist" is were unconstitutional. We now turn to a discussion of several new definitions that caused ire among civil liberties groups.

DOMESTIC TERRORISTS

As noted in Chapter 4, Section 802 changed the meaning of terrorism to include "domestic" terrorism. Any American who acts in a manner that

---

904. See "House approves Patriot Act renewal" (2006–03–07). *Politics,* CNN. Retrieved on 2008–02–04.
905. See Jeff Bliss & James Rowley. "Bush Logs Victory as USA Patriot Act Passes Congress" (2006–03–08). *Bloomberg.* Retrieved on 2008–02–04.
906. See The White House. President's Statement on H.R. 199, the "USA PATRIOT Improvement and Reauthorization Act of 2005" (2006–03–09). *Press release.* Retrieved on 2008–03–14.
907. Charlie Savage. "Bush shuns Patriot Act Requirement: In Addendum to Law, He says oversight rules are not binding" (2006–03–26). *The Boston Globe.* Retrieved on 2008–03–15.
908. Ibid.

could be considered dangerous to others is violating the criminal statutes of each individual state or of the federal government. This is so when the individual behaves in a way that: (i) intimidates or coerces a civilian population; (ii) influences the policy of a government by intimidation or coercion; or (iii) to affect the conduct of a government by mass destruction, assassination, or kidnapping. In addition, the act(s) must take place chiefly within the legal jurisdiction of the U.S.; otherwise, the behavior could be construed as international or global terrorism.[909]

> Groups like Greenpeace, the Environment Liberation Front or the WTO protesters like those in Seattle on November 30, 1999, could be classified as terrorists, thus incurring any and all punishment meted out by the government.

While a new meaning has been generated, it is still the same crime; on the other hand, the types of "terrorist" behavior that can be investigated by law enforcement personnel have greatly expanded. For instance, groups like Greenpeace, the Environmental Liberation Front, or WTO protesters like those seen in Seattle on November 30, 1999, could be classified as terrorists, thus incurring any and all punishment meted out by the government.

One apropos example, in addition to the 1999 incident in Seattle, is the Vieques Island protests which occurred on April 28, 2001 in Vieques, Puerto Rico. On that day, Puerto Ricans, along with a number of well-known Americans, joined in civil disobedience regarding an American military base where the U.S. conducted training for its military, which the Puerto Ricans protested.[910] The activists unlawfully gained access into the compound and tried to impede the Navy's bombing exercises. After the Patriot Act, this type of behavior would classify as domestic terrorism. How so? The protesters intentionally disregarded federal statutes by illegally entering the base and their actions centered on coercing the government to change its policy. Furthermore, the protesters, in their attempt to halt bombing exercises, possibly caused a threat to life–their own and those of military personnel.

The Patriot Act gives the federal government enhanced power to determine, locate, and prosecute terrorists and/or presumed terrorists. American citizens could face the following if they are found to be Domestic Terrorists.

---

909. See Section 802. The USA PATRIOT ACT.
910. See Pedro A. Sanjuan. The Navy doesn't Need Vieques (2000–05–02). *The New York Times.* Retrieved on 2007–12–02.

SEIZURE OF ASSETS–SECTION 806

Section 806 is a civil proceeding that states, in essence, someone could lose his/her belongings, home, automobile, etc. without any consideration and without the individual being found guilty of a crime in a court of law.[911] Section 806 changed the law in such a way so that the U.S. government now has the power to seize:

> all assets, foreign or domestic (i) of any individual, entity, or organization engaged in planning or perpetrating any act of domestic or international terrorism against the United States, or their property, and all assets, foreign or domestic, affording any person a source of influence over any such entity or organization or (ii) acquired or maintained by any person with the intent and for the purpose of supporting, planning, conducting, or concealing an act of domestic or international terrorism against the United States, citizens or residents of the United States or their property or (iii) derived from, involved in, or used or intended to be used to commit any act of domestic or international terrorism against the United States, citizens or residents of the United States, or their property.[912]

The language used is expansive and thus, in the example of the Vieques Island protests of 1999, any of the individuals or groups involved could have their assets seized by the government. This includes any secondary backers of the protests, including political action groups, or religious organizations that housed and/or fed the protesters. This allows Uncle Sam the right to seize someone's assets if there is "probable cause" that the individual is a domestic terrorist; likewise, the suspected individual could lose his/her assets before he/she is given a hearing before a judge.

As Section 806 is a civil proceeding, the government need only show that the individual was involved in terrorism by the weight of the evidence, not because a jury of his/her peers has decided so. Because the section is civil and not criminal, an individual is not permitted to a court appointed lawyer if he/she lacks the funds to pay for a private attorney. The length of time between when someone's property is seized and when everything is declared forfeited could be several months; however, during that time, the person or group that had assets seized will have to function without them.[913]

---

911. See 115 STAT. 378 PUBLIC LAW 107–56–OCT. 26, 2001 Section 806 Assets of Terrorist Organizations.
912. Ibid.
913. Ibid.

DISCLOSURE OF EDUCATIONAL RECORDS–SECTION 507

Section 507 of the PA mandates that a judge issue a directive allowing the government to acquire confidential educational documents if the Attorney General and/or his designee publicly state that the documents are needed for investigating domestic or international terrorism.[914] No autonomous judicial ruling is needed to certify that the documents are pertinent. This translates into the fact that the AG may acquire the confidential educational documents of students taking part in the Vieques protests (and many did) by stating that the documents are applicable to a domestic terrorism investigation. These documents may contain data such as grades, confidential medical information (sexually transmitted diseases, visits to a staff psychologist), any groups in which the student was a member, and any other data that schools gather regarding its students.

DISCLOSURE OF INFORMATION FROM NATIONAL EDUCATION STATISTICS ACT–SEC. 508

This section of Patriot Act mandates that a judge issue a directive for the government to acquire educational data gathered in accordance with the National Education Statistics Act.[915] NESA contains an enormous quantity of specialized student data from grades to confidential data concerning health, family SES, and race. Until the Patriot Act, this data was held in the strictest confidentiality, without exception. A student taking part in the Vieques protests could find out that once private information has been distributed to functionaries in the federal government, there is little he/she can do about it.

SINGLE-JURISDICTION SEARCH WARRANTS (SECTION 219)

This segment of the Patriot Act alters Rule 41(a) of the Federal Rules of Criminal Procedure to sanction the government to stand before a federal magistrate judge in any court district in which activity involving terrorism may have taken place, to acquire a warrant to investigate property or an individual either within the district or outside of it.[916,917] What this means is that a

---

914. See 115 STAT. 378 PUBLIC LAW 107–56–OCT. 26, 2001, Section 507 Disclosure of Educational Records.
915. See 115 STAT. 378 PUBLIC LAW 107–56–OCT. 26, 2001, Section 508, Disclosure of Information from National Statistics Act.
916. See 115 STAT. 378 PUBLIC LAW 107–56–OCT. 26, 2001, Section 219, Jurisdiction Search Warrants.
917. See 26 U.S.C.A. Sec. 6103(i)(3)(C).

federal magistrate in Atlanta could OK a warrant for an individual involved with the Vieques protests to have his/her property to be searched in Oregon. If he/she wants the warrant nullified, he/she needs to travel to Atlanta in order to do it.

TAXPAYER INFORMATION

The law[918] requires the Secretary of the Internal Revenue Service to supply data regarding any taxpayer to any federal law enforcement agency investigating a terrorist incident. If used incorrectly, law enforcement personnel could obtain the private, taxpayer data of political protesters.

SECTION 215

Before the Patriot Act, the FBI could only acquire business documents from a few sources, but Section 215 permits Uncle Sam to acquire "any tangible things," which can include library records, medical information, specific details regarding the use of the Internet, and any other documents considered important. Specifically the Act states that: "Upon application . . . the judge shall enter an ex parte (in the interest of one side only) order as requested, or as modified, approving the release of records if the judge finds that the application meets the requirements of this section").[919]

While the section states that judicial supervision is mandatory concerning FBI appeals for data,[920] a difference of opinion exists between Uncle Sam and civil liberties groups over how the exact wording of the Act should be interpreted. The requirements for "tangible things" likely means that the proviso would contain assurances that ". . . such investigation of a United States person is not conducted solely upon the basis of activities protected by the First Amendment to the Constitution."[921] While this sounds promising, many civil liberties groups feel that the FISA court is nothing more than a conduit for FBI investigation, as the court gives approval for the Bureau to do practically whatever it wants.[922]

---

918. See 50 USC 1861, at (c)(1).
919. See 115 STAT. 378 PUBLIC LAW 107–56–OCT. 26, 2001, Section 215 Access to records and other items under the Foreign Intelligence Surveillance Act.
920. See (50 USC 1861–at (a)(1).
921. See David Hudson, Jr. Patriot Act: Overview (2006–November). *First Amendment Center.* Retrieved on 2007–12–03.
922. Ibid.

The manner in which Section 215 was written permits a great deal of discretionary review for law enforcement, and a judge who examines an application has little space to maneuver when it comes to rejecting the appeal for a warrant. Moreover, no requirement is needed to show probable cause, meaning that the FBI does not have to give any rationale concerning why it thinks the objective of the surveillance is a terrorist; thus, the person could be innocent of any crime.[923]

The Section also provides: "No person shall disclose to any other person (other than those persons necessary to produce the tangible things under this section) that the Federal Bureau of Investigation has sought or obtained tangible things under this section."[924] In addition, Section 215 would not allow a library to tell its clients that the government has asked for information regarding their reading habits and choices under Section 215, a move that is patently unconstitutional, so wrote the ACLU.[925]

Most protests regarding the Patriot Act focus on the Fourth Amendment, but many legal scholars state that the PA also abridges First Amendment rights. In July, 2003, the ACLU, acting for six different groups (Muslim Community Association of Ann Arbor; American-Arab-Anti-Discrimination Committee; Arab Community Center for Economic and Social Services; Bridge Refugee & Sponsorship Services, Inc.; Council on American-Islamic Relations; Islamic Center of Portland, Masjed As-Saber) sued the government in *Muslim Community Association of Ann Arbor v. Ashcroft*,[926] where the plaintiffs argued that the Patriot Act violated:

1. the Fourth Amendment by authorizing the FBI to execute searches without criminal or foreign intelligence probable cause;
2. the Fourth Amendment by authorizing the FBI to execute searches without providing targeted individuals with notice or an opportunity to be heard;
3. the Fifth Amendment by authorizing the FBI to deprive individuals of property without due process;
4. the First Amendment by categorically and permanently prohibiting any person from disclosing to any other person that the FBI has sought records or personal belongings;

---

923. Ibid.
924. Op. cit. number 162.
925. Amy Beeson & Jameel Jaffer. "Unpatriot Acts: The FBI's Power to Rifle Through your Records and Personal Belongings Without Telling You" (2003–July). *The American Civil Liberties Union.* Retrieved on 2007–11–29.
926. See CA No. 03–72913, filed July 30, 2003. The ACLU's suit alleged that section using 215 to acquire private documents without probable cause or disclosure, contravened the First, Fourth, and Fifth Amendments of the Constitution.

5. the First Amendment by authorizing the FBI to investigate individuals based on their exercise of First Amendment rights, including the rights of free expression, free association, and free exercise of religion.[927]

The government tried to have the case thrown out of court, stating that the plaintiffs lacked standing to dispute the section. In December, 2003, U.S. District Judge Denise P. Hood in the Eastern District of Michigan heard the arguments from both sides; however, she did not make a ruling until Sept. 29, 2006, when Hood rejected the government's arguments for dismissal.[928]

During the interim between December, 2003 and September, 2006, Congress made substantive alterations to Section 215.[929] Under the new statutes, any person receiving a request for private documents may engage the services of an attorney. Furthermore, the new law states that the FBI, when submitting a records request before a judge, must show that it is reasonable to assume, due to the facts and evidence that the "tangible things" required are significant to an official investigation.[930]

After Judge Hood rejected the government's arguments, she allowed the plaintiffs an extra 30 days to make a decision regarding whether they wanted to change their first grievance in light of the newer version of Section 215. On Oct. 27, 2006, the ACLU proclaimed that it would remove its civil suit concerning Section 215, stating that the changes Congress had initiated had taken away much that was disagreeable.

---

927. Ibid.
928. See Muslim Community Association of Ann Arbor, American-Arab Antidiscrimination Committee, Arab Community Center for Economic and Social Services, Bridge Refugee and Sponsorship Services, Incorporated, Council on American-Islamic Relations, and Islamic Center of Portland, Masjed As-Saber. v. John Ashcroft, United States Attorney General, and Robert Mueller, Director of the Federal Bureau of Investigation. September 29, 2006.
929. See 50 U.S.C. 1861(a).
930. Ibid.

Chapter 6

THE LAW

A primary complaint voiced by foes of the Patriot Act is that it treads upon each American's inherent civil liberties as articulated in the Bill of Rights. The question is not whether the ACLU and other groups are correct—without doubt, they are. Rather, the question should be, "If the Patriot Act contravenes civil liberties, how does it do so, and does surrendering one's inalienable rights increase each citizen's security from terrorist attacks?" Chapter 6 will discuss these questions.

THE BILL OF RIGHTS

America is different from most countries (even those considered democratic) in that the Bill of Rights, the title given to the first ten amendments to the United States Constitution, guarantees that each American citizen receive certain civil liberties just because he/she is an American. James Madison introduced them in 1789, at the First United States Congress, as a sequence of constitutional amendments that became the law of the land on December 15, 1791, when they were ratified by the mandatory three-fourths of the states. The Bill of Rights restricts the federal government's power over American citizens, permanent residents, and/or visitors, making sure that each individual has protected rights which cannot be infringed upon.

The Bill of Rights safeguards our freedom in a number of ways. In America, we have freedom of speech, press, and religion; the right to own guns, if we choose to; the freedom of assembly; the freedom to petition; we are free from unreasonable searches and seizures as was common in England in the eighteenth century; we are guaranteed freedom from cruel and unusual punishment; and we cannot be made to incriminate ourselves in a court of law. Moreover, the Bill of Rights prevents Congress from establishing a state sponsored religion; likewise, the federal government cannot deprive any individual of his/her life, liberty, or property, without due process of law. In federal cases involving criminal law, an indictment by a federal grand jury is required for any crime considered capital or "infamous," guarantees that each defendant receives a speedy public trial (once again, unlike England in the eighteenth century) with an unbiased and objective jury made up of individuals that are residents of the state or jurisdiction where the illegal act occurred, and once someone has been tried and found not guilty, he/she cannot be tried again for the same crime—commonly known as "double jeopardy."

The Ninth Amendment states that Constitution shall not deny any rights not enumerated within it, and that the powers not given to the federal government are within the domain of each individual state and its citizens. Madison put forward the Bill of Rights during a period when disagreement regarding ideology was commonplace between Federalists and anti-Federalists. It began with the heated debates that took place during the 1787 Philadelphia Convention and seemed, at times, to threaten the ratification of the Constitution. In general, the Constitution answered eloquently to its prominent and influential adversaries, including well-known Founding Fathers, who stated that the Constitution should be done away with as it neglected the fundamental standards of human liberty and decency. The Bill of Rights was inspired by natural philosophers like Thomas Hobbes, John Locke, and Thomas Paine, as well as the much earlier Magna Carta, written in 1215 and forced upon King John of England, which was itself preceded by the Charter of Liberties in 1100 when Henry I admitted he was subject to the law.

Other influences included George Mason's 1776 Virginia Declaration of Rights where it was stated that citizens had the right to rebel to inadequate or oppressive government. Also influential was the 1689 English Bill of Rights, where it was enumerated that the citizens and permanent residents had certain rights such as petitioning the king and the right to bear arms for defense.

AMENDMENTS TO THE UNITED STATES CONSTITUTION

#	Amendments	Proposal date	Enactment date
1st	Freedom of religion, speech, press, petition, and assembly	September 25, 1789	December 15, 1791
2nd	The right to keep and bear arms	September 25, 1789	December 15, 1791

Continued on next page

3rd	No quartering of soldiers in private houses during peace time, i.e., no Declaration of War has been announced	September 25, 1789	December 15, 1791
4th	Searches and seizures; warrants	September 25, 1789	December 15, 1791
5th	Due process; Self-incrimination; Double jeopardy (Can't be tried for the same crime twice), and rules for Eminent Domain	September 25, 1789	December 15, 1791
6th	Rights of the accused, Right to a speedy public trial	September 25, 1789	December 15, 1791
7th	Right to trial by jury in civil cases	September 25, 1789	December 15, 1791
8th	No excessive bail & fines or cruel & unusual punishment	September 25, 1789	December 15, 1791
9th	Specifying that "the enumeration . . . of certain rights shall not be construed to deny or disparage others retained by the people." In other words, just because a certain right is not specifically listed or explicitly protected by the Constitution does not mean that right does not exist. Rather this amendment explicates the principle of government power as a grant from the people, rather than individual rights being a grant from the government.	September 25, 1789	December 15, 1791
10th	Unenumerated rights (i.e., rights not listed) are reserved to the states or to the people	September 25, 1789	December 15, 1791
11th	Immunity of states from suits from out-of-state citizens and foreigners not living within the state borders. Lays the foundation for sovereign immunity.	March 4, 1794	February 7, 1795
12th	Revision of presidential election procedures	December 9, 1803	June 15, 1804
13th	Abolition of slavery and punishment without conviction	January 31, 1865	December 6, 1865
14th	Citizenship, state due process, state equal protection, applies Bill of Rights to the States	June 13, 1866	July 9, 1868

Continued on next page

15th	Racial suffrage	February 26, 1869	February 3, 1870
16th	Allows federal income tax	July 12, 1909	February 3, 1913
17th	Direct election to the United States Senate	May 13, 1912	April 8, 1913
18th	Prohibition of alcohol (Repealed by 21st amendment)	December 18, 1917	January 16, 1919
19th	Women's suffrage	June 4, 1919	August 18, 1920
20th	Term Commencement for congress (January 3) and president (January 20). (This amendment is also known as the "lame duck amendment.")	March 2, 1932	January 23, 1933
21st	Repeal of Eighteenth Amendment; state and local prohibition permitted	February 20, 1933	December 5, 1933
22nd	Limits the president to two terms	March 24, 1947	February 27, 1951
23rd	Representation of Washington, D.C. in Electoral College	June 16, 1960	March 29, 1961
24th	Prohibition of the restriction of voting rights due to the non-payment of poll taxes	September 14, 1962	January 23, 1964
25th	Presidential disabilities	July 6, 1965	February 23, 1967
26th	Voting age nationally established as age 18	March 23, 1971	July 1, 1971
27th	Variance of congressional compensation	September 25, 1789	May 7, 1992

THE PATRIOT ACT AND THE FIRST AMENDMENT RIGHT TO FREE SPEECH

The Patriot Act attempts to abridge the First Amendment rights of free speech and the right of Americans to assemble together into groups. Over the decades, the Supreme Court has upheld these rights and allowed broadly the terms of free "speech," stating unequivocally that in a free society, each citizen must be free to speak his/her mind.[931] As mentioned in Chapter 5, section 411 gives a new meaning to terrorism (i.e., acts that are potentially dangerous . . . using intimidation or coercion to persuade the government to change its policies), as well as a new meaning regarding "engaging in terrorist activity" (i.e., it now means all one needs to do is attempt to collect money or something else of value for any group the AG feels contributes to the undercutting of American policy). If an American citizen does this, he/she is "Guilty by Association"; thus, raising money for one's cause or coming together in a group to express one's dissatisfaction with governmental policy is now illegal, which is in direct contravention of the First Amendment.

> Sections 215 and 505 of the Act prevent citizens like physicians, bank tellers, etc. who are visited by FBI special agents from saying anything–a gag order.

As mentioned in Chapter 5, Sections 215 and 505 of the Act prevent citizens like physicians, bank tellers, etc. who are visited by FBI special agents from saying anything–a gag order. Section 411 permits for the jailing and/or expulsion of an émigré who vocally states his/her support of a terrorist group, even if he/she does not support its methods. Section 802 has a meaning for domestic terrorism that is so vague that many mainstream groups like Greenpeace could be construed as terrorist. In addition, due to the Act's vagueness, Uncle Sam was able to wiretap and listen in to groups that before the Patriot Act were considered mainstream.[932]

THE FOURTH AMENDMENT

The Amendment reads:

The right of the people to be secure in their persons, houses, papers, and effects, against unreasonable searches and seizures, shall not be violated, and no warrants shall issue, but upon probable cause, supported by Oath or affirmation, and particularly describing the place to be searched, and the persons or things to be seized.

Since 1890, the right to privacy has been a right that the U.S. Supreme Court has declared to be "self-evident" and constitutionally implied in the

---

931. Of course, this precludes the slandering of someone's reputation and character.
932. See ACLU. *The SAFE Act of 2005.*

Fourth Amendment to the U.S. Constitution. A number of statutes have been established under the Fourth Amendment that necessitate the government to create confirmation for eavesdropping and search and seizure. With the Patriot Act, this norm is made exceedingly thin, which in turn creates headaches for anyone concerned with the Fourth Amendment. As much detail was written about the Fourth Amendment here and elsewhere, we now proceed to other amendments just as important, but less written about.

THE FIFTH AMENDMENT

The Fifth Amendment is concerned with the requirements of due process, which states that Uncle Sam must act in a manner free from arbitrariness. This includes each individual's constitutional right for being assumed innocent until demonstrated otherwise, as well as having the accusers establish a defendant's guilt beyond reasonable doubt.

"No person shall be . . . deprived of life, liberty, or property, without due process of law . . ." is the main gist of the Amendment. Due to various television shows and movies, the right to "plead the fifth" is thought to be one of the bedrock principles of American democracy; however, the Patriot Act infringes upon the Amendment. Section 412 allows the Attorney General to incarcerate non-Americans up to seven days, up to a period of 180 days without the individual ever being charged with criminal and/or immigration noncompliance. Moreover, any contravention regarding immigration law results immediately in compulsory arrests without discharge up until the time the AG decides they are not terrorists. In addition, neither the Department of Justice nor Homeland Security is required to give proof that the individual detained is a terrorist; rather, all the AG need do is to have "reasonable grounds" for the detainment.

Title I, section 106 of the PA significantly enhances Executive power over the belongings of non-Americans and/or any agencies by altering section 203 of the International Emergency Powers Act.[933] This particular segment endows the President with wide-ranging influence during war or any military conflict.[934] It also permits the President to instruct other organizations or individuals to utilize or move such assets as he wants.

The AG discussed the recognized necessity for this specific provision, saying that:

---

933. See 50 U.S.C. § 1702 (1977).
934. See USA Patriot Act § 106, 115 Stat. at 277.

law enforcement must be able to "follow the money' in order to identify and neutralize terrorist networks. We need the capacity for more than a freeze. We must be able to seize. Consistent with the President's action yesterday [seizing aspects of identified groups and individuals allegedly associated with *al-Qaida*], our proposal gives law enforcement the ability to seize their terrorist assets.[935]

Both transitory and permanent aliens within American borders benefit from the Fifth Amendment guarantee to due process, which includes the right to possess both individual and real property. President Bush utilized section 106 of the Patriot Act to command the apprehension of various financial records and goods of suspected terrorist groups and the people affiliated with them.[936] It should be noted that the President may cite the statute whenever the U.S. is involved militarily with a foreign country, or whenever the U.S. is singly attacked by a foreigner.[937]

Moreover, the law does not grant judicial oversight for these confiscations, and any judicial review of the President's actions will occur ex parte.[938] While judicial oversight is obtainable under section 316 of the Patriot Act, that specific section allows only the proprietor of seized property the entitlement to file a lawsuit against Uncle Sam when the idea that the goods were the property of terrorists and/or their organizations is contested.[939] In addition, the Federal Rules of Evidence can be shelved if the court rules that conformity with the Federal Rules could endanger the security of the U.S.[940]

THE SIXTH AMENDMENT

The Sixth Amendment states that all people charged with criminal behavior have the right to a speedy trial. While this right originates in the U.S. Constitution, it has been used in individual state criminal cases due to the Supreme Court's understanding of the Due Process and Equal Protection Clauses found in the Fourteenth Amendment.

The right to a speedy trial is one that dates back hundreds of years. Henry II (1154–1189) disseminated the Assize of Clarendon, a legal code made up of 22 commentaries, one that stated that each person is guaranteed swift justice to all parties. Later, in 1215, the Magna Carta prevented the regent from

---

935. See *Homeland Defense Before the Senate Comm. on the Judiciary,* 107th Cong. (2001) (Sept. 25, 2001) (written testimony of John Ashcroft, Attorney General).

936. See A. Jeff Ifrah et al., Casting a Wide Net, *Legal Times* (2001-11-19). Retrieved on 2008-02-01.

937. See USA Patriot Act § 106, 115 Stat. at 278.

938. Ibid.

939. Ibid. 106, 115 Stat. at 278.

940. Ibid.

hindering justice to any individuals living within the kingdom. Within the original 13 colonies, their charters defended the right to a speedy trial.

Under the Patriot Act, the government has the authority to use material gathered covertly against American citizens and/or immigrants. Unlike the Alien and Seditions act (see Chapter 3) which required the government to produce each piece of evidence in a public courtroom, the Patriot Act allows individuals to be charged with terrorism without the benefit of a public trial. This contravenes the Sixth Amendment, as its purpose is to safeguard the constitutional rights of citizens and immigrants to meet their accusers in a public arena. The government, depending upon facts gained secretly, explicitly violates the Amendment.

Covert proof was allowed under the 1996 antiterrorism statutes, but a number of federal judges stated it violated the Constitution. In addition, more than 100 members of Congress agreed and affixed their signatures in support of the Secret Evidence Repeal Act (H.R. 2121) of 2000[941]–a potential law that was forgotten due to 9/11. As one U.S. District Court judge wrote: "The [Immigration and Naturalization Service's] reliance on secret evidence raises serious issues about the integrity of the adversarial process, the impossibility of self-defense against undisclosed charges, and the reliability of governmental processes initiated and prosecuted in darkness."[942]

In 1950, Supreme Court Justice Robert H. Jackson stated in a case centering on secret evidence against a defendant that "the plea that evidence of guilt must be secret is abhorrent to free men, because it provides a cloak for the malevolent, the misinformed, the meddlesome, and the corrupt to play the role of informer undetected and uncorrected."[943]

The Sixth Amendment Right to Counsel

When an individual is charged with a crime, he/she has the right to have a court-appointed attorney represent him/her; with the Patriot Act, however, immigrants lack this basic right. It should be noted that this does not mean that the immigrant cannot hire a private attorney, for they can. The difference is that if they are poor, they will not be supplied a lawyer, as would an American citizen.

A bedrock principle of law now being ignored centers on the confidentiality that a prisoner enjoys when speaking to his/her attorney.[944] After September 11 (October 30, 2001 to be precise), the DOJ, on its own initia-

---

941. See HR 2121.
942. See Al Najjar v. Reno, 97 F.Supp.2d 1329 (S.D. Fla. 2000).
943. See U.S. ex rel. Knauff v. Shaughnessy, 338 U.S. 537, 551.
944. See *United States v. Levy*, 577 F.2d 200, 209 (3d Cir. 1978) and *Flaherty v. Warden of Conn. State Prison*, 229 A.2d 362 (Conn. 1967).

tive, stated that henceforward, at all federal prisons, lawyers speaking to their clients could be subject to monitoring.[945] Quickly thereafter, Attorney General Ashcroft put the new rule into use–without notifying the public, an act that ran counter to the Administrative Procedures Act.[946] The new rule was posted in the Federal Register on October 31, 2001, the day after it went into effect. Further, the rule is not limited to alleged terrorists; rather, it extends to all incarcerated individuals.[947] Under the rule, communications or mail between prisoners and their attorneys may be monitored if the Attorney General "has certified that reasonable suspicion exists to believe that an inmate may use communications with attorneys or their agents to further or facilitate acts of violence or terrorism."[948]

As the expression "acts of violence" is so expansive and allows for the AG's good judgment, no safeguards are in place to make sure that the monitoring will not grow to comprise a huge number of federal inmates.[949] The American Bar Association wrote that this type of observing infringes upon the basic attorney-client relationship and severely contravenes upon an individual's Sixth Amendment right to an attorney.[950] Before the directive passed, only a judicial command could legally allow the listening in or close observation of attorney-client contact, and even then, the government had to show that it was likely that criminal behavior was transpiring.[951] In essence, the lawyer finds himself/herself in a ticklish situation. He/she could violate basic ethics involving a lawyer and client, or sacrifice a communications with his/her client, likely causing the client harm in terms of legal representation.[952]

Each second year law student finds out that whenever a suspect invokes his/her right to a lawyer, any further questioning by the authorities is precluded. Any pertinent data attained from a suspect by the legal authorities, including the admission of guilt, gathered after his/her rights to legal representation is invoked, is not allowed in court.

---

945. See Final Rule, 66 Fed. Reg. 55,061, 55,063 (Oct. 31, 2001) [hereinafter National Security] (amending C.F.R. pts. 500 & 501); see also George Lardner, Jr., U.S. Will Monitor Calls to Lawyers: Rule on Detainees Called 'Terrifying,' *Wash. Post,* Nov. 9, 2001, at A1.
946. See 5 U.S.C. § 553 (1966).
947. See Andrew Miga, Court Demands to See Clinton Lawyer, Boston Herald, Aug. 5, 1998, at 4.
948. See *United States v. Proctor & Gamble Co.,* 356 U.S. 677, 682 n.6, 684 (1958).
949. See Patriot Act, § 203a, 115 Stat. 272, 280 (2001).
950. See ABA Leadership Statement of Robert E. Hirshorn, President (Nov. 9, 2001) (on file with the American University Law Review); see, e.g., *Black v. United States,* 385.
951. Ibid.
952. See Model Code of Prof'l Responsibility DR 4–101 (1986); Model Rules of Professionall Conduct R. 1.6 (1992).

The Sixth Amendment Right to a Jury Trial

On November 13, 2001, the President delivered an Executive Order shelving a suspect's rights of indictment, trial by jury, appellate relief, and habeas corpus; that is, if the suspect was a non-American accused of helping or supporting terrorist groups.[953] The Order, released in accordance with the President's lawful ability as Commander in Chief of the Armed Forces, remarked that the 9/11 terrorist depredations had initiated an armed conflict calling for the military to flex its muscles. The President stated that in order to "protect the United States and its citizens, and for the effective conduct of military operations and prevention of terrorist attacks, it is necessary for individuals subject to this Order . . . to be detained, and, when tried, to be tried for violations of the laws of war and other applicable laws" in military tribunals.[954]

The Order allows the Chief Executive to treat non-Americans as if he/she (1) was a member of al-Qaeda; (2) "engaged in, aided or abetted, or conspired to commit, acts of international terrorism, or acts in preparation therefore, that have caused, threaten to cause, or have as their aim to cause, injury to or adverse effects on the United States, its citizens, national security, foreign policy, or economy"; or (3) had housed terrorists and knew the fact at the time, and that it would serve the interests of the U.S. by utilizing the Order to the individual.[955]

The Order gives the Secretary of Defense the authority to issue rules and directives for the selection and management of the military tribunals that will sit and judge alleged terrorists.[956] Incidentally, the Order states that since international terrorism is so hideous, the tribunals will not bother attempting to use basic principles of jurisprudence; that is, the laws and/or rules of evidence will not apply to terrorists.[957] The rules only allow evidence that the Defense Secretary feels does not infringe upon national security.[958] What this means in plain language is that the military will act as both the trier of facts and sole say-so regarding the law. Moreover, each tribunal has the vested ability to sentence someone to death,[959] but unlike that which is found in civilian trials, the vote needed for death is only a 2/3 majority (in civilian trials, the vote must be unanimous).[960]

---

953. See Military Order of Nov. 11, 2001, Detention, Treatment, and Trial of Certain Non-Citizens in the War Against Terror, 66 Fed. Reg. 57,833 (Nov. 13, 2001).
954. Ibid.
955. Ibid.
956. Ibid.
957. Ibid.
958. Ibid.
959. Ibid.
960. Ibid.

THE EIGHTH AMENDMENT

The Eighth Amendment safeguards each American citizen from experiencing either cruel and/or unusual punishment. After the initiation of the Patriot Act, the federal government took into custody people that were then transported across the country, incarcerating them for months at a time with absolutely no contact with friends or family members.[961]

Specifically, section 412 permits expulsion to areas where torture is allowed. In these areas, the standards of law outlined in the Geneva conventions are done away with. The stipulations, possessing the ability to arrest terrorists, permit the mistreatment of resident aliens who have done nothing wrong. Section 411 makes it legal to expel resident aliens for affiliating with anything that Uncle Sam feels is terrorist in nature. Section 412 hands power to the AG to incarcerate anyone that he thinks could be a danger to American security. Aliens can be incarcerated up to seven days without ever being charged with any criminal offense. If the alien is unlucky enough not to have a nation that will accept him/her, he/she could be held ad infinitum, without ever seeing the inside of a court room.[962] The PA mandates that bi-annual account be given to Congress; however, the account does not need to possess data concerning the names of anyone incarcerated, nor does it need any information concerning when they were captured, where they were held, or the reasons why the government thinks they are terrorists.[963]

THE FOURTEENTH AMENDMENT

The Supreme Court wrote ". . . the Fourteenth Amendment protects every one of these persons from deprivation of life, liberty, or property without due process of law. Even one whose presence in this country is unlawful, involuntary, or transitory is entitled to that constitutional protection."[964] One example typifies this. In *Plyler v. Doe*,[965] the Supreme Court ruled that when a public school in Texas did not allow Mexicans illegally living in America the right to a public education, it was violating the immigrants' Fourteenth Amendment. Thus, the civil liberties guaranteed by the U.S. Constitution are also valid for illegal immigrants living within the United States.[966] Moreover,

---

961. See The Patriot Act, Section 411–412.
962. Ibid.
963. Ibid.
964. See *Mathews v. Diaz,* 426 U.S. 67, 77 (1976).
965. See *Plyler v. Doe,* 457 U.S. 202 (1982).
966. See *Zadvydas v. Davis,* 533 U.S. 678, 121 S. Ct. 2491, 2500 (2001) (citing *Plyler v. Doe,* 457 U.S. 202, 210 (1982)).

the Supreme Court has elucidated this issue by saying that once an individual crosses into American territory, regardless of the reasons, he/she enjoys the protections given to American citizens.[967] Due to these legal protections, when an illegal immigrant is deported back to his/her mother country, the authorities must ensure that due process is followed.[968]

Before 9/11, federal law ensured that any person held in custody due to thinking that he/she had violated immigration rules, had be accused of a crime within 24 hours or he/she was released.[969] On Sept. 20, 2001, DOJ released a temporary directive, without allowing the general public the chance to speak about it, expanding the 24 hours to 48 hours, while permitting a vague expansion of that time if the circumstances warranted it.[970] In addition, the directives give no direction on what precisely these circumstances will be.

Once the Patriot Act became law, the authority to keep in custody noncitizens, though they were not charged, was again lengthened. The Patriot Act gave John Ashcroft, or any other AG, the wherewithal to designate any non-American citizen the label of terrorist if he thinks that individual is a terrorist or has been involved in terrorist activity.[971] Once someone receives the label of "terrorist," he/she can be held up to seven days, even if he/she has not been charged with a crime.[972]

Once a person is labeled "terrorist" and receives a charge of violating immigration law, he/she is subject to obligatory imprisonment for the entire time of his/her proceedings, regardless of whether or not he/she has been charged with any terrorist acts.[973] The PA gives no rules or regulations regarding the reasons why someone should receive charges of terrorism and gives no rules concerning whether or not the "terrorist" and his/her attorney can review the AG's decision.

Before the PA, any non-American citizen, including long-term resident aliens that had never broken the law, could be deported or be denied admission into the U.S. if he/she was found to be involved with terrorists or involved in any terrorist activity.[974] Terrorist activity was declared as being a participant in aggressive acts (i.e., sabotage of facilities, plane hijacking, killing of foreign leaders, etc.) or giving substantive aid when the individual

---

967. See *Kwong Hai Chew,* 344 U.S. at 596–98, and *Yick Wo v. Hopkins,* 118 U.S. 356, 369 (1886).
968. See *Shaughnessy v. United States ex rel. Mezei,* 345 U.S. 206, 212 (1953).
969. See 8 CFR Part 287.3(d).
970. See Interim Rule 8 CFR part 287.3(d).
971. See the USA Patriot Act: sections 212(a)93)(A)9i), 212(a)(3)(A)(iii), 212(a)(3)(B), 237(a)(4)(A)(i), 237(a)(4)(A)(iii), or 237(a)(4)(B).
972. Ibid.
973. Op. cit no. 41.
974. See 8 USC§ 1182(a)(3)(B)(i).

knew that the aid would lead to terrorist activity.[975] The reasons why some-one was denied entrance and/or deported out of the country increased due to the PA. For instance, raising money for charitable ventures sponsored by groups labeled as terrorist,[976] supporting terrorist acts or terrorist groups in a manner that the Secretary of State decides harms the U.S.[977]

The Secretary of State has the authority to label a group a "terrorist" organization; however, before 9/11, the list of such groups considered ter-rorist was 28. By 1–28–2002, this had grown to 168 groups and individuals. On October 21, 2001, the DOJ issued a provisional directive, taking effect the day after its issuance, and gave wide range authority to the Federal Bureau of Prisons, their facilities, and other organizations within the De-partment to watch closely any mail and/or other communications between the detainees and their lawyers.[978] On September 21, 2001, immigration judges throughout the United States received a note from the DOJ directing them to apply precise security measures for specific cases.

These measures consisted of having closed hearings in which neither fam-ily nor the press could attend, and making sure that no information about the case was released; that is, to any individuals not inside the immigration court.[979] The measures were put into place, even though regulations existed that removal hearings would be open to the public.[980]

FREEDOM OF INFORMATION ACT

One issue affected by the Patriot Act is the Freedom of Information Act (FOIA), which was the legislation that allowed the public to gain access to governmental information. Lyndon B. Johnson affixed his signature to the law back on July 4, 1966 and it took effect January 1, 1967. FOIA permitted for the entire or partial release of prior, withheld data and papers restricted by the U.S. Government. The Act spells out which organizational documents are subject for disclosure, details obligatory release procedures, and allows for nine exemptions to the law.[981]

---

975. See 8 USC§ 1182(a)(3)(B)(ii).
976. See Patriot Act, Section 411.
977. Ibid.
978. See Interim Rule 28 CFR Part 501.3(d).
979. See Memorandum from Michael Creppy to All Immigration Judges; Court Administrators, dated 9/21/2001, *Instructions for cases requiring additional security.* Retrieved on 2008–01–20.
980. See 8 CFR Part 3.27.
981. See Branscomb, Anne (1994). *Who Owns Information?: From Privacy To Public Access.* Section 552–(a)4(F): BasicBooks.

The potential problems arising from FOIA are usually due to the exemptions, as they deal with matters regarding personal rights. They are:[982] (A) exclusively endorsed under measures created by a Presidential command to be kept confidential due to matters of national interest and (B) are kept confidential in accordance with a Presidential order;

1. Connected exclusively to the in-house personnel regulations and performance of an organization;
2. Specifically free from public release by law, that is, if such law (A) mandates that the issues be kept private from the public in a way that leaves no discretion regarding the matter, or (B) creates specific rules withholding data or alludes to certain sorts of issues to be kept secret;
3. Confidential trade, business, and/or banking data gained form someone or something that is privileged;
4. Inter-agency or intra-agency memos or messages that normally would not be accessible by statute to someone other than an organization in a legal action with the agency;
5. Any files from which the release of information would represent an invasion of one's privacy;
6. Data or documents assembled for the purpose of aiding law enforcement, but only to the degree that the manufacture of such law enforcement data or documents:
   (A) could plausibly be expected to obstruct with enforcement procedures,
   (B) would likely deny an individual of his/her vested right to a fair trial or an unbiased adjudication,
   (C) could plausibly be expected to represent a gratuitous invasion of one's privacy,
   (D) could plausibly be expected to divulge the identification of a secret source, and, in the case of a document or data amassed by law enforcement authorities during a criminal investigation, or by an organization carrying out a legal national security intelligence inquiry, data given by a secret source,
   (E) would divulge methods for law enforcement, or would divulge rules regarding law enforcement if such revelation could rationally be predicted to risk breaking the law, or
   (F) could rationally be predicted to put in danger an individual's life or his/her bodily safety,
7. Anything pertaining to the investigation, use, or condition reports writ-

---

982. See Title 5 of the United States Code, section 552.

ten by or for the use of any organization accountable for the guidelines or administration of banks; or

8. Geological and/or geophysical facts and statistics, including charts or diagrams, regarding wells.

Executive Order 13233, penned by Alberto R. Gonzales and released by President Bush on November 1, 2001, mere weeks after 9/11, limited right of entry for citizens to view data of former Presidents. Section 13 rescinded Executive Order 12667 of January 18, 1989. Order 13233 was partially struck down in October, 2007, and in his first day as President of the United States, Barack Obama completely revoked it with Executive Order 13489.[983]

During 1974, the U.S. Congress approved legislation regarding the presidential records of Richard Nixon being placed in federal safekeeping to thwart their being destroyed. This law was meant to diminish concealment, while permitting scholars to study the records. In 1972, upon the death of FBI czar J. Edgar Hoover, his secretary obliterated years of authorized and unauthorized records.[984] The Presidential Records Act of 1978 extended such safeguards concerning historical data by making it obligatory that the data of prior Chief Executives would routinely become the possession of Uncle Sam upon his leaving the Presidency. At that point, the material would transfer to the archivist of the United States, and would become accessible to the American public no more than 12 years after the President left office.[985]

Hence, the official records of Ronald Reagan were to be made viewable to John Q. Citizen in January, 2001, Counsel for President George W. Bush wrote a memo to John W. Carlin, U.S. Archivist, saying:

> Section 2(b) of Executive Order 12667, issued by former President Ronald Reagan on January 16, 1989, requires the Archivist of the United States to delay President, I instruct you to extend for 90 days (until June 21, 2001) the time in which President Bush may claim a constitutionally based privilege over the Presidential records that former President Reagan, acting under Section 2204(a) of Title 4, has protected from disclosure for the 12 years since the end of his Presidency. This directive applies as well to the Vice Presidential records of former Vice President George H.W. Bush.[986]

---

983. See *Executive Order no. 13489, Presidential Records,* 74 F.R. 4669.
984. See Curt Gentry (1991). *J. Edgar Hoover: The Man and the Secrets.* New York: W.W. Norton.
985. See 44 U.S.C. § 2201–2207.
986. See Alberto R. Gonzalez (2001, March 23). Memo to John W. Carlin halting Presidential Records release. Retrieved 2009–01–12.

This directive was reissued after three months.[987] After six months, Alberto Gonzales directed Carlin to wait longer.[988] On 11-01-2001, Bush released Executive Order 13233, which limited the ability for the public to view the official papers of prior American Presidents, including records dealing with the military, ambassadorial, or information thought to relate to national security and in addition, details concerning presidential communications, any legal counsel and/or legal work, or the procedures used by the President and his advisors when faced with questions confronting the country. Any release of data to the public should be carried out in a fashion following the guidelines issued in accordance with the Supreme Court's rulings in *Nixon v. Administrator of General Services.*[989]

On 03-01-2007, the Presidential Records Act Amendments of 2007 was debated.[990] At the hearing, a number of scholars stated that Order 13233 had all but stopped public contact with presidential records. The bill received the imprimatur of the entire committee, and on 3-14-2007, the House voted 333-93 on the bill, a strong sign of bipartisan support. On 06-13-2007, the bill passed the Senate committee, but thus far has not been voted in the full Senate, due to the machinations of Senator Jim Bunning (R-KY).[991] President Bush stated unequivocally that he would veto the bill, but the House tally made his remark worthless, especially with the Senate Committee's vote being unanimous.

In 2002, Congress passed the Intelligence Authorization Act for Fiscal Year 2003.[992] A major issue with the legislation centered on the inclusion of various changes to the FOIA (primarily those dealing with intelligence organizations) entitled "Prohibition on Compliance with Requests for Information Submitted by Foreign Governments":

Section 552(a)(3) of title 5, United States Code, is amended:
(1) in subparagraph (A) by inserting "and except as provided in subparagraph (E)," after "of this subsection,"; and (2) by adding at the end the following: "(E) An agency, or part of an agency, that is an element of the intelligence community (as that term is defined in section 3(4) of the National Security Act of 1947 (50 U.S.C. 401a(4))) shall not make any record available under this paragraph to—"(i) any government entity, other than a State, territory, common-

987. See Alberto R. Gonzalez (2001, June 6). Second memo to John W. Carlin halting Presidential Records release. Retrieved 2009–01–12.
988. Alberto R. Gonzalez (2001, August 31). Third memo to John W. Carlin halting Presidential Records release. Retrieved 2009–01–12.
989. See 433 U.S. 425 (1977).
990. See http://www.govtrack.us/congress/bill.xpd?bill=h110-1255. Retrieved on 2008–12–29.
991. The bill was brought to the Senate floor in late September, 2007 but Sen. Bunning objected to the request under his own name, thus the bill was held off.
992. See Public Law 107–306.

wealth, or district of the United States, or any subdivision thereof; or "(ii) a representative of a government entity described in clause (i)."[993]

What this meant was that any sheltered U.S. intelligence organization did not need to disclose any data in pursuant to FOIA demands made by alien governments or international legislative agencies. In addition, it prohibited any release of information even if the calls for data were made by non-U.S. governmental agencies either directly or through an agent representing the agency.[994]

The organizations affected by this change are any that are part of governmental intelligence, including the CIA, the NSA, the DIA, the NIMA (National Imagery and Mapping Agency), the NRO (National Reconnaissance Office), the intelligence parts of the U.S. military, the FBI, the Department of the Treasury, the Department of Energy, the Coast Guard, the Department of Homeland Security, the Bureau of Intelligence and Research in the Department of State, and any other group determined by the President to belong.[995]

EPIC, the well-known civil liberties group, brought a lawsuit against the Federal Bureau of Investigation for alleged bad behavior that the Bureau exhibited toward an intelligence oversight board. In November, 2005, a federal judge commanded the Bureau to openly release all information or every 15 days, would need to respond to the request with 1,500 pages.[996]

* * * * * *

The future of the Patriot Act is not as opaque as one might first think; that is, the life or death of the Act depends upon the behavior of terrorists. The more time that elapses between 9/11 and any new predatory attack will likely mean that the PA will continue to be defanged and declawed until it is completely acceptable by all civil liberties groups. Does that mean it will lose much of its punch? Unequivocally, the answer is yes, and it depends upon which side of the aisle one agrees with whether that is good or not.

One thing to remember is that immediately after the attacks, most Americans wanted revenge against the terrorists and the more noxious aspects of the Patriot Act was OK. It was only after no new attacks that the populace debated whether having legislation like the PA was conducive to American democracy. What would have happened if after 9/11, another

---

993. The Intelligence Authorization Act of 2003 amended the Freedom of Information Act (FOIA) by adding new language under 5 U.S.C. 552(a)(3)(E).
994. See 5 U.S.C. § 552(a)(3)(E)(ii) (as amended).
995. See 50 U.S.C. § 401a(4) (2000).
996. See EPIC v. Department of Justice Civ. No. 05–845 (D.D.C. 2005 ESH).

attack occurred only a few weeks later? What if al-Qaeda operatives had smuggled a nuclear device into the country and detonated it, killing thousands, perhaps millions, of citizens? Would the majority of American citizens preached about the cruelty the U.S. is a symbol for, or would shouts of revenge against Islamists been the norm?

Only Russ Feingold voted against the PA's ratification, which showed an amazing amount of moral courage, since both parties were on the bandwagon concerning catching terrorists, no matter what the costs. Would he have held out a second time? What if a weapon of mass destruction had been set off in the nation's capital or one of the major metropolitan areas? Would he have still voted no? Probably not because it would have been political suicide.

If the United States is attacked again, will it mean that we will become a fascist dictatorship due to our longing for security? The answer is no. While many in the media excoriated Bush for the Patriot Act, at no point were we close to fascism. Political cartoons comparing Bush to Hitler were common, but even the most diehard conspiracists admit that if Bush were trying to gain control of the U.S., he was a putz that failed. This is not to say that America will always remain a democratic republic, for in times of great stress, the public is willing to cede some of its civil rights for security. However, the way in which our government was established by the Founders, makes this highly unlikely.

GLOSSARY OF STATUTES AND LAWS
AFFECTED BY THE PATRIOT ACT

ACLU and EPIC v. Department of Justice, Civil Action No. 02-2077–EPIC along with the ACLU, and various library and booksellers' organizations, brought a lawsuit against the DOJ on October 24, 2002 under the Freedom of Information Act asking for the disclosure of data regarding the implementation of the PA. The lawsuit covered some of the information the Justice Department withheld from the House Judiciary Committee in response to a set of detailed questions. On November 26, 2002, U.S. District Judge Ellen Huvelle ordered the Justice Department to complete its processing of the EPIC/ACLU information request by January 15, 2003. DOJ and the FBI released some responsive material, but withheld a substantial amount of information asserting national security classification.

ACLU and EPIC v. Department of Justice, Civil Action No. 03-2522–On October 23, 2003, EPIC, the ACLU, and various library and booksellers' organizations submitted a FOIA request to the FBI seeking information about Section 215 of the USA PATRIOT Act. When FBI denied expedited processing, EPIC and the ACLU filed suit in federal court seeking the immediate release of the requested records. On May 10, 2004, U.S. District Judge Ellen Huvelle ordered the FBI to expeditiously process the request. Some responsive records were released in June 2004, and more documents were released in July.

Atomic Energy Act of 1946 (McMahon Act)–decided the methods from which the U.S. would manage and organize the scientific know-how it had developed regarding nuclear weapons. Most importantly, it declared that the development of nuclear weapons and/or nuclear power in general, would be in the hands of civilians, not the military; thus, the United States Atomic Energy Commission was created. It was originally sponsored by Senator Brien McMahon (D-CT), the chair of the United States Senate Special Committee on Atomic Energy whose hearings led to the passage of the Act.

Atomic Energy Act of 1954 42 U.S.C. § 2011 et seq.–United States federal law controls nuclear materials within the United States. It was an amendment to the Atomic Energy Act of 1946 and significantly improved specific areas of the law, including additional aid for the likelihood of a civilian nuclear industry.

5 U.S.C. § 102–Military Departments: The Department of the Army, The Department of the Navy, and The Department of the Air Force.

5 U.S.C. § 105–"Executive agency" means an Executive department, a Government corporation, and an independent establishment.

5 U.S.C. § 552–Freedom of Information Act

5 U.S.C. § 553–Rule Making

7 U.S.C.A.–Statute dealing with agriculture

8 CFR Part 3.27–Rule that determined who could and could not attend "public" hearings. Specifically, "All hearings other than exclusion hearings, shall be open to the public except that: (a) Depending upon physical facilities, the IJ may place reasonable limitations upon the number in attendance at any one time with priority being given to the press over the general public; (b) For the purpose of protecting witnesses, parties, or the public interest the Immigration Judge may limit attendance of hold a closed hearing; (c) In any proceedings before an Immigration Judge concerning an abused alien spouse, the hearing and the Record of Proceedings shall be closed to the public unless the abused spouse agrees that the hearing and the Record of Proceedings shall be open to the public. In any proceedings concerning an abused alien child, the hearing the Record of Proceedings shall be closed to the public."

8 CFR Part 287.3(d)–Custody procedures. Unless voluntary departure has been granted pursuant to subpart C of 8 CFR Part 240, a determination will be made within 24 hours of the arrest whether the alien will be continued in custody or released on bond or recognizance and whether a notice to appear and warrant of arrest as prescribed in 8 CFR Parts 236 and 239 will be issued. Interim rule declared that unless voluntary departure has been granted pursuant to subpart C of 8 CFR Part 240, a determination will be made within 48 hours of the arrest, except in the event of an emergency or other extraordinary circumstance in which case a determination will be made within an additional reasonable period of time, whether the alien will be continued in custody or released on bond or recognizance and whether a notice to appear and warrant of arrest as prescribed in 8 CFR Parts 236 and 239 will be issued.

8 U.S.C. § 1105–Liaison with internal security officers; data exchange

8 U.S.C. § 1151–Worldwide level of immigration
  (b) Aliens not subject to direct numerical limitations
  (2)(A)(i) Immediate relatives

8 U.S.C. § 1154–Procedure for granting immigrant status

8 U.S.C. § 1182–Inadmissible aliens
  (a) Classes of aliens ineligible for visas or admission
  (3) Ineligible due to security and related grounds

8 U.S.C. § 1187–Visa waiver support for certain visitors
  (a)(3)–Elimination of pilot program status

8 U.S.C. § 1189–Designation of foreign terrorist organizations

8 U.S.C. § 1202–Applications for visa

8 U.S.C. § 1226–Apprehension and detention of aliens

8 U.S.C. § 1232–Detention and removal of aliens ordered removed

8 U.S.C. § 1372–Program to collect information relating to nonimmigrant foreign students and other exchange program participants

10 U.S.C. § 47–Uniform Code of Military Justice

10 U.S.C. § 375–Restriction on direct participation by military personnel

10 U.S.C. § 382–Authority for the use of the military in a broader role to respond to terrorist acts expired September 30, 2004

10 U.S.C. § 1565–Armed Forces DNA identification information: collection from certain offenders;
    d–Qualifying military offenses

12 U.S.C. §248–Federal Reserve Act

12 U.S.C. § 1828–The Federal Deposit Insurance Act
    W–Written employment references may contain suspicions of involvement in illegal activity

12 U.S.C. § 1829–Penalty for unauthorized participation by convicted individual

12 U.S.C. § 1953–Recordkeeping and procedures

12 U.S.C. § 3412–Use of information
    a–Transfer of financial records to other agencies or departments; certification

12 U.S.C. §3414–Special procedures
    a–Access to financial records for certain intelligence and protective purposes

15 Kan. App. 2d 365 (rev. denied 248 Kan. 998 [1991]. *State v. Horn*–Kansas law stating that warrants authorizing the search of all persons present at a location are not per se invalid

15 U.S.C. §1681–Congressional findings and statement of purpose

15 U.S.C. §6102–Telemarketing rules

15 U.S.C. § 6106–Definitions for Attorney General and Commission

15 CFR 730-774–Export Administration Regulations

17 F. Cas. 144 (C.C.D. Md. 1861)–Lincoln's suspension of habeas corpus

18 U.S.C. § 7–Special maritime and territorial jurisdiction of the United States defined

18 U.S.C. § 16--Crime of violence defined

18 U.S.C. § 32–Destruction of aircraft or aircraft facilities

18 U.S.C. § 37–Violence at international airports

18 U.S.C. § 81–defines arson, attempted arson, or conspiracy to commit arson

18 U.S.C. § 97–Railroad carriers and mass transportation systems on land, on water, or through the air

18 U.S.C. § 113–Assaults within maritime and territorial jurisdiction

18 U.S.C. §121–Stored Wire and Electronic Communications and Transactional Records Access

18 U. S. C. § 175–Prohibitions with respect to biological weapons
(**a**)–In general
(**b**)–Additional offense
(**c**)–Definition

18 U.S.C. § 229–Prohibited activities that include chemical weapons

18 U. S. C. § 351–Congressional, Cabinet, and Supreme Court assassination, kidnapping, and assault; penalties

18 U.S.C. § 470–Counterfeit acts committed outside the United States

18 U.S.C. § 471–Obligations or securities of United States

18 U.S.C. § 472–Uttering counterfeit obligations or securities

18 U.S.C. § 473–Dealing in counterfeit obligations or securities

18 U.S.C. § 476–Taking impressions of tools used for obligations or securities

18 U.S.C. §477–Possessing or selling impressions of tools used for obligations or securities

18 U.S.C. § 478–Foreign obligations or securities

18 U.S.C. § 479–Uttering counterfeit foreign obligations or securities

18 U.S.C. §480–Possession of counterfeit obligations or securities of foreign countries

18 U.S.C. §481–Possession of plates for counterfeiting obligations or securities o foreign countries

18 U.S.C. § 482–Forgery of foreign bank notes

18 U.S.C. § 483–Falsely making or materially altering a document with the intent to defraud. Includes such falsification with intent to pass off as genuine

18 U.S.C. § 484–Connecting parts of different notes

18 U.S.C. § 493–Bonds and obligations of certain lending agencies

18 U.S.C. § 541–Entry of goods falsely classified

18 U.S.C. § 831–Prohibited transactions involving nuclear materials
(**e**)–The Attorney General can ask for aid from the Secretary of Defense

18 U.S.C. § 832–Participation in nuclear and weapons of mass destruction threats to the United States

18 U.S.C. § 842–Unlawful acts involving importation, manufacture, distribution, and storage of explosive materials
(**m**)–It is unlawful to bring plastic explosives into the United States
(**n**)–It is unlawful to transport any plastic explosive without a detection agent.

18 U.S.C. § 844–Penalties
(**f**)–Anyone attempting to destroy U.S. property in whole, or property leased or rented, as well as receiving financial assistance from the government, can be imprisoned for not less than five years, but not more than 20
(**2**)–Anyone causing the death, or the proximate death of someone, or causes someone to be seriously injured, can be imprisoned for not less than seven years, but not more than 40
(**3**)–Anyone causing the death of any person, including a safety officer, shall be subject to the death penalty, or imprisoned for no less than 20 years, fined, or both

18 U.S.C. §917–It is also a federal felony for anyone to falsely or fraudulently hold himself or herself out as a member of or an agent for the American Red Cross for the purpose of soliciting or collecting money.

18 U.S.C. § 922–Unlawful acts involving firearms

18 U.S.C. § 925–Exceptions: Relief from disabilities
(**d**)–Details what the Attorney General can do regarding firearms

18 U.S.C. § 930–Possession of firearms and dangerous weapons in Federal facilities
(**c**)–Details the punishment of anyone using a firearm in the attack on a federal facility

18 U.S.C. § 956–Conspiracy to kill, kidnap, maim, or injure persons or damage property in a foreign country

18 U.S.C. § 981–Civil forfeiture

18 U.S.C. § 983–General rules for civil forfeiture proceedings

18 U.S.C. § 1029–Fraud and related activity in connection with access devices

18 U.S.C. § 1030–Fraud and related activity in connection with computers

18 U.S.C. § 1114–Protection of officers and employees of the United States

18 U.S.C. § 1116–Murder or manslaughter of foreign officials, official guests, or internationally protected persons

18 U.S.C. § 1203–Hostage taking

18 U.S.C. § 1361–Malicious mischief involving Government property or contracts

18 U.S.C. § 1362–Malicious mischief involving communication lines, stations or systems

18 U.S.C. § 1363–Malicious mischief involving buildings or property within special maritime and territorial jurisdiction

18 U.S.C. § 1366–Malicious mischief involving the destruction of an energy facility

18 U.S.C. 1385–Use of Army and Air Force as posse comitatus

18 U.S.C. § 1751–Presidential and Presidential staff assassination, kidnapping, and assault; penalties

18 U.S.C. § 1956–Laundering of monetary instruments

18 U.S.C. § 1960–Prohibition of unlicensed money transmitting businesses

18 U.S.C. §1961–Definitions of racketeering

18 U.S.C. § 1992–Entering train to commit crime

18 U.S.C. § 1993–Attacking a mass transit is a crime. Was repealed.

18 U.S.C. § 2152–Sabotage involving fortifications, harbor defenses, or defensive sea areas

18 U.S.C. § 2155–Sabotage involving the destruction of national-defense materials, national-defense premises, or national-defense utilities

18 U.S.C. § 2156–Sabotage involving the production of defective national-defense material, national-defense premises, or national-defense utilities

18 U.S.C. § 2280–Violence against maritime navigation

18 U.S.C. § 2281–Violence against maritime fixed platforms

18 U.S.C. §2325–Definition of telemarketing

18 U.S.C. § 2331–Definitions of terrorism

18 U.S.C. § 2332–Criminal penalties for terrorism
  a–Homicide
  b–Attempt or conspiracy with respect to homicide
  c–Other conduct
  d–Limitation on prosecution

18 U.S.C. 2339–Harboring or concealing terrorists
  a–Providing material support to terrorists
  b–Providing material support or resources to designated foreign terrorist organizations
  c–Prohibitions against the financing of terrorism

d–Receiving military-type training from a foreign terrorist organization

18 U.S.C. § 2340–Definitions of torture

18 U.S.C. § 2510–Definitions of "communications"

18 U.S.C. §2511–Interception and disclosure of wire, oral, or electronic communications prohibited

18 U.S.C. §2516–Authorization for interception of wire, oral, or electronic communications

18 U.S.C. §2517–Authorization for disclosure and use of intercepted wire, oral, or electronic communications

18 USC § 2518–Procedure for interception of wire, oral, or electronic communications

18 U.S.C. §2520–Recovery of civil damages authorized

18 USC § 2701; *ECPA Title II*–Also known as the ***Stored Communications Act*** Unlawful access to stored communications.

18 U.S.C. §2702–Voluntary disclosure of customer communications or records

18 U.S.C. § 2703–Required disclosure of customer communications or records

18 U.S.C. § 2705–Delayed notice

18 U.S.C. §2707–Civil action

18 U.S.C. § 2709–Counterintelligence access to telephone toll and transactional records

18 U.S.C. §2711–Definitions for chapter

18 U.S.C. §2712–Civil actions against the United States

18 U.S.C. § 3056–Powers, authorities, and duties of United States Secret Service

18 U.S.C. §3077–Definitions of terrorism

18 U.S.C. §3103–Single jurisdiction search warrants and sneak and peak warrants may be issued.

18 U.S.C. § 3121; *ECPA Title III*–also known as the ***Pen Register Act*.** General prohibition on pen register and trap and trace device use; exception.

18 USC § 3122–Application for an order for a pen register or a trap and trace device

18 USC § 3123–Issuance of an order for a pen register or a trap and trace device

18 USC § 3124–Assistance in installation and use of a pen register or a trap and trace device

18 U.S.C. § 3127–Definitions involving pen registers and trap and trace devices

18 U.S.C. § 3286–Limitations involving extension of statute of limitation for certain terrorism offenses

18 U.S.C. § 3583–Inclusion of a term of supervised release after imprisonment

19 Kan. App. 2d 786 (1994). *State v. Vandiver*–When the facts material to a decision of the court on a motion to suppress evidence are not in dispute, the question of whether to suppress becomes a question of law

20 U.S.C. § 1232–Regulations

20 U.S.C. §9007–Confidentiality

22 CFR 40.5–Limitations on the use of National Crime Information Center (NCIC) criminal history information

22 U.S.C. § 1474–Non-US Citizens that are employees

22 U.S.C. § 2656–Functions of President respecting certain facilities constructed and maintained on United States borders delegated to Secretary of State,
> **f(d)(2)j**–states, "terrorism" as "premeditated, politically motivated violence, perpetrated against noncombatant targets by subnational groups or clandestine agents"

22 U.S.C. § 2708–A program for the payment of rewards to carry out the purposes of this section

22 U.S.C. 2778 and 27947 *Arms Export Control Act of 1976*–gives the President of the United States the authority to control the import and export of defense articles and defense services. It requires governments that receive weapons from the United States to use them for legitimate self-defense. Exports are prohibited to a country that "contribute to an arms race, aid in the development of weapons of mass destruction, support international terrorism, increase the possibility of outbreak or escalation of conflict, or prejudice the development of bilateral or multilateral arms control or nonproliferation agreements or other arrangements." It also places certain restrictions on American arms traders and manufacturers, prohibiting them from the sale of certain sensitive technologies to certain parties and requiring thorough documentation of such trades to trusted parties.

22 U.S.C. § 2778 *United States Munitions List,* **which is part of the** *Arms Export Control Act*–is a list of articles, services, and related technology designated as defense-related by the United States federal government. These articles fall under the export and temporary import jurisdiction of the Department of State.

22 U.S.C. § 4024–Functions of the Secretary of State

22 U.S.C. § 2656–Management of foreign affairs

26 U.S.C. § 6103–Confidentiality and disclosure of returns and return information

28 U.S.C. § 2467–Enforcement of foreign judgments

28 C.F.R. Part 0.85–Definition of terrorism

28 CFR Part 501.3–authorizes the imposition of special administrative measures on a particular inmate based on a written determination by the Attorney General. In addition, at the Attorney General's discretion, the head of a federal law enforcement or intelligence agency that there is a substantial risk that an inmate's communications or contacts with other persons could result in death or serious bodily injury to persons, or substantial damage to property that would entail the risk of death or serious bodily injury to persons.

31 CFR 100–Regulation regarding information sharing between law enforcement and financial institutions. Implements Section 314 of the Patriot Act.

31 CFR 103–Financial recordkeeping and reporting of currency And foreign transactions

31 U.S.C. § 310–an authorization for the President to appoint an Assistant General Counsel in the U.S. Department of the Treasury to be the Chief Counsel for the IRS

31 U.S.C. § 5311–require certain reports or records where they have a high degree of usefulness in criminal, tax, or regulatory investigations or proceedings, or in the conduct of intelligence or counterintelligence activities, including analysis, to protect against international terrorism

31 U.S.C. §5312–Definitions of financial institution

31 U.S.C. § 5313–Reports on domestic coins and currency transactions

31 U.S.C. § 5316–Reports on exporting and importing monetary instruments

31 U.S.C. § 5317–Search and forfeiture of monetary instruments

31 U.S.C. § 5318–Compliance, exemptions, and summons authority for the Secretary of the Treasury

31 U.S.C. § 5319–Availability of reports regarding monetary transactions

31 U.S.C. § 5321–Civil penalties for banking institutions or individual involved in banking for money laundering

31 U.S.C. § 5322–Criminal penalties for banking institutions or individual involved in banking for money laundering

31 U.S.C. § 5324–Structuring transaction to evade reporting requirement prohibited

31 USC 5325–Identification required to purchase certain monetary instruments

31 USC 5326–Records of certain domestic coin and currency transactions

31 U.S.C. § 5327–statute imposed on banks that required them to identify their depositor or their account holder and determine if that person was a money service business. Was repealed.

31 U.S.C. § 5328–Whistleblower protections

31 U.S.C. § 5329–Staff commentaries

31 U.S.C. § 5330–Registration of money transmitting businesses

31 U.S.C. §5331–Authorizes the Treasury to require that a separate report of the transaction also be filed with the Financial Crimes Enforcement Network (FinCEN) at such time and in such manner as the Secretary prescribes by regulation.

31 U.S.C. §5332–Bulk cash smuggling into or out of the United States

31 U.S.C. §5341–National money laundering and related financial crimes strategy

72.6 of title 42, C.F.R.–Additional requirements for facilities transferring or receiving select agents.

42 U.S.C. § 2284–Sabotage of nuclear facilities or fuel

42 U.S.C. § 3711; *The Omnibus Crime Control and Safe Streets Act of 1968*–also known as the Wiretap Act. Legislation passed by Congress that established the Law Enforcement Assistance Administration (LEAA). Title III of the Act set rules for obtaining wiretap orders in the United States.

42 U.S.C. § 3796–Payment of death benefits to public safety officer

42 U.S.C. § 10601–*Crime Victims Fund*

42 U.S.C. § 10602–*Crime Victim Compensation*

42 U.S.C. § 10603 *Victims of Crime Act of 1984*–The fund dollars come from criminal fines, penalties and special assessments, bequests or donations from private entities. VOCA funds are utilized to provide direct services to victims of sexual assault, domestic violence, child abuse, drunk driving, homicide, and other crimes.

42 U.S.C. § 14135 *DNA Analysis Backlog Elimination Act of 2000*–Legislation that allowed states comprising the union to carry out DNA analyses for use in the FBI's Combined DNA Index System and to collect and analyze DNA samples.

42 U.S.C. §14601 *Crime Identification Technology Act of 1998*–A bill that provide for the enhancement of interstate criminal justice identification, information, communications, and forensics.

42 U.S.C. § 2284 *The Atomic Energy Act of 1954*–It covers the laws for the "development and the regulation of the uses of nuclear materials and facilities in the United States"

42 U.S.C.–The title of the United States Code dealing with public health, social welfare, and civil rights

47 U.S.C. § 151–Purposes of chapter; Federal Communications Commission created

47 U.S.C. 551 *et. seq Cable Communications Policy Act of 1984 (the Cable Act)*–Established a comprehensive framework for cable regulation and sets forth strong protections for subscriber privacy by restricting the collection, maintenance, and dissemination of subscriber data.

47 U.S.C. 1001 *et seq Communications Assistance for Law Enforcement Act*–The Law that defined the existing statutory obligation of telecommunications carriers to assist law enforcement in executing electronic surveillance pursuant to court order or other lawful authorization.

49 U.S.C. § 31305–minimum standards for written and driving tests of an individual operating a motor vehicle

49 U.S.C. § 46502–Aircraft piracy

49 U.S.C. § 46504–Interference with flight crew members and attendants

49 U.S.C. § 46505–Carrying a weapon or explosive on an aircraft

49 U.S.C. § 46506–Certain crimes aboard aircraft in flight

49 U.S.C. § 60123–Criminal penalties for damaging or destroying U.S. property

50 U.S.C. §401–Congressional declaration of purpose

50 U.S.C. § 403–Office of the Director of Central Intelligence

50 F.3d 285, 292 (1995) *Brown v. Waddell*–The contents of a network account are the actual files stored in the account. The contents, when used with respect to any wire, oral, or electronic communication, includes any information concerning the substance, purport, or meaning of that communication. For example, stored e-mails or voice mails are "contents," as are word processing files stored in employee network accounts. The subject headers of e-mails are also contents.

50 U.S.C. ch.36, The complete text of the *Foreign Intelligence Surveillance Act*

50 U.S.C. § 403 *The National Security Act of 1947*–Pub. L. No. 235, 80 Cong., 61 Stat. 496 (July 26, 1947), was signed into law by President Harry S. Truman and both brought into line and restructured America's international relations, the U.S. Military, and created the CIA from William Donovan's Office of Strategic Services in the years after WWII. The bulk of the Act's provisions started on September 18, 1947, exactly 24 hours after James V. Forrestal became the country's first Secretary of Defense.

50 U.S.C. §1702–Presidential authorities

50 U.S.C. §1801–Definitions regarding the meanings of Foreign Power, Agent of a Foreign Power, Sabotage, International Terrorism, Foreign Intelligence Information, Electronic Surveillance, Attorney General, Minimization Procedures, United States Person, United States, Aggrieved Person, Wire Communication, Person, Contents, and State.

50 U.S.C. § 1802–Electronic surveillance authorization without court order; certification by Attorney General; reports to Congressional committees; transmittal under seal; duties and compensation of communication common carrier; applications; jurisdiction of court

50 U.S.C. § 1803–Designation of judges

50 U.S.C. § 1804–Applications for court orders

50 U.S.C. § 1805–Issuance of order

50 U.S.C. § 1806–Use of privileged or confidential information

50 U.S.C. § 1811–Authorizing electronic surveillance during war time

50 U.S.C. §1823–Explains the process regarding attaining a search order

50 U.S.C. 1824–Issuance of order

50 U.S.C. 1825–Use of privileged or confidential information

50 U.S.C. 1842–Pen registers and trap and trace devices for foreign intelligence and international terrorism investigations

50 U.S.C. 1843–Authorization during emergencies

50 U.S.C. 1861–Access to certain business records for foreign intelligence and international terrorism investigations

50 U.S.C. 1862–Congressional oversight

50 U.S.C. 1863–Repealed: Foreign intelligence surveillance. Access to certain business records for foreign intelligence purposes

51 U.S.C. §5103–General regulatory authority and limitation on Hazmat licenses

61 U. S. C. § 496 *National Security Act of 1947*–Reorganized the United States' armed forces, foreign policy, and Intelligence Community apparatus in the aftermath of World War II. The Act merged the Department of War and the Department of the Navy into the National Military Establishment (NME) headed by the Secretary of Defense. It was also responsible for the creation of a separate Department of the Air Force from the existing United States Army Air Forces.

Final Rule, 66 Fed. Reg. 55,061, 55,06–Limited or restricted the right to counsel pursuant to the Sixth Amendment, by allowing monitoring of attorney-client conversations and denying certain suspects the right to counsel.

66 Fed. Reg. 57,833 *(Nov. 13, 2001). Military Order of Nov. 11, 2001*–Detention, Treatment, and Trial of Certain Non-Citizens in the War Against Terror. Primarily, it it instructed the Secretary of Defense to establish one or more "military commissions" for the trial of captured al-Qaeda members, has generally been accepted, in light of the Supreme Court's 1942 decision in *Ex parte Quirin,* as legal under U.S. domestic law.

71 U.S. 2 (1866) *Ex-parte Milligan*–U.S. Supreme Court case that stated suspension of Habeas Corpus when civilian courts are still operating is unconstitutional.

92 §1783 *The Foreign Intelligence Surveillance Act of 1978*–an Act of Congress that prescribes procedures for the physical and electronic surveillance and collection of "foreign intelligence information" between "foreign powers" and "agents of foreign powers" (which may include American citizens and permanent residents suspected of being engaged in espionage and violating U.S. law on territory under United States control).

97 F.Supp.2d 1329 (S.D. Fla. 2000) *Al Najjar v. Reno*–A lawsuit, filed by the Center for Constitutional Rights, the Nationalities Service Center, Tampa attorney Martin Schwartz, and the American Civil Liberties Union (ACLU) of Florida. It argued that the Immigration and Naturalization Service (INS) practice of detaining people on the basis of secret evidence is unconstitutional and that there is no authority under immigration law for the current government policy of detaining aliens on the basis of secret evidence. Al Najjar, a Palestinian, was held for 21/2 years in a Florida jail and argued that his detention on secret evidence was unconstitutional.

114 §1549 *The Trade Sanctions Reform and Export Enhancement Act of 2000*–was amended by Section 221 of the Patriot Act. The Act prohibits, except under certain specific circumstances, the President from imposing a unilateral agricultural sanction or unilateral medical sanction against a foreign country or foreign entity.

116 § 2135; Pub. L. No. 107-296, 116 *The Homeland Security Act of 2002*–introduced in the aftermath 9/11, created the United States Department of Homeland Security in the largest federal government reorganization since the Department of Defense was created via the National Security Act of 1947 (as amended in 1949). The HSA includes many of the organizations under which the powers of the USA PATRIOT Act are exercised. Among other things, it created the new cabinet-level position of Secretary of Homeland Security.

118 U.S. 356, 369 (1886) *Yick Wo v. Hopkins*–Supreme court ruled that a municipal ordinance to regulate the carrying on of public laundries within the city limits was unconstitutional. That is, if it conferred upon the municipal authorities arbitrary power, at their own will, and without regard to discretion in the legal sense of the term, to give or withhold consent as to persons or places, without regard to the competency of the persons applying, or the propriety of the place selected, for the carrying on of the business.

147 *Congressional Record.* H7197–October 23, 2001, the Second Circuit ruled that the validity of sneak and peek warrants and of delayed notice are better judged by Rule 41 standards, rather than the Fourth Amendment.

155 F.3d 1050, 1055-56 *United States v. Smith*–Ninth Circuit court case that stated getting a warrant for voice mail had to follow a strict set of guidelines, otherwise law enforcement could not invade an individual's privacy.

158 F.Supp.2d 644 (D.Md. 2001) *In re Application of U.S.A. for an Order Pursuant to 18 U.S.C. 2703(d)*–Court case that examined whether law enforcement access to their customers records was to be governed by the standards applicable to the communications industry or by the earlier cable standards. The court held that the cable provisions implicitly repealed and summarizing existing ambivalent case law.

229 A.2d 362 (Conn. 1967). *Flaherty v. Warden of Conn. State Prison–* Connecticut case in which it was found that individuals have the right to counsel, including the right to consult in private.

277 U.S. 438 (1928) *Olmstead v. United States–*A 1928 opinion of the Supreme Court of the United States, in which the Court reviewed whether the use of wire-tapped private telephone conversations, obtained by federal agents without judicial approval and subsequently used evidence, constituted a violation of the defendant's rights provided by the Fourth and Fifth Amendments. In a 5-4 decision, the Court held that neither the Fourth Amendment nor the Fifth Amendment rights of the defendant were violated.

310 F.3d 717, 742 *In re Sealed Case, Foreign Intel. Surv. Ct. of Rev. 2002–*A case where the FISA court of review stated that the President had the natural ability to carry out warrantless searches to attain foreign intelligence data and that FISA did not have the right to impinge upon that power

320. U.S. 81 (1941) *Hirabayashi v. United States–*U.S. Supreme Court case that held that the application of curfews against members of a minority group were constitutional when the nation was at war with the country from which that group originated

323 U.S. 214 (1944) *Korematsu v. United States–*Concerning the constitutionality of Executive Order 9066, which required Japanese-Americans in the western United States to be excluded from a described West Coast military area. In a 6-3 decision, the Court sided with the government, ruling that the exclusion order was constitutional.

334 F.Supp.2d 471(2004) *Doe v. Ashcroft–*Case where the constitutionality of 18 U.S.C. § 2709 was argued. The statute authorized the FBI to force Communications firms, such as ISPs or telephone companies, to produce specific customer records whenever the FBI certified that those records were relevant to an authorized investigation to protect against international terrorism or clandestine intelligence activities. The FBI's demands under the statute were issued in the form of NSLs which constituted a form of administrative subpoena covered in secrecy and pertaining to national security issues. The statute barred all NSL recipients from ever disclosing that the FBI had issued an NSL.

338 U.S. 537, 551 *U.S. ex rel. Knauff v. Shaughnessy–*Case in which the alien wife of a citizen who had served honorably in the armed forces of the United States during World War II sought admission to the United States. Due to confidential information, the disclosure of which, in his judgment, would endanger the public security, the Attorney General denied a hearing, finding that her admission would be prejudicial to the interests of the United States, and ordered her excluded. The Court ruled that this action was authorized by the Act of June 21, 1941, 22 U.S.C. § 223, and the proclamations and regulations issued thereunder.

343 U.S. 717 (1952) *Kawakita v. United States*–A case in which the United States Supreme Court reviewed a treason accusation against the defendant Tomoya Kawakita, a dual U.S./Japanese citizen. Kawakita was found guilty of torturing American prisoners of war while living in Japan during World War II. The court found that Kawakita owed allegiance to the United States during his time in Japan. He was found guilty of eight overt acts, his U.S. citizenship was revoked, and he was sentenced to death, but received life imprisonment from President Dwight D. Eisenhower.

344 U.S. 590 (1953) *Kwong Hai Chew v. Colding*–Under 8 CFR § 175.57(b), a regulation pertaining to the entry of aliens into the United States, the Attorney General had no authority to deny to an alien who is a lawful permanent resident of the United States a chance to be heard in opposition to an order for his "permanent exclusion." In this specific case, the petitioner was an alien and a lawful permanent resident of the United States, who maintained his residence in the United States and was usually physically present. While returning from a voyage to foreign ports as a seaman on a vessel of American registry with its home port in the United States, he was detained on board by an order of the Attorney General and ordered "temporarily excluded" from the United States under 8 CFR § 175.57, as an alien whose entry was deemed prejudicial to the public interest. The Attorney General denied him a hearing on the ground that the order was based on information of a confidential nature, the disclosure of which would be prejudicial to the public interest, and he was ordered to be permanently excluded from the United States. The Court of Appeals ruled that the petitioner's detention, without notice of any charges against him and without opportunity to be heard in opposition to them, was not authorized by 8 CFR § 175.57.

***Shaughnessy v. United States ex rel. Mezei,* 345 U.S. 206, 212 (1953)**–An alien resident of the U.S. traveled overseas, staying in Hungary for 19 months. Upon his return to the U.S., the Attorney General, in accordance with 22 U.S.C. § 223, directed that the alien not be allowed back into the country, without a hearing. The directive centered on the fact that "information of a confidential nature, the disclosure of which would be prejudicial to the public interest," and on a judgment that the individual's return would be detrimental to the American public for safety measures. As no other country would allow him entry, he stayed at Ellis Island for almost two years, exactly 21 months. A federal district court in habeas corpus proceedings allowed for his provisional parole into U.S. on bond. The court held that the AG's holding the alien with the benefit of a hearing was not an illegal incarceration, and federal courts did not have the authority to momentarily allow him into the country.

356 U.S. 677, 682 n.6, 684 (1958) *United States v. Proctor & Gamble Co.*–After a criminal investigation against Procter & Gamble for Sherman Act violations, the grand jury chose not to bring an indictment. However, the Department of Justice brought a subsequent civil suit against the company and, despite the absence of an indictment, used the grand jury transcripts in that suit. The Supreme Court affirmed the lower court's denial of Proctor & Gamble's discovery request for the transcript, finding no "compelling necessity" to set aside the "indispensable secrecy of grand jury proceedings."

376 U.S. 254, 276 (1964) *New York Times v. Sullivan*–U.S. Supreme Court ruled that a specific malice standard had to be met, before what the press writes about a public individual can be construed as defamation and/or libel.

381 U.S. 479 (1965) *Griswold v. Connecticut*–A milestone in which the United States Supreme Court stated that there was a Constitutional right to privacy. The case centered on a Connecticut statute that did not allow the use of contraceptives. By a vote of 7-2, the Supreme Court found that the law violated the "right to marital privacy." Although the Bill of Rights does not explicitly mention "privacy," Justice William O. Douglas wrote for the majority that the right was to be found in the "penumbras" and "emanations" of other constitutional protections. Justice Arthur Goldberg wrote a concurring opinion in which he used the Ninth Amendment to defend the Supreme Court's ruling. Justice John Marshall Harlan II wrote a concurring opinion in which he argued that privacy is protected by the due process clause of the Fourteenth Amendment. Justice Byron White also wrote a concurrence based on the due process clause.

389 U.S. 347 (1967) *Katz v. United States*–U.S. Supreme court extended the Fourth Amendment protection from unreasonable search and seizure to protect individuals in a telephone booth from wiretaps by authorities without a warrant.

407 U.S. 297 (1972) *United States v. U.S. District Court*–also known as the **Keith case**, was a groundbreaking United States Supreme Court ruling that supported, in a unanimous 8-0 count, the prerequisites of the Fourth Amendment in cases of domestic surveillance targeting a domestic threat.

426 U.S. 67, 77 (1976). *Mathews v. Diaz*–Title 42 U.S.C. § 1395o(2) states enrollment in the Medicare supplemental medical insurance program residents of the United States who are 65 or older, but in subsection (b) denies eligibility to aliens unless they have been admitted for permanent residence and also have resided in the United States for at least five years. Diaz filed a class action suit in the District Court attacking the constitutionality of § 1395o(2)(b), and thereafter the District Court granted leave to add appellees Clara and Espinosa as plaintiffs and to file an amended complaint, which alleged that Clara had been disqualified for the same reasons as Diaz (lack of citizenship, nonadmission for permanent residence, and inability to meet the five-year residence requirement), but explained that Espinosa, though lawfully admitted for permanent residence, had not attempted to enroll because he could not meet the durational residence requirement. Appellant filed a motion to dismiss on the ground that appellees had not exhausted their administrative remedies. Two days later, Espinosa applied for enrollment, and so advised the court. Though none of the appellees completely exhausted available avenues for administrative review, appellant acknowledged that the applications of Diaz and Clara raised no disputed factual issues, and that the interlocutory denials of their applications should be treated as final for purposes of this litigation, and conceded that Espinosa's application could not be allowed under the statute. The District Court overruled appellant's motion and held that the five-year residence requirement violated due process and that, since it could not be severed from the requirement of admission for permanent residence, the alien eligibility provisions of § 1395o(2)(B) were entirely unenforceable.

433 U.S. 425 (1977) *Nixon v. Administrator of General Services*–After Nixon resigned as President of the United States, he executed a depository agreement with the Administrator of General Services that provided for the storage near his California home of Presidential materials (an estimated 42 million pages of documents and 880 tape recordings) accumulated during his terms in office. Under this agreement, neither he nor the General Services Administration (GSA) could gain access to the materials without the other's consent. He was not to withdraw any original writing for three years, although he could make and withdraw copies. After the initial three-year period, he could withdraw any of the materials except tape recordings. With respect to the tape recordings, he agreed not to withdraw the originals for five years, and to make reproductions only by mutual agreement. Following this five-year period, the Administrator would destroy such tapes as the former president directed, and all of the tapes were to be destroyed at his death or after the expiration of 10 years, whichever occurred first. Shortly after the public announcement of this agreement, a bill was introduced in Congress designed to abrogate it, and, about three months later, this bill was enacted as the Presidential Recordings and Materials Preservation Act (Act), and was signed into law by President Ford. The Act directed the Administrator of GSA to take custody of Nixon's Presidential materials and have them screened by government archivists in order to return to him those personal and private in nature and to preserve those having historical value and to make the materials available for use in judicial proceedings subject to "any rights, defenses or privileges which the Federal Government or any person may invoke." Nixon sued that the act violated (1) the principle of separation of powers; (2) the Presidential privilege; (3) appellant's privacy interests; (4) his First Amendment associational rights; and (5) the Bill of Attainder Clause, and seeking declaratory and injunctive relief against enforcement of the Act. Concluding that, since no public access regulations had yet taken effect, it could consider only the injury to appellant's constitutionally protected interests allegedly caused by the taking of the Presidential materials into custody and their screening by Government archivists, the District Court held that appellant's constitutional challenges were without merit, and dismissed the complaint.

434 U.S. 159, 167 (1977) *United States v. New York Tel. Co.*–On the basis of an FBI affidavit stating that certain individuals were conducting an illegal gambling enterprise at a specified New York City address and that there was probable cause to believe that two telephones with different numbers were being used there to further the illegal activity, the District Court authorized the FBI to install and use pen registers with respect to the two telephones. It directed respondent telephone company to furnish the FBI "all information, facilities and technical assistance" necessary to employ the devices, which (without overhearing oral communications or indicating whether calls are completed) record the numbers dialed. The Supreme Court affirmed the opinion of the Court of Appeals, stating that the District Court abused its discretion in ordering the phone company to help the FBI.

442 U.S. 735, 744 (1979) *Smith v. Maryland*–the Supreme Court held that a pen register is not a search because the "petitioner voluntarily conveyed numerical information to the telephone company. Since the defendant had disclosed the dialed numbers to the telephone company so they could connect his call, he did not have a reasonable expectation of privacy in the numbers he dialed. The court did not distinguish between disclosing the numbers to a human operator or just the automatic equipment used by the telephone company. *Smith v. Maryland* decision left pen registers completely outside constitutional protection. If there was to be any privacy protection, it would have to be enacted by Congress as statutory privacy law.

457 U.S. 202 (1982) *Plyler v. Doe*–was a case in which the Supreme Court of the United States struck down a state statute denying funding for education to children who were illegal immigrants. The Court found that where states limit the rights afforded to people based on their status as aliens, this limitation must be examined under an intermediate scrutiny standard to determine whether it furthers a substantial goal of the State.

484 F.2d 418 (5th Cir. 1973), *United States v. Brown*–A case where the Fifth Circuit upheld the legitimacy of the Attorney General sanctioning the use of warrantless wiretaps for foreign intelligence purposes; here, a conversation made by Brown, an American citizen, was accidentally overheard.

494 F.2d 593 (3rd Cir. 1974), *United States v. Butenko*–The Third Circuit Court stated that electronic surveillance without a warrant was not illegal under the law, as it violated neither Section 605 of the Communications Act, nor did it violate the Fourth Amendment–with the proviso that the primary aim of the surveillance was the acquire foreign intelligence data.

516 F.2d 594 *Zweibon v. Mitchell*–Zweibon v. Mitchell involved a FBI wiretap of the Jewish Defense League. The tap was installed without prior judicial approval and, according to the Attorney General, had been installed to "provide advance knowledge of any activities of JDL causing international embarrassment to this country." The court rejected the argument that the wiretap was proper notwithstanding the government's failure to obtain prior judicial approval, basing its argument principally on the finding that a warrant procedure would not fetter the legitimate intelligence-gathering functions of the Executive Branch. The court also noted the risk that expansive and unchecked executive surveillance powers might chill protected speech.

533 U.S. 678, 121 S. Ct. 2491, 2500 (2001) *Zadvydas v. Davis*–case where the Supreme Court avoided constitutional concerns by interpreting 8 U.S.C. 1231(a)(6) to limit to a "reasonable time" the period that permanent resident aliens may be detained following final orders directing their removal from the United States.

Applying that standard, the Court held that a resident alien generally may not be detained under Section 1231(a)(6) for more than six months after being ordered removed, if the alien demonstrates that there is not a significant likelihood of removal in the reasonably foreseeable future.

542 U.S. 507 (2004) *Hamdi v. Rumsfeld*–Supreme Court decision reversing the dismissal of a *habeas corpus* petition brought on behalf of Yaser Esam Hamdi, a U.S. citizen being detained indefinitely as an "illegal enemy combatant." The Court recognized the power of the government to detain unlawful combatants, but ruled that detainees who are U.S. citizens must have the ability to challenge their detention before an impartial judge.

548 U.S. 557 (2006) *Hamdan v. Rumsfeld*–Supreme Court ruled that the military commissions created by the Bush administration to try detainees at Guantanamo Bay lack "the power to proceed because its structures and procedures violate both the Uniform Code of Military Justice and the four Geneva Conventions signed in 1949." Specifically, the ruling says that Common Article 3 of the Third Geneva Convention was violated.

577 F.2d 200, 209 (3d Cir. 1978) *United States v. Levy*–The Circuit Court of Appeals ruled that the Sixth Amendment right to counsel protects the integrity of the adversarial system of criminal justice by ensuring that all persons accused of crimes have access to effective assistance of counsel for their defense. The right is grounded in "the presumed inability of a defendant to make informed choices about the preparation and conduct of his defense." Although the Sixth Amendment right to counsel is distinguishable from the attorney-client privilege, the court ruled that the two concepts overlapped in a number of ways. In essence, the right to counsel would be meaningless without the protection of free and open communication between client and counsel.

743 F.2d 59 (2nd Cir., 1984) *United States US v. Duggan*–A Case where the court found that FISA was legislated to establish a safe means by which the President could engage in legal, electronic surveillance of foreign operatives while maintaining America's preeminent commitment to the Fourth Amendment. FISA was found to meet the constitutional prerequisites of the Fourth Amendment concerning a reasonable balance between what the government needs and each American's protected civil liberties.

955 F.Supp. 588 (Va. 1997) *United States v. Nicholson*–Jack Lavelton Nicholson was a federal inmate in Virginia, who had filed a Writ of Habeas Corpus, which was turned down by the Eastern District Court of Virginia. The United States Court of Appeals for the Fourth Circuit awarded Nicholson a Certificate of Appealability, agreeing with the defendant in stating that his attorney at the original hearing had a conflict of interest and thus, Nicholson's Sixth Amendment rights were violated.

983 F.2d 449 (2d Cir. 1993) *United States v. Pangburn*–A search warrant's violation of notice requirement of Rule 41 did not require suppression.

1870 Force Act–Legislation where the government banned the use of terror, force, or bribery to prevent someone from voting because of their race. Helped fight the Ku Klux Klan in the South after the Civil War.

***Civil Rights Act of 1871, also known as the 1871 Ku Klux Klan Act*–**stated that "Every person who under color of any statute, ordinance, regulation, custom, or usage, of any State or Territory or the District of Columbia, subjects, or causes to be subjected, any citizen of the United States or other person within the jurisdiction thereof to the deprivation of any rights, privileges, or immunities secured by the Constitution and laws, shall be liable to the party injured in an action at law, Suit in equity, or other proper proceeding for redress, except that in any action brought against a judicial officer for an act or omission taken in such officer's judicial capacity, injunctive relief shall not be granted unless a declaratory decree was violated or declaratory relief was unavailable."

Alien Registration Act of 1940–commonly referred to as the **Smith Act**. Law stated that it is a criminal offense to knowingly or willfully advocate, abet, advise, or teach the duty, necessity, desirability or propriety of overthrowing the Government of the United States or of any State by force or violence. Moreover, it is illegal for anyone to organize any association that teaches, advises, or encourages such an overthrow, or for anyone to become a member of or to affiliate with any such association.

American Civil Liberties Union v. Ashcroft (2004)–an unknown party, with the help of the Civil Liberties Union, sued the U.S. federal government. The unknown party, an Internet service provider, was subject to National Security Letters (NSLs) from the Federal Bureau of Investigation requiring the release of private information and under a gag order forbidding any public discussion of the issues. In September 2004, Judge Victor Marrero of the United States District Court for the Southern District of New York struck down the NSL provisions of the Patriot Act. This prompted Congress to amend the law to allow limited judicial review of NSLs, and prompted the government to appeal the case to the United States Court of Appeals for the Second Circuit. On the recommendation of the Second Circuit, the district court considered the amended law in 2007, in *Doe v. Gonzales*. On September 6, 2007, Judge Marrero struck down the NSL provision of the revised Act, ruling that even with limited judicial review granted in the amended law, it was still a violation of separation of powers under the United States Constitution and the First Amendment. This is not yet enforced, pending a possible government appeal.

Anti-Terrorism Act of 2001–The Patriot Act was a compromise version of the Anti-Terrorism Act of 2001 (ATA), a far-reaching legislative package intended to strengthen the nation's defense against terrorism. The ATA contained several provisions vastly expanding the authority of law enforcement and intelligence agencies to monitor private communications and access personal information. The final legislation included a few beneficial additions from the Administration's initial proposal. For instance, the "sunset" provisions (which provided that several sections of the act automatically expire after a certain period, unless they are explicitly renewed by

Congress) on some of the electronic surveillance provisions, and an amendment providing judicial oversight of law enforcement's use of the FBI's Carnivore system.

Antiterrorism and Effective Death Penalty Act of 1996–(also known as *AEDPA*) An Act of Congress signed into law on April 24, 1996 to "deter terrorism, provide justice for victims, provide for an effective death penalty, and for other purposes." It was passed with broad bipartisan support by Congress (91–8–1 in the United States Senate, 293-133-7 in the House of Representatives) following the Oklahoma City bombing and signed into law by President Bill Clinton.

Bank Secrecy Act of 1970–commonly referred to as "BSA," and the "Currency, and Foreign Transactions Reporting Act." It requires financial institutions to assist U.S. government agencies to detect and prevent money laundering. Specifically, the act requires financial institutions to keep records of cash purchases of negotiable instruments, and file reports of cash purchases of these negotiable instruments of $3,000 or more (daily aggregate amount), and to report suspicious activity that might signify money laundering, tax evasion, or other criminal activities.

Boumediene v. Bush (2008)–a writ of habeas corpus submission made in a civilian court of the United States on behalf of Lakhdar Boumediene, a naturalized citizen of Bosnia and Herzegovina, held by the U.S. at the Guantanamo Bay detention camps in Cuba. The case was consolidated with habeas petition *Al Odah v. United States*. The case challenged the legality of Boumediene's detention at the Guantanamo Bay military base as well as the constitutionality of the Military Commissions Act (MCA) of 2006. Oral arguments on the combined case were heard by the Supreme Court on December 5, 2007. On June 12, 2008, Justice Kennedy wrote the opinion for the 5-4 majority holding that the prisoners had a right to the habeas corpus under the United States Constitution and that the MCA was an unconstitutional suspension of that right.

Center for National Security Studies v. Department of Justice–On June 7, 2003, the U.S. Court of Appeals for the District of Columbia Circuit overturned a lower court order requiring the federal government to disclose the names of all those detained in connection with its post-September 11 anti-terrorism investigation. The decision was a victory for the Washington Legal Foundation which had filed two briefs with the court, arguing that such disclosure could well interfere with the investigation by providing valuable information to al-Qaeda and by making detainees less likely to cooperate with the government.

Civilian Exclusion Order No. 346–order stating that, after 12 o'clock May 8, 1942, all persons of Japanese ancestry, both alien and non-alien, were to be excluded from a described portion of Military Area No. 1, which included the County of Alameda, California.

Commerce, Justice, State Appropriations Bill of 2005–The Commerce, Justice, State appropriations bill reported to the House on 1 July 2004 (HR 4754; H.Rept. 108–576) provides new budget authority equal to the 302(b) suballocation for the Appropriations Subcommittee on Commerce, Justice, State, and Related Agencies.

H.R. 4754 provided $39.815 billion in new budget authority and $40.428 billion in outlays for 2005–an increase of $878 million in BA and $1.679 billion in outlays from fiscal year 2004. The increase in outlays includes the effect of budget authority approved in the previous years in addition to the increase for 2005. Budget authority in the bill is $240 million above the President's budget request.

The Crime Victim Compensation Fund–Fund that reimburses victims of crime occurring within a state (including victims of federal crimes) for crime-related expenses. Crimes covered include violent crimes such as homicide, rape, drunk driving, domestic violence, and child sexual abuse and neglect. Expenses covered are medical costs, mental health counseling, funeral and burial costs, and lost wages or loss of support. Crime victim assistance programs provide a range of services, including crisis intervention, counseling, emergency shelter, criminal justice advocacy, and emergency transportation. Although compensation and assistance are provided most often to individuals, in certain instances, entire communities may be eligible to receive assistance for a multiple victimization.

Departments of Commerce, Justice, and State, the Judiciary, and Related Agencies Appropriations Act, 2002–On November 28, 2001, the appropriations made for the United States up to September 30, 2002.

Department of Defense Appropriations Act, 2006–Authorization by the government regarding the amount of money the Department of Defense could spent during 2006.

Department of Defense, Military Commission Order No. 1, March 21, 2002–A military order established by President Bush that allowed a military tribunal to hear cases against suspected terrorists. The Order was overturned by the Supreme Court.

Department of Homeland Security 8 CFR Part 264–the suspension of the 30-Day and Annual Interview Requirements from the Special Registration Process for Certain Nonimmigrants.

Detainee Treatment Act of 2005–An Act of the United States Congress that prohibits inhumane treatment of prisoners, including prisoners at Guantanamo Bay and requires military interrogations to be performed according to the U.S. Army Field Manual for Human Intelligence Collector Operations. In addition, it strips federal courts of jurisdiction to consider habeas corpus petitions filed by prisoners in Guantanamo, or other claims asserted by Guantanamo detainees against the U.S. government, as well as limiting appellate review of decisions of the Combatant Status Review Tribunals and Military Commissions.

DHS REAL ID Final Rule (2008-01-11)–The Department of Homeland Security issued a final rule to establish minimum standards for state-issued driver's licenses and identification cards in accordance with the REAL ID Act of 2005. These regulations set standards for states to meet the requirements of the REAL ID Act, including:
   • information and security features that must be incorporated into each card;
   • proof of identity and U.S. citizenship or legal status of an applicant;

• verification of the source documents provided by an applicant; and

• security standards for the offices that issue licenses and identification cards. This final rule also provides a process for States to seek an additional extension of the compliance deadline to May 11, 2011, by demonstrating material compliance with the core requirements of the Act and this rule.

The Controlled Substances Act–Was enacted into law by the Congress of the United States as Title II of the Comprehensive Drug Abuse Prevention and Control Act of 1970. The CSA is the federal U.S. drug policy under which the manufacture, importation, possession, and distribution of certain drugs is regulated.

The Department of Justice Appropriations Act, 2001–Also known as the 21st Century Department of Justice Appropriations Authorization Act. The appropriations set by the U.S. Congress for the D.O.J. for fiscal year 2002.

18 USC 3121 et seq; ECPA Pub. L. 99-508; 100 Stat. 1848 ***The Electronic Communications Privacy Act of 1986***–enacted by the United States Congress to extend government restrictions on wire taps from telephone calls to include transmissions of electronic data by computer. Specifically, ECPA was an amendment to Title III of the Omnibus Crime Control and Safe Streets Act of 1968 (the Wire Tap Statute), which was primarily designed to prevent unauthorized government access to private electronic communications. Later, the ECPA was amended, and weakened to some extent, by some provisions of the Patriot Act.

(H.R. 5825) ***Electronic Surveillance Modernization Act***–A bill designed to address a number of different areas concerning the Terrorist Surveillance Program, a top secret venture that had been initiated by the National Security Agency to conduct surveillance on American citizens. The bill was also designed to augment elasticity in electronic surveillance to obtain foreign intelligence data, while mandating greater reporting and congressional oversight. The bill was introduced on 07–18–2006, and passed the House on 09–28–2006.

Emergency Supplemental Appropriations Act for Defense–Money that was voted for by Congress to increase the amount given for defense against terrorism.

Executive Order 9066–A presidential executive order issued during World War II by U.S. President Franklin D. Roosevelt on February 19, 1942, using his authority as Commander-in-Chief to exercise war powers to send ethnic groups to internment camps. This order authorized the Secretary of War and U.S. armed forces commanders to declare areas of the United States as military areas "from which any or all persons may be excluded," although it did not name any nationality or ethnic group. It was eventually applied to one-third of the land area of the U.S. (mostly in the West) and was used against those with "Foreign Enemy Ancestry"–Japanese, Italians, and Germans. The order led to the Japanese American internment in which some 120,000 ethnic Japanese people were held in internment camps for the duration of the war.

Executive Order 9095–Created the Office of the Alien Property Custodian.

Executive Order 12667–Established a procedure for former United States Presidents to limit access to certain records which would otherwise have been released by the National Archives and Records Administration under the Presidential Records Act of 1978. It was issued by President Ronald Reagan on 18 January 1989.

Executive Order 13233–On November 1, 2001, President Bush released this Executive Order that superceded Executive Order 12667. The new Order allowed former Presidents to have greater control over which records are released by the National Archives and Records Administration.

Executive Order 13489–On January 21, 2009, Barack Obama, in the first act as President of the United States overturned his predecessor's Executive Order 13233.

Federal Rules of Criminal Procedure Rule 6–Rules regarding the Grand Jury

Federal Rules of Criminal Procedure 17–Subpoena

Federal Rules of Criminal Procedure 41–Search and seizure

Fair Credit Reporting Act–An American federal law (codified at 15 U.S.C. § 1681 et seq.) that regulates the collection, dissemination, and use of consumer credit information. Along with the Fair Debt Collection Practices Act (FDCPA), it forms the base of consumer credit rights in the United States. It was originally passed in 1970, and is enforced by the US Federal Trade Commission. It established consumer reporting agencies, which are entities that collect and disseminate information about consumers to be used for credit evaluation and other purposes. In addition, it established information furnishers which, as defined by the FCRA, are companies that provide information to consumer reporting agencies. Typically, these are creditors, with which a consumer has some sort of credit agreement (credit card companies, auto finance companies and mortgage banking institutions, to name a few). However, other examples of information furnishers are collection agencies (third-party collectors), state or municipal courts reporting a judgment of some kind, past and present employers and bonders.

Family Educational Rights and Privacy Act–(**FERPA** or the **Buckley Amendment**) A United States federal law codified at 20 U.S.C. § 1232g, with implementing regulations in title 34, part 99 of the Code of Federal Regulations. The regulations provide that educational agencies and institutions that receive funding under a program administered by the U. S. Department of Education must provide students with access to their education records, an opportunity to seek to have the records amended, and some control over the disclosure of information from the records. With several exceptions, schools must have a student's consent prior to the disclosure of education records. Examples of situations affected by FERPA include school employees divulging information to someone other than the child's parents about a child's grades or behavior, and school work posted on a bulletin board with a grade. This privacy policy also governs how state agencies transmit testing data to federal agencies. The law allows students who apply to an educational institution such as graduate school permission to view recommendations submitted by others as part of the application. However, on standard application forms, students are given the option to waive this right.FERPA specifically excludes employees of an educational institution if they are not students. The act is also referred to as the *Buckley Amendment,* named for one of its proponents, Senator James L. Buckley of New York.

Foreign Agents Registration Act of 1938–U.S. law passed in 1938 requiring information from foreign sources to be properly identified to the American public. The act was passed in response to German propaganda in the lead-up to World War II. The Foreign Agent Registration Unit within the Criminal Division of the Department of Justice is charged with handling the execution of the law

Foreign Intelligence Surveillance Improvement and Enhancement Act of 2006–A bill to ensure that all electronic surveillance of United States persons for foreign intelligence purposes is conducted pursuant to individualized court-issued orders, to streamline the procedures of the Foreign Intelligence Surveillance Act of 1978, and for other purposes.

The Foreign Relations Authorization Act–To authorize appropriations for the Department of State, to authorize appropriations under the Arms Export Control Act and the Foreign Assistance Act of 1961 for security assistance for a fiscal year, and for other purposes.

General Education Provisions Act–This section requires each applicant for federal funds (other than an individual person) to include in its application a description of the steps the applicant proposes to take to ensure equitable access to, and participation in, its federally assisted program for students, teachers, and other program beneficiaries with special needs. This provision allows applicants discretion in developing the required description. The statute highlights six types of barriers that can impede equitable access or participation: gender, race, national origin, color, disability, or age.

Geneva Conventions–The Geneva Conventions consist of four treaties formulated in Geneva, Switzerland, that set the standards for international law for humanitarian concerns. They chiefly concern the treatment of noncombatants and prisoners of war. They do not affect the use of weapons in war, which are covered by the Hague Conventions of 1899 and 1907 and the Geneva Protocol on the use of gas and biological weapons of 1925. The Conventions were the results of efforts by Henry Dunant, who was motivated by the horrors of war he witnessed at the Battle of Solferino in 1859. In 1977 and 2005, three separate amendments were made part of the Geneva Conventions.

H. AMDT 489–Amendment that required the Director of the FBI to personally approve any library or bookstore request for records by the FBI under section 215 of the Patriot Act. An amendment numbered 2 printed in part B of House Report 109–178 to state that the Director of the FBI must personally approve any library or bookstore request for records by the FBI under section 215.

H. AMDT 490–Amendment requires the Agency for Health Care Policy and Research internet web site to provide linkages to consumer satisfaction agencies that perform evaluations on health care quality. An amendment no. 12 printed in the Congressional Record to establish linkages on the World Wide Web site maintained by the Director to consumer satisfaction agencies or other entities that perform evaluations on health care quality, HMOs, and includes a link to the National Committee for Quality Assurance.

H. AMDT 491–An amendment consisting of the new text reported by the Committee on Education and Labor currently printed in the bill and made in order as original text for the purpose of further amendment pursuant to the provisions of H. Res. 531.An amendment to H.R. 2669: College Cost Reduction and Access Act.

H. AMDT 492–Amendment in the nature of a substitute sought to replace the language of the bill with the text of the "Pell Grant Enhancement Act." An amendment to H.R. 2669 [110th]: College Cost Reduction and Access Act. An amendment in the nature of a substitute printed in part B of House Report 110-224 to reduce subsidies in the loan programs an d invests the majority of the savings in the Pell Grant program by providing increases of $350 in 2008 and $100 each year thereafter. It also provides a plan for improved consumer information and public accountability with respect to college costs.

H. AMDT 493–Amendment sought to remove the emergency designation requirement for FBI funding amending H.R. 4775 [107th].

H. AMDT 495–Amendment sought to change the calculation of toll credits by basing them on the proportion of non-federal investment in toll projects. An amendment to H.R. 3550 [108th]: Safe, Accountable, Flexible, and Efficient Transportation Equity Act of 2004. An amendment numbered four printed in part B of House Report 108–456 to allow states to receive toll credits for any local, state or private funds contributed to a toll project that exceeds the minimum non-federal 20 percent threshold required for federal match.

H. AMDT 497–Amendment sought to strike the authorization of funds for the creation of 100,000 new vouchers over five years. An amendment to H.R. 1851 [110th]: Section 8 Voucher Reform Act of 2007. An amendment numbered 5 printed in House Report 110–227 to strike the authorization of appropriations for the creation of 20,000 new vouchers each year for years FY 2008 through FY 2012.

H. AMDT 498–Amendment adds to the list of predicates used for obtaining electronic surveillance, certain crimes which are related to terrorism. The amendment changed H.R. 3199 [109th]: USA PATRIOT Improvement and Reauthorization Act of 2005.

Homeland Security Presidential Directive-2–On October 29, 2001, President Bush released the statement: Combating Terrorism Through Immigration Policies. He stated that America's policy toward immigrants had changed due to 9/11. Changes included: (1) Foreign Terrorist Tracking Task Force, (2) Enhanced INS and Customs Enforcement Capability, (3) Abuse of International Student Status, (4) North American Complementary Immigration Policies, (5) Use of Advanced Technologies for Data Sharing and Enforcement Efforts, and (6) Budgetary Support.

H.R. 107-236–An amended version of H.R. 2975, which was the Patriot Act in the House of Representatives.

H.R. 107-256–Section in the Patriot Act that permitted the court to issue a generic order that can be presented to the new carrier, landlord or custodian directing their assistance to assure that the surveillance may be undertaken as soon as technically feasible.

HR 1268, *Making Emergency Supplemental Appropriations*–Emergency supplemental appropriations for the fiscal year ending September 30, 2005. It established and rapidly implemented regulations for State driver's license and identification document security standards, to prevent terrorists from abusing the asylum laws of the United States, to unify terrorism-related grounds for inadmissibility and removal, to ensure expeditious construction of the San Diego border fence, and for other purposes.

H.R. 2121–To amend the Internal Revenue Code of 1986 to allow individuals to defer recognition of reinvested capital gains distributions from regulated investment companies. This bill was proposed in a previous session of Congress. Sessions of Congress last two years, and at the end of each session all proposed bills and resolutions that haven't passed are cleared from the books. Members often reintroduce bills that did not come up for debate under a new number in the next session.

H.R. 2862 THOMAS–Known as the Science, State, Justice & Commerce Appropriations Act for FY 2006, that prohibited federal funds from being used to acquire library circulation records, library patron lists, or bookstore sales records without judicial approval. The House adopted the amendment by a vote of 238 to 187. Despite its support in both the House and Senate, this language was subsequently removed from the final Conference Report on H.R. 2862.

H.R. 2975–*USA Patriot Act*

H.R. 3171–the *Benjamin Franklin True Patriot Act.* To provide for an appropriate review of recently enacted legislation relating to terrorism to assure that powers granted in it do not inappropriately undermine civil liberties. Never became law.

H.R. 3801–*Education Sciences Reform Act of 2002.* would restructure and reauthorize programs authorized under the National Education Statistics Act of 1994, and the Educational Research, Development, Dissemination, and Improvement Act of 1994. These programs currently were through 2002. H.R. 3801 would reorganize and reauthorize these programs through 2008.

H.R. 4754–An amendment to HR 4754 sponsored by Bernard Sanders (Vermont) required that no funds would be provided to that portion of the Patriot Act which allows federal agencies to attain lists from booksellers, libraries, etc. without a warrant. If the book seller or librarian informs you that an agency is asking about you, he/she may be fined and/or jailed. The amendment was defeated in the House 210–210.

Humanitarian Law Project v. John Ashcroft–Was a suit brought in the United

States District Court for the Central District of California by various individuals and organizations challenging the constitutionality of the Antiterrorism and Effective Death Penalty Act of 1996. Plaintiffs were two United States citizens and six organizations. One citizen (Nagalingam Jeyalingam) and five of the organizations wanted to provide cash and various other types of support to the Liberation Tigers of Tamil Eelam ("LTTE" or "Tamil Tigers"), a terrorist organization that caused great lost of life in Sri-Lanka. The other citizen plaintiff (Ralph Fertig) and the remaining plaintiff organization (the Humanitarian Law Project) wanted to give money cash and other support to the Kurdistan Workers' Party ("PKK"), a foreign entity that carries out deadly terrorist acts in Turkey and elsewhere. These plaintiffs sued the Secretary of State and the United States Department of State, as well as the Attorney General and the United States Department of Justice, claiming that the Antiterrorism Act violates the First and Fifth Amendments. On appeal, the Appeals Court affirmed the district court's decision. In particular, the Court held that the Antiterrorism Act is constitutional, with the possible exception of the terms "personnel" and "training." With respect to these terms, the Court determined that the district court had not abused its discretion in issuing a limited preliminary injunction against enforcement. This case then resumed in the district court. That court again largely denied plaintiffs' constitutional claims. However, the district court issued a limited final injunction against the "personnel" and "training" provisions of the Antiterrorism Act as to the plaintiffs and the two terrorist organizations involved.

***Illegal Immigration Reform and Immigrant Responsibility Act of 1996**–Pub.L. 104–208, Div. C, 110 Stat. 3009–546. Act that made it much easier for individuals to be deported. Prior to the act, instant deportation occurred only for crimes that could potentially lead to jail time (5 years or more). The act stated that even with minor offenses, a foreigner could be deported. Moreover, the Act also applied to residents who had an American for a spouse and/or had American-born children.

***Immigration and Nationality Act of 1952**–Also known as the **McCarran-Walter Act**, it restricted immigration into the U.S. and is codified under Title 8 of the United States Code. The Act governs primarily immigration and citizenship in the United States. Before the INA, a variety of statutes governed immigration law but were not organized within one body of text. As a result of the September 11, 2001 attacks, the INA has undergone a major restructuring beginning in March 2003 and its provisions regarding the admissibility and removability of terrorist suspects has received much media and scholarly attention.

***Immigration and Naturalization Service Data Management Improvement Act of 2000**–System that would document the entry and departure of "every alien" arriving and leaving the United States. Thus, people entering the leaving the United States to and from Canada and Mexico would need to be stopped by the INS in each direction to have information collected from them. The California Chamber of Commerce believed that Section 110 could cause harm to California's trade and tourism with Canada and Mexico.

***Intelligence Authorization Act of 2003**–To authorize appropriations for fiscal year

2003 for intelligence and intelligence-related activities of the United States Government, the Community Management Account, and the Central Intelligence Agency Retirement and Disability System, and for other purposes.

Joint Congressional Resolution 107-40–Authorization for use of Military Force Against Iraq Resolution of 2002.

Joint Pub 1-02, *Department of Defense Dictionary of Military and Associated Terms 12 April 2001, as amended through 9 June 2004*–sets forth standard US military and associated terminology to encompass the joint activity of the Armed Forces of the United States in both US joint and allied joint operations, as well as to encompass the Department of Defense (DOD) as a whole. These military and associated terms, together with their definitions, constitute approved DOD terminology for general use by all components of the Department of Defense.

KSA 22-2509 L. 1970, ch. 129, § 22-2509–Kansas law that states In the execution of a search warrant the person executing the same may reasonably detain and search any person in the place at the time:
(a) To protect himself from attack, or
(b) To prevent the disposal or concealment of any things particularly described in the warrant.

Pub. L. No. 109-366 *Military Commissions Act of 2006*–Also known as HR-6166, was an Act of Congress signed by President George W. Bush on October 17, 2006. Drafted in the wake of the Supreme Court's decision on *Hamdan v. Rumsfeld,* the Act's stated purpose was "To authorize trial by military commission for violations of the law of war, and for other purposes." Section 7 of the MCA was found to be unconstitutional by the Supreme Court on June 12, 2008.

Military Commission Order No. 1–Commission's procedures, set forth in Commission Order No. 1, provide, among other things, that an accused and his civilian counsel may be excluded from, and precluded from ever learning what evidence was presented during, any part of the proceeding the official who appointed the commission or the presiding officer decides to "close." Grounds for closure include the protection of classified information, the physical safety of participants and witnesses, the protection of intelligence and law enforcement sources, methods, or activities, and "other national security interests." Appointed military defense counsel must be privy to these closed sessions, but may, at the presiding officer's discretion, be forbidden to reveal to the client what took place therein. Held as unconstitutional in *Hamdan v. Rumsfeld.*

Model Code of Professional Responsibility DR 4-101 (1986)–Rules governing how a lawyer should treat any information obtained from his/her client. In essence, rule states that:
A. "Confidence" refers to information protected by the attorney-client privilege under applicable law, and "secret" refers to other information gained in the professional relationship that the client has requested be held inviolate or the disclosure of which would be embarrassing or would be likely to be detrimen-

tal to the client.

B. Except when permitted under DR 4-101 [1200.19] (C), a lawyer shall not knowingly:

1. Reveal a confidence or secret of a client.
2. Use a confidence or secret of a client to the disadvantage of the client.
3. Use a confidence or secret of a client for the advantage of the lawyer or of a third person, unless the client consents after full disclosure.

C. A lawyer may reveal:

1. Confidences or secrets with the consent of the client or clients affected, but only after a full disclosure to them.
2. Confidences or secrets when permitted under Disciplinary Rules or required by law or court order.
3. The intention of a client to commit a crime and the information necessary to prevent the crime.
4. Confidences or secrets necessary to establish or collect the lawyer's fee or to defend the lawyer or his or her employees or associates against an accusation of wrongful conduct.
5. Confidences or secrets to the extent implicit in withdrawing a written or oral opinion or representation previously given by the lawyer and believed by the lawyer still to be relied upon by a third person where the lawyer has discovered that the opinion or representation was based on materially inaccurate information or is being used to further a crime or fraud.

D. A lawyer shall exercise reasonable care to prevent his or her employees, associates, and others whose services are utilized by the lawyer from disclosing or using confidences or secrets of a client, except that a lawyer may reveal the information allowed by DR 4-101 [1200.19] (C) through an employee.[997]

Model Rules of Professional Conduct R. 1.6 (1992)–Rules governing how a lawyer should treat any information obtained from his/her client. In essence, rule states that:

(a) Except when required under Rule 1.6(b) or permitted under Rule 1.6(c), a lawyer shall not, during or after termination of the professional relationship with the client, use or reveal a confidence or secret of the client known to the lawyer unless the client consents after disclosure.

(b) A lawyer shall reveal information about a client to the extent it appears necessary to prevent the client from committing an act that would result in death or serious bodily harm.

(c) A lawyer may use or reveal:

(1) Confidences or secrets when permitted under these Rules or required by law or court order,

(2) The intention of a client to commit a crime in circumstances other than those enumerated in Rule 1.6(b); or

(3) Confidences or secrets necessary to establish or collect the lawyer's fee or to

---

997. American Bar Association.

defend the lawyer or the lawyer's employees or associates against an accusation of wrongful conduct.

(d) The relationship of trained intervenor and a lawyer, judge, or a law student who seeks or receives assistance through the Lawyers' Assistance Program, Inc., shall be the same as that of lawyer and client for purposes of the application of Rule 8.1, Rule 8.3 and Rule 1.6.

(e) Any information received by a lawyer in a formal proceeding before a trained intervenor, or panel of intervenors, of the Lawyers' Assistance Program, Inc., or in an intermediary program approved by a circuit court in which nondisciplinary complaints against judges or lawyers can be referred shall be deemed to have been received from a client for purposes of the application of Rules 1.6, 8.1 and 8.3.

Adopted February 8, 1990; effective August 1, 1990; amended February 2, 1994, effective immediately; amended May 24, 2006.[998]

Money Laundering Control Act of 1986–(Public Law 99-570) A United States Act of Congress that made money laundering a Federal crime. It was passed in 1984. It consists of two sections, 18 U.S.C. § 1956 and 18 U.S.C. § 1957. It enhanced the Bank Secrecy Act by making it a crime to structure transactions in such a way as to avoid the reporting requirements of that Act. It enhanced the Bank Secrecy Act by making it a crime to structure transactions in such a way as to avoid the reporting requirements of that Act.

Muslim Community Association of Ann Arbor v. Ashcroft–A legal challenge to Section 215 of the Patriot Act, which amends the business records provision of the Foreign Intelligence Surveillance Act to permit FBI agents to obtain all types of records, including library records, without a showing of probable cause.

The National Education Statistics Act of 1994–The primary federal entity for collecting, analyzing, and reporting data related to education in the United States and other nations. It fulfills a congressional mandate to collect, collate, analyze, and report full and complete statistics on the condition of education in the United States; conduct and publish reports and specialized analyses of the meaning and significance of such statistics; assist state and local education agencies in improving their statistical systems; and review and report on education activities in foreign countries.

National Security Surveillance Act of 2006–A bill in Congress that would have created guidelines for the assessment of electronic surveillance programs. Was introducted by Senator Arlen Specter (R-PA).

Presidential Executive Order 13224–On September 23, 2001, President Bush ordered the Blocking of property and the prohibition of transactions with persons who commit, threaten to commit, or support terrorism.

The Presidential Records Act of 1978–governs the official records of Presidents and Vice Presidents created or received after January 20, 1981 and mandates the preservation of all presidential records. The PRA changed the legal ownership of the

---

998. Ibid.

official records of the President from private to public, and established a new statutory structure under which Presidents must manage their records.

Presidential Records Act Amendments of 2007–On March 1, 2007, Rep. Henry A. Waxman along with Reps. Platts, Clay, and Burton introduced H.R. 1255, the Presidential Records Act Amendments of 2007, to nullify a 2001 presidential executive order and restore public access to presidential records. The Subcommittee on Information Policy, Census, and National Archives reported this bill favorably to the full committee on March 6.

The Privacy Act of 1974–Public Law No. 93-579, 88 Stat. 1897 (Dec. 31, 1974), codified in part at 5 U.S.C. § 552a,[999] was passed by the United States Congress following revelations of the abuse of privacy during the administration of President Richard Nixon. The Privacy Act states in part:

> No agency shall disclose any record which is contained in a system of records by any means of communication to any person, or to another agency, except pursuant to a written request by, or with the prior written consent of, the individual to whom the record pertains. . . .

Protecting the Rights of Individuals Act (2003)–A bill to amend title 18, United States Code, and the Foreign Intelligence Surveillance Act of 1978 to strengthen protections of civil liberties in the exercise of the foreign intelligence surveillance authorities under Federal law, and for other purposes. Its primary goal was to limit the number of searches allowed under the Patriot Act only to individuals who were foreign agents and/or engaged in terrorism. Americans who had no history of terrorist acts would not have any of their background checked by the FBI.

The Protect America Act of 2007–The bill amended FISA to replace the prerequisite of a warrant to carry out surveillance with a network of NSA in-house controls. The bill mandated that announcement to the FISA Court of surveillance absent a warrant occur within 72 hours of any authorization. The bill also required that "a sealed copy of the certification" be sent which would "remain sealed unless the certification is needed to determine the legality of the acquisition." The bill allowed the monitoring of all electronic communications of people in the United States without a court's order or oversight, so long as it is not targeted at one particular person "reasonably believed to be" inside the country. The bill clarified confusion in current law by allowing the National Security Agency to collect communications between people in foreign countries without a warrant, regardless of whether or not the communications travel through telecommunication equipment located in the United States.

Public Law 90-351–Repealed law that related to establishment of Office of Justice Assistance, Research, and Statistics.

Public Law 91-508 ***The Fair Credit Reporting Act***–An American federal law that regulates the collection, dissemination, and use of consumer credit information.

---

999. See 5 U.S.C. § 552a.

Along with the Fair Debt Collection Practices Act (FDCPA), it forms the base of consumer credit rights in the United States. It was originally passed in 1970, and is enforced by the US Federal Trade Commission.

Public Law 95-511 *Foreign Intelligence Surveillance Act of 1978*–An Act of Congress which prescribes procedures for the physical and electronic surveillance and collection of "foreign intelligence information" between "foreign powers" and "agents of foreign powers" (which may include American citizens and permanent residents suspected of being engaged in espionage and violating U.S. law on territory under United States control).

Public Law 99-508 Oct. 21, 1986, 100 Stat. 1848, 18 U.S.C. § 2510, *Electronic Communications Privacy Act of 1986*–An act created by Congress to expand governmental constraints on wire taps on telephones to include transmissions of digital information using a computer. Specifically, ECPA altered Title III of the Omnibus Crime Control and Safe Streets Act of 1968 (the Wire Tap Statute) that was chiefly calculated to avert illegal governmental access to confidential electronic communications. The USA Patriot Act changed the ECPA. For instance, section 2709 which permitted law enforcement agencies (primarily the FBI) to issue National Security Letters to Internet service providers (ISPs) commanding them to release confidential data regarding their patrons, was ruled unconstitutional under the First (and possibly Fourth) Amendment in ACLU v. Ashcroft (2004). The line of reasoning was thought to be applicable toward other uses of NSLs.

Public Law 103-382 *Improving America's Schools Act (IASA) of 1994*–A major part of the Clinton administration's efforts to reform education. It was signed in the gymnasium of Framingham High School (MA). It reauthorized the Elementary and Secondary Education Act of 1965.

It included provisions or reforms for:
- The Title 1 program, providing extra help to disadvantaged students and holding schools accountable for their results at the same level as other students
- charter schools
- Safe and Drug-free schools
- Eisenhower Professional Development
- Major increases in bilingual and immigrant education funding
- Impact aid
- Education technology and other programs.

Public Law 104-19. 109 Stat. 249 (1995)–After the attack on the Alfred P. Murrah Federal Building in 1995, Congress established a **Counterterrorism Fund** to compensate the DOJ for the price of recreating the operating ability that was lost due to the bombing. It took a comparable course in order to reimburse the Justice Department for the costs of (1) reestablishing the operating capacity of facilities damaged or destroyed by terrorists; (2) preventing, investigating and prosecuting terrorism by various means including the payment of rewards (without limitation); and (3) conducting terrorism threat assessments of federal facilities. The Fund is also available to reimburse federal agencies for costs associated with overseas detention of individuals accused of terrorism in violation of United States law.

Public Law 104-132, 110 Stat. 1314 (1996) *Antiterrorism and Effective Death Penalty Act of 1996*–(also known as *AEDPA*) An Act of Congress that became federal law on 04-24-1996, due to the Oklahoma City bombing. Its major emphasis was to "deter terrorism, provide justice for victims, provide for an effective death penalty, and for other purposes." Both sides of the aisle supported the law: in the Senate, the vote was 91-8-1, whereas in the House the vote was 293–133–7.

The AEDPA impacted greatly upon habeas corpus within the US. One proviso of the AEDPA restrained the authority of federal judges to grant relief; that is, unless the state court's arbitration of the claim resulted in a ruling that was:

1. contrary to, or involved an unreasonable application of clearly established federal law as determined by the Supreme Court of the United States; or
2. based on an unreasonable determination of the facts in light of the evidence presented in the state court proceeding.

Opponents stated that this restriction efficiently shuts out the authority of federal courts to remedy unfair guilty verdicts; however, federal judges have granted relief to inmates in habeas cases regardless of the restrictions.

Public Law 104-208, Div. C, 110 Stat. 3009-546 *Illegal Immigration Reform and Immigrant Responsibility Act of 1996*–Often referred to as "Ira-Ira", and sometimes abbreviated to IIRIRA, it vastly changed the immigration laws of the United States. It was passed on September 30, 1996. Previously, immediate deportation was triggered only for offences that could lead to five years or more in jail. Under the Act, minor offences such as shoplifting, may make an individual eligible for deportation. The Act also applies to residents who have married American citizens and have American-born children. When IIRIRA was passed in 1996, it was applied retroactively to all those convicted of deportable offenses. This included US residents who committed minor offences decades ago. However, in 2001, the Supreme Court decided that Congress did not intend IIRIRA to be applied retroactively to those who pleaded guilty to a crime prior to the enactment of IIRIRA, if that person would not have been deportable at the time that he pleaded guilty.

Public Law 105-277–*the Omnibus Consolidated and Emergency Supplemental Appropriations Act.* Provides a total of $486.7 billion in funding for FY 1999. It combined eight of the thirteen regular appropriations bills, including: Agriculture; Commerce, Justice and State; District of Columbia; Foreign Operations; Interior; Labor, Health and Human Services; Transportation; and Treasury and General Government. The Omnibus bill also contains $20.8 billion in funding for supplemental emergency requests, and a $9.2 billion tax extender package.

Public Law 106-113–*Medicare, Medicaid, and SCHIP Balanced Budget Refinement Act of 1999* provided a very modest increase for oxygen supplies - amounting to .3% increase in fiscal year (FY) 2001 and .6% in FY 2002.

Public Law 106-387 *The Agriculture, Rural Development, Food and Drug Administration, and Related Agencies Appropriations Act, 2001*–An act that included several provisions affecting the Food Stamp Program. This memorandum describes the two provisions of the act that increased the maximum excess shelter expense deduction, and allowed States to substitute their Temporary Assistance for Needy Families (TANF) vehicle rules for the food stamp vehicle rules where doing so would result in a lower attribution of resources to food stamp households.

Public Law 107-306 *Intelligence Authorization Act for Fiscal Year 2003*–H.R. 4628 would authorize appropriations for FY 2003 for intelligence activities of the United States government, the Intelligence Community Management Account, and the Central Intelligence Agency Retirement and Disability System (CIARDS). The estimate addressed only the unclassified portion of the bill. On that limited basis, CBO estimated that implementing certain provisions of the bill would cost $221 million over the 2003-2007 period, assuming appropriation of the necessary funds.

Public Law 107-42 *The Air Transportation Safety and System Stabilization Act*– The Air Transportation Stabilization Board (ATSB) was created to assist U.S. airlines after the terrorist attacks occurred on 9/11 and Act was signed into law September 22, 2001. It authorized the board to issue up to $10 billion in federal loan guarantees to air carriers for which credit is not otherwise available.

Public Law 107-56 *Uniting and Strengthening America By Providing Appropriate Tools Required to Intercept and Obstruct Terrorism Act of 2001.* The Patriot Act.

Public Law 107-296, 116 Stat. 2135 *Homeland Security Act of 2002*–introduced in the after effects of 9/11. It established the United States Department of Homeland Security, the single largest federal government reorganization since the Department of Defense was created via the National Security Act of 1947 (as amended in 1949). The Act includes many of the organizations under which the powers of the USA PATRIOT Act are exercised.

Public Law 109-13 *The Emergency Supplemental Appropriations Act for Defense, the Global War on Terror, and Tsunami Relief, 2005*–This law provides emergency supplemental appropriations for the fiscal year ending September 30, 2005 for defense, the global war on terror, and tsunami relief. The law establishes and implements regulations for State driver's license and identification security standards. The law prohibits funds from being used by a Federal agency to produce any prepackaged news story, unless the story includes a clear notification that it was prepared or funded by that Federal agency.

Public Law 885, August 1, 1956; 22 U.S.C. 2708 *State Department Basic Authorities Act of 1956*–Act that states the roles of the United States Department of State.

Public Proclamation No. 1 (1942)–General John L. DeWitt, Western Defense Commander, was assigned to administer Executive Order 9066. By its authority, he issued a series of proclamations. Public Proclamation No. 1 was issued on March 2, 1942. It expanded the restricted area established by the U.S. the Justice Department by designating the western halves of California, Oregon, Washington and the southern part of Arizona as Military Area No. 1. Japanese-Americans as well as Japanese, German, and Italian aliens were excluded from it. Voluntary removal to the interior of the U.S. was advised.

Public Proclamation No. 2–DeWitt issued Public Proclamation No. 2 on March 16, 1942, creating Military Areas 3 to 6 in Idaho, Montana, Nevada, and Utah, respectively.

Public Proclamation No. 3–On March 24, 1942, Dewitt issued Public Proclamation No. 3 that included Japanese American citizens among "enemy aliens" who must obey travel restrictions, curfew, and contraband regulations.

Public Proclamation No. 4–On March 27, 1942, Dewitt issued Public Proclamation No. 4 which prohibited Japanese aliens from voluntary evacuation of Military Area No. 1.2.

Public Safety and Cyber Security Enhancement Act–Amended the federal criminal code to offer an exemption to wiretapping restrictions for an individual acting legally to catch either wire or digital communications of a "computer trespasser" under specific conditions. It established a foreign intelligence exemption regarding the seizure of digital communications. It allowed a governmental organization authorized to utilize pen registers and/or trap and trace devices to use modern equipment reasonably obtainable that limits the copying or decoding of electronic and/or other signals to the dialing, routing, addressing, and signaling data used in the processing and transmitting of wire and electronic communications.

Right to Financial Privacy Act of 1978–also known as the **RFPA** is a United States Act that gives the customers of financial institutions the right to some level of privacy from government searches. Before the Act was passed, the United States government did not have to tell customers that they were accessing their records, and customers did not have the right to prevent such actions. It came about after the United States Supreme Court, in *United States v. Miller,* 425 U.S. 435(1976), held that financial records are the property of the financial institution with which they are held, rather than the property of the customer.

Terrorist Surveillance Act of 2006–Bill that would authorize warrantless surveillance at any time the President determined that such surveillance was necessary to the country, its citizens, or its interests, either in the country or out.

The National Security Surveillance Act of 2006–Redefined surveillance so that only an agenda specifically designed to catch the gravamen of a communication need oversight. Any governmental surveillance program that seizes, studies, and amasses patterns of communication data such as phone records, or e-mail and website addresses, is no longer thought to be "surveillance." It enlarged the area of law that permitted the Attorney General to approve spying on foreign embassies, with the understanding that it would be unlikely that an American citizen's communication would be caught.

The Protect America Act of 2007–It took away the warrant prerequisite for governmental surveillance of foreign intelligence operatives thought to be outside American borders. The FISA Amendments Act of 2008 reauthorized many provisions of the Protect America Act.

The Right to Financial Privacy Act of 1978–Also known as the RFPA is a United States Act that gives the customers of financial institutions the right to some level of privacy from government searches. Before the Act was passed, the United States government did not have to tell customers that they were accessing their records, and customers did not have the right to prevent such actions. It came about after the United States Supreme Court, in *United States v. Miller,* 425 U.S. 435(1976), held that financial records are the property of the financial institution with which they are held, rather than the property of the customer.

The SAFE Act of 2005–The Security and Freedom Enhancement Act was introduced in the 109th Congress to provide commonsense safeguards for intrusive Patriot Act powers and was created by a diverse group of members led by Republican Senator Larry Craig from Idaho. It was felt that the SAFE Act would give Congress a chance to bring the Patriot Act in line with the Constitution. The SAFE Act safeguarded a number of intrusive Patriot Act powers that shared certain common themes. As a result of gag orders, or delayed notification, these powers permit surveillance with a far greater degree of secrecy than is common in most government investigations. They do not allow affected parties the opportunity to challenge government orders before a judge. Because the substantive standards for some forms of surveillance have been modified, weakened, or even eliminated, the role of a judge in checking government abuse has been made less meaningful.

Secret Evidence Repeal Act of 1999 (HR 2121)–Written in order that the government would cease using secret evidence in immigration proceedings. In regular removal proceedings where the Government is attempting to prove deportability, but HR2121 would expand this rule to all deportation cases, including those involving aliens accused of being terrorists, and to proceedings involving denial of bond, immigration benefits, and to certain persons seeking admission. Died after 9/11.

Security and Freedom Ensured Act of 2003–a bipartisan act that was felt to be a measured, informed response that added safeguards against the Patriot Act, including enhanced judicial oversight for the provisions.

Tools to Fight Terrorism Act–Bill that never became law. Was initiated by Senator Jon Kyl, Republican Senator from Arizona.

Tsunami Relief, 2005–Refers to the effort made by Congress to lend aid to the different countries involved in the massive tsunami of December 2004.

Uniform Code of Military Justice–The foundation of military law in the United States. The UCMJ applies to all members of the Uniformed Services of the United States (i.e., U.S. Army, U.S. Navy, U.S. Marine Corps and U.S. Air Force. It also applies to non-Department of Defense military or other uniformed services, such as the U.S. Coast Guard, which is administered under Title 14 of the United States Code when not operating as part of the U.S. Navy. The UCMJ also includes the National Oceanic and Atmospheric Administration Commissioned Corps, and the United States Public Health Service Commissioned Corps. However, commissioned members of the NOAA and PHS are only subject to the UCMJ when attached or detailed to a military unit or are militarized by presidential executive order.

United States Constitution–The supreme law of the United States. It provides the framework for the organization of the United States Government. The document defines the three main branches of the government: The legislative branch with a bicameral Congress, an executive branch led by the President, and a judicial branch headed by the Supreme Court. Besides providing for the organization of these branches, the Constitution carefully outlines which powers each branch may exercise. It also reserves numerous rights for the individual states, thereby establishing the United States' federal system of government. It is the shortest and oldest written constitution of any major sovereign state.

USA Patriot and Terrorism Prevention Reauthorization Act of 2005–The first, the USA Patriot and Terrorism Prevent Reauthorization Act of 2005 was a passed by both houses of Congress in July 2005. It reauthorized provisions of the Patriot Act and the Intelligence Reform and Terrorism Prevention Act of 2004. It created new provisions relating to the death penalty for terrorists, enhancing security at seaports, new measures to combat the financing of terrorism, new powers for the Secret Service, anti-Methamphetamine initiatives, and a number of other miscellaneous provisions.

United States v. United States District Court, Plamondon–Also known as the **Keith Case**. This was a momentous decision for the Supreme Court as the justices decided, in a unanimous 8-0 ruling, that the requirements of the Fourth Amendment in cases of domestic surveillance targeting a domestic threat are valid.

Victims of Terrorism Compensation Act–Correct title is Omnibus Diplomatic Security and Antiterrorism Act of 1986 and it amended the Victims of Crime Act of 1984. Motions for Review of Orders of the United States Foreign Intelligence Surveillance Court (Nos. 02–662 and 02–968). In re: Sealed Case No. 02–001.

REFERENCES

9/11 Death Toll. *CNN* (2006, April 26). Retrieved on 2008-02-07.

9/11 Commission Report. National Commission on Terrorist Attacks Upon the United States (2004).

ABA Leadership Statement of Robert E. Hirshorn, President (Nov. 9, 2001).

Abrams, Floyd. The First Amendment and the war against terrorism. *University of Pennsylvania Journal of Constitutional Law,* vol. 5 (Oct. 2002).

Adams, Cecil M. (2003-05-02). Was Martin Luther King, Jr. a plagiarist? *Washington Post.* Retrieved on 2008-01-22.

Adams, Mike. (2001-09-21). INS unable to track millions in the US. *The Baltimore Sun.* Retrieved from www.rense.com on 2008-06-06.

Allen, Mike. (2005-06-11). Panel Chairman Leaves Hearing. Politics. *The Washington Post.*

Alpern, David M., Marro, Anthony, & Lesher, Stephan. This is your new FBI. *Newsweek,* Jan. 5, 1976, p. 14.

Al-Qaeda: Funding in Afghanistan. Global Security.org. Retrieved on 2008-07-23. Website: http://www.globalsecurity.org/military/world/para/al-qaida.htm.

Al-Qaida tape finally claims responsibility for attacks. *The Guardian* (2002-09-10).

American Civil Liberties Union (2007-09-06). *Federal court strikes down national security letter provision of Patriot Act.*

Americans Consider Powers of Investigation. (2006-08-19). *Angus Reid Global Monitor: Polls & Research.* Retrieved on 2008-04-20.

Americans ponder censure, impeachment for Bush. (2006-05-19). *Angus Reid Global Monitor: Polls and Research.* Retrieved on 2008-02-20.

Andrews, Tim. (2002-06-28). *Half of Americans are willing to give up personal freedoms guaranteed by the Constitution to protect country, study finds.* Colonial Williamsburg.

Apology Note from the United States Government. (2006-11-29). *The Washington Post.*

Ashcroft: Bush would veto bill scaling back Patriot Act. (2004-01-29). Washington/ Politics, *USA Today.*

Associated Press. (2004-09-02). Bin Laden's wealth not the force behind terror attacks. *USA Today.* Retrieved on 2008-01-23.

Associated Press. (2007-05-19). "List of attacks on U.S. embassies" *USA Today.* Retrieved on 2008-01-06.

Averill, Jason D. et al. (2005). Occupant Behavior, Egress, and Emergency Communications. *Final Reports of the Federal Building and Fire Investigation of the World Trade Center Disaster* (PDF). National Institute of Standards and Technology (NIST). Retrieved on 2008-05-20.

Beeson, Amy, & Jaffer, Jameel. (2003-July). Unpatriot acts: The FBI's power to rifle through your records and personal belongings without telling you. *The American Civil Liberties Union.*

Benson, Robert L. *The Venona story.* National Security Agency. Retrieved on 2007-12-20.

Berger, Peter. (2001). *Holy war, inc. Inside the secret world of Bin Laden.* New York: Free Press.

Bin Laden claims responsibility for 9/11. (2004-10-29). CBC News. Retrieved on 2008-01-08 from: http://www.cbc.ca/world/story/2004/10/29/binladen_mes sage041029.html.

Blackstock, Nelson. (1975). *COINTELPRO: The FBI's secret war on political freedom.* Pathfinder: New York.

Bliss, Jeff, & Rowley, James. (2006-03-08). Bush logs victory as USA Patriot Act passes Congress. *Bloomberg.*

Bowden, Mark. (1997-11-16). Black Hawk down. *The Philadelphia Inquirer.* Retrieved on 2008-01-11.

Branscomb, Anne. (1994). *Who owns information?: From privacy to public access.* Section 552-(a)4(F): BasicBooks.

Brezinski, Matthew. (2002-01-02). Operation Bojinka's bombshell. *Toronto Star.* Retrieved on 2007-12-20.

Broach, Ann. (2008-04-02). *Big brother: Homeland security blinks on read ID: No hassles on May 11.* www.newscom. Retrieved on 2008-05-11.

Brown v. Waddell, 50 F.3d 285, 292 (4th Cir. 1995).

Buckley, Jr. William F. (2002-05-20). Exit Gun Control. *The National Review.*

Butterfield, Jeanne A. (2001-10-17). Executive Director, American Immigration Lawyers Association. *Antiterrorism border controls,* Congressional Hearing, Senate Judiciary, Subcommittee on Immigration (2001-10-17).

Camarota, Steven A. (2002). *The open door: How militant Islamic terrorists entered and remained in the United States, 1993-2001.* Center for Immigration Studies Retrieved on 2008-02-23.

Camarota, Steven A. (2005-10-23). Use enforcement to ease situation. *The Arizona Republic.*

Carbonara, Peter. (2001-12-24). *Following the al Qaeda money trail.* CNN.com Community. Retrieved on 2008-01-23.

Cauchon, Dennis, & Moore, Martha. (September 2, 2002). Desperation forced a horrific decision. *USA Today.*

Canadian Security Intelligence Service (CSIS), Security Intelligence Report concerning Mohamed Harkat, February 22, 2008.

CDT's Analysis of S. 2092: Amending the pen register and trap and trace statute in response to recent Internet denial of service attacks and to establish meaningful privacy protections. (2000-04-04). Center of Democracy and Technology. Retrieved on 2008-01-20.

Center for Democracy and Technology. United States Congress, Senate Amendment 1562, September 13, 2001.

Churchill, Ward, & and Vander Wall, Jim. (1990). *The COINTELPRO Papers: Documents from the FBI's secret wars against domestic dissent.* Boston: South End Press, pp. xii, 303.

Citing improvements to law, ACLU withdraws Section 215 Case but vows to fight individual orders. (2006–10–26). *ACLU.*

Cohen, David B., & Wells, John W. (2004). *American national security and civil liberties in an era of terrorism.* New York: Palgrave MacMillan.

Combating terrorism: Law enforcement agencies lack directives to assist foreign nations to identify, disrupt, and prosecute terrorists. (2007–06–25). General Accounting Office. Retrieved on 2008–04–05.

Comprehensive Immigration Reform Act of 2007, S. 1348 (proposed). Council on Foreign Relations, Retrieved on 2008–06–15.

Comras, Victor. (January 2005). Al Qaeda financing and funding to affiliated groups. *Strategic Insights (4),* 1, Retrieved on 2007–12–29.

Coppolo, George. (2005–06–03). *State police arrests of people who break federal law.* Retrieved on 2008–01–20.

Corallo, Mark, spokesman for the United States Department of Justice. Cited in: Frieden, Terry (2004–01–27). Federal judge rules part of Patriot Act unconstitutional. Law Center, CNN.

Creppy, Michael. (9–21–2001). Memorandum All Immigration Judges and Court Administrators. *Instructions for cases requiring additional security.*

Critical nature of the J-1 Visa Waiver Program for foreign medical graduates. (2002). The American College of Healthcare Executives.

CRS Report for Congress. *Border security: The role of the US Border Patrol.* (2005–5–10). Retrieved on 2008–02–04.

Cumming, Alfred, & Masse, Todd. (2004–04–06). RL32336: *FBI intelligence reform since September 11, 2001–Issues and Options for Congress.* Retrieved on 2008–05–24.

Dempsey, Jim. (2007–10–10). *CDT's analysis of S. 2092: Amending the pen register and trap and trace statute in response to recent Internet denial of service attacks and to establish meaningful privacy protections.* Center for Democracy and Technology. Retrieved on 2008–03–22.

Diamond, John. Senate passes Patriot Act changes. Washington/Politics, *USA Today.*

Dillard, III, Wilson P. (2002–04–26). *House votes to abolish INS, creates two new agencies.* Government Computer News. Retrieved on 2008–02–02.

Dolfman, Michael L., & Wasser, Solidelle F. (2004). 9/11 and the New York City economy. *Monthly Labor Review,* 127.

Dunham, Richard. H. (2005–11–10). The Patriot Act: Business balks. *Business Week.*

Duvall, Lindsay. (Spring 2002). The guest worker program. Earned legalization and reform: The best solution. Chicago-Kent College of Law. *Honors Seminar.* Retrieved on 2008–01–20.

Dwyer, Jim et al. (2002–05–26). Last words at the Trade Center; Fighting to live as the towers die. *The New York Times.*

EFF: Analysis of the SAFE Act, *Electronic Frontiers Foundation* website.

EFF: EFF analysis of the provisions of the USA PATRIOT Act that relate to online activities, Were our Freedoms the Problem? *Electronic Frontiers Foundation* website.

EFF: EFF analysis of the provisions of the USA PATRIOT Act that relate to online activities, B. Computer Crimes under CFAA Defined as Terrorist Offenses. *Electronic Frontiers Foundation* website.

EFF: Let the sun set on PATRIOT–Section 202: Section 202, Authority to intercept wire, oral, and electronic communications relating to computer fraud and abuse offenses and Section 217, Interception of computer trespasser communications. *Electronic Frontiers Foundation* website.

EFF: Let the sun set on Patriot: Section 206. *Electronic Frontiers Foundation* website.

EFF: Let the sun set on PATRIOT–Section 207: Duration of FISA surveillance of non-United States persons who are agents of a foreign power. *Electronic Frontiers Foundation* website.

EFF: Let the sun set on PATRIOT–Section 209: Seizure of voicemail messages pursuant to warrants. *Electronic Frontiers Foundation* website.

EFF: Let the sun set on PATRIOT–Section 212 and Homeland Security Act Section 225: Emergency disclosure of electronic communications to protect life and limb. *Electronic Frontiers Foundation* website.

EFF: Let the Sun Set on PATRIOT–Section 214: Pen register and trap and trace authority under FISA. *Electronic Frontiers Foundation* website.

EFF: Let the sun set on PATRIOT–Section 215: Access to records and other items under the Foreign Intelligence Surveillance Act. *Electronic Frontiers Foundation* website.

EFF: Let the sun set on PATRIOT–Section 220: Nationwide service of search warrants for electronic evidence. *Electronic Frontiers Foundation* website.

EFF: Let the sun set on PATRIOT–Section 223: Civil liability for certain unauthorized disclosures. *Electronic Frontiers Foundation* website.

EFF: Let the sun set on PATRIOT–Section 225: Immunity for compliance with FISA wiretap. *Electronic Frontiers Foundation* website.

EFF: Section 204: Clarification of intelligence exceptions from limitations on interception and disclosure of wire, oral, and electronic communications. *Electronic Frontiers Foundation* website.

Eggen, Dan. (September 7, 2007). Judge invalidates Patriot Act provisions. *The Washington Post.*

Ehrlich, Dorothy M. (2005–07–04). Patriotism vs. the USA Patriot Act. *Open Forum, San Francisco Herald.*

Fact Sheet: United States Marshals Service. www.usmarshals.gov. Retrieved on 2007–11–08.

Farah, Douglas. (2004). *Blood from stones: The secret financial network of terror.* New York: Broadway Publishers.

FBI charges Florida professor with terrorist activities. (2003–02–20). *CNN.*

FBI Intelligence Investigations: Coordination within Justice on counterintelligence matters is limited. General Accounting Office: *Report to the Ranking Minority Member, Committee on Governmental Affairs,* US Senate (July 2001). Retrieved 2008–03–22.

FBI Report. *Counterterrorism progress since September 2001.* April 14, 2004 p. 20. Retrieved 2008–12–20.

FBI. Terrorism. http://denver.fbi.gov/nfip.htm. Retrieved on 2008–01–08.

The Federal Bureau of Investigation's Compliance with the Attorney General's Investigative Guidelines (Redacted). *Special Report.* September 2005. Retrieved on 2008–01–22.

Feingold, Russ. (2001). Address given October 12, 2001, to the Associated Press Managing Editors Conference at the Milwaukee Art Museum, Milwaukee, Wisconsin.

Fick, Bob. (2004–06–11). Jury acquits Saudi graduate student of charges he used computer skills to promote terrorism. *Associated Press.*

FISA Applied to Secret Foreign Intelligence Physical Searches in 1994 (Counterintelligence and Security Enhancements Act of 1994, Public Law 103–359, Sec. 9).

Flight 93 Hijacker: We have a bomb on board. *Fox News* (2006–04–13). Retrieved on 2008–02–23.

Fotis, James J. (2004). *Actions speak louder than words.* Law Enforcement Alliance of America. Retrieved on 2008–05–09.

FM 100–20. *Military Operations in Low Intensity Conflict,* 5 December 1990.

Freedberg, Louis, & McLeod, Ramon G. (1998–10–13). The other side of the law: Despite all US efforts to curb it, immigration is rising. *SF Gate. Com.* Retrieved on 2008–02–19.

Freeh, Louis. The complete transcript of Louis Freeh's testimony. *The Star Ledger* (2004–04–13). Retrieved on 2008–04–03.

Gaouette, Nicole. (2008–01–12). States get more time on national ID law. *The LA Times.* Retrieved on 2008–08–20.

Gentry, Curt. (1991). *J. Edgar Hoover: The man and the secrets.* New York: W.W. Norton.

Goldberg, Maurice R., Wechsler, William F., &. Wolosky, Leo S. (2002–11–25). *Terrorist financing: Report of an independent task force sponsored the Council on Foreign Relations.* Retrieved on 2008–02–08.

Gordon, Jane. (2005–04–24). In patriot's cradle, the Patriot Act faces scrutiny. *New York Times.*

Grady, Denise, & Revkin, Andrew C. (2002–09–10). Threats and responses: Rescuer's health: Lung ailments may force 500 firefighters off job. *The New York Times.*

Grissom, Brandi. (2007–05–23). Bill to give sheriffs bulk of funds to fight border crime. *El Paso Times.* Retrieved 2007–12–20.

Hertzberg, Hendrik. (2006–09–11). Lost love. *The New Yorker.*

Hersh, Seymour. (1974–12–22). Huge C.I.A. operation reported in U.S. against anti-war forces, other dissidents in Nixon years. *New York Times,* p. 1.

Hijacked planes used in coordinated attacks upon New York, Washington. *Fox News* (2001–09–11). Retrieved on 2008–2–24.

History of the FBI: Byte out of history–Solving a complex case of international terrorism. (2003–12–19). Retrieved on 2008–02–02.

History of the FBI: Rise of international crimes–1980s. Federal Bureau of Investigation

Website. Retrieved on 2008–02–02.

Holland, Jesse J. (2005–11–27). Bipartisan group of senators threatens to hold up Patriot Act reauthorization. *The America's Intelligence Wire.*

Homeland Defense Before the Senate Comm. on the Judiciary, 107th Cong. (2001) (Sept. 25, 2001) (written testimony of John Ashcroft, Attorney General).

Homeland Security Presidential Directive–2 (2001–10–29). Retrieved on 2008–06–09.

House approves Patriot Act renewal. (2006–03–07). *Politics,* CNN.

House GOP defends Patriot Act powers. Politics in Congress (July 9, 2004). *The Washington Post.*

Hudson Jr., David. (2006–November). Patriot Act: Overview. *First Amendment Center.*

Ifrah A. Jeff et al. (2001–11–19). Casting a wide net. *Legal Times.*

The Immigration and Naturalization Service's Removal of Aliens Issued Final Orders. (2003–02).

Internet denial of service attacks and the federal response. (2007–10–07). Center for Democracy and Technology. Retrieved on 2007–12–20.

INS Commissioner Doris Meissner announces retirement. (2000–10–18). *Immigration and Naturalization Service, News Release.* Retrieved on 2008–01–08.

International reaction. September 11 News.com. Retrieved on 2008–02–08.

An Interview with Judge Royce C. Lamberth. http://www.uscourts.gov/ttb/june 02ttb/interview.html. Retrieved on 2007–01–03.

Jehangir, S. P., Ciesinger, R., & Young, M. (2006–9–10). 9/11: Five years later. World views of attacks varied. *San Francisco Chronicle.* Retrieved 02–02–08.

Jordan attacks are likely to backfire. (2005–05–21). *Intelligence Briefing.* Retrieved on 2008–01–06.

Kellman, Laurie. (2006–02–02). Congress closer to extending Patriot Act. *San Francisco Herald.*

Keller, Susan Jo. Judge rules provisions in Patriot Act to be illegal. (September 27, 2007). *The New York Times.*

Kershaw, Sarah. (2005–04–23). In Portland, Ore., a bid to pull out of terror task force. *The New York Times.* Retrieved on 2008–07–23.

The Keystone terrorists (2005–7–21). *Flynn Files.* Retrieved on 2007–12–08.

Kohlmann. Evan F. (2004–11–25). *Al-Qaida's Jihad in Europe.* Oxford: Berg Publishers.

Kyl, Jon. (September 20, 2004). Giving law enforcement some overdue tools in the fight against terrorism. *Truth News.*

Law enforcement, counterterrorism, and intelligence collection in the United States prior to 9/11. *National Committee on Terrorist Attacks: Staff Statement No. 9.*

Leahy, Patrick. (February 10, 2003). Comments of Senator Patrick Leahy ranking Democratic member, Senate Judiciary Committee, on the Justice Department's secrecy in drafting a sequel to the USA PATRIOT Act. Office of Patrick Leahy, Senator for Vermont.

Lewis, John E. (2004–09–29). *Statement of John E. Lewis Deputy Assistant Director, Counterterrorism Division Federal Bureau of Investigation before the Senate Committee on Banking, Housing and Urban Affairs.* Retrieved on 2008–02–23.

Lichtblau, Eric. (2003–09–08). Ashcroft's tour rallies supporters and detractors. *The*

New York Times.

Liptak, Adam. (2007–09–07). Judge voids F.B.I. tool granted by Patriot Act. *The New York Times.*

Lipton, Eric. (2004–07–22). Study maps the location of deaths in the Twin Towers. *The New York Times.*

McCarthy, Andrew C. The wall truth. *National Review Online* (2004–04–19). Retrieved on 12–3–07.

McGirk, Tim. (2003–1–20). Terrorism's missing link: Khalid Shaikh Mohammed, al Qaeda's deadliest agent, is still at large–and more threatening than ever. *Time.*

MacDonald, Heather. Sneak-and-peek in the full light of day. *American Bar Association.*

Maintaining your immigration status while a student or exchange visitor. (2008). USCIS. Retrieved on 2008–04–08.

Marinucci, Carla. (2001–02–16). Mexico prepares for Bush visit: "Cowboy Summit" to be first trip abroad as President. *The San Francisco Chronicle.* Retrieved on 2008–01–09.

Miga, Andrew. (Aug. 5, 1998). Court demands to see Clinton lawyer. *Boston Herald.*

Miller, Sarah B. (2003–08–20). In defense of the Patriot Act. *Christian Science Monitor.* Retrieved on 2008–02–23.

Mixed response from Arab world (2001–9–11). BBC. Retrieved on 1–03–08.

Monograph on terrorist financing. (2004). National Commission on Terrorist Attacks upon the United States: Staff Report to the Commission.

Morahan, Lawrence. (2003–02–13). Patriot 2 raises concerns for civil liberties groups. *The Nation,* CNS News. Retrieved on 2007–12–20.

Morrison, Jane Ann, & Puit Puit, Glenn. (2003–08–27). Ashcroft touts Patriot Act's virtues. *Las Vegas Review-Journal.*

Most Americans decry NSA surveillance. (2006–5–17). *Gallup/USA Today.*

Mulhausen, Robert. (2002–10–19). *Finding funds to fight terrorism.* The Heritage Foundation. Retrieved on 2008–02–02.

Myers, Joseph M. (Winter/Spring 2004). The silent struggle against terrorist financing. *Georgetown Journal of International Affairs* (6.1).

Mylroie, Laurie. (Winter, 1995–1996). The World Trade Center bomb: Who is Ramzi Yousef and why it matters. *The National Interest.*

National Commission on Terrorist Attacks Upon the United States. (2004). Chapter 5, *9/11 Commission Report,* Government Printing Office.

Neilan, Terence. (2001–09–11). 2 Planes crash into World Trade Center. *The New York Times.*

Nichols, Nicole. (2003). *Domestic terrorism 101: Timothy James McVeigh (The boy next door).* http://www.eyeonhate.com/mcveigh/mcveigh6.html. Retrieved on 2008–06–29.

Nieves, Evelyn. (2003–04–21). Local officials rise up to defy The Patriot Act. *Washington Post,* p. A01.

Office of the Inspector General, DOJ. (2002–05–20). *The Immigration and Naturalization Service's contacts with two September 11 Terrorists: A review of the INS's admissions of Mohamed Atta and Marwan Alshehhi, its processing of their change of status applications, and its effort to track foreign students in the United States.* Retrieved on 2008–02–08.

Official US-VISIT fact sheet. (2008–06–05). U.S. Department of Homeland Security. Retrieved on 2008–07–29.

O'Harrow, Jr., Robert. (2002–10–27). Six weeks in autumn. *The Washington Post,* pp. W06.

Ottley, Ted. (2005–04–14). *License tag snag.*

Owen III, Henry. (January 2007). The Life and Liberty.gov Web site review. *Government Information Quarterly, 24* (1): 229–229.

Panel to weigh beefed-up Patriot Act. *Nation, Washington.* (2005–06–05). *The Boston Globe.*

Part of Patriot Act struck down. (2004–09–29). *Politics: Law, Wired.*

Peace group infiltrated by government agent. (2003–10–9). Retrieved on 2007–12–12.

Pear, Robert. (2001–10–18). Egypt, Saudi Airlines won't share passenger list data. *The New York Times.*

PBS: Frontline–*Interview with Robert M. "Bear" Bryant: The man who knew.* Retrieved on 12–20–07.

Peters, Jr., Ronald M. (1978). *The Massachusetts Constitution of 1780: A Social Compact.* Amherst, MA: University of Massachusetts Press.

Pistole, John S. (2004–4–14). Federal Bureau of Investigation: *Congressional testimony.* Retrieved on 2007–12–20.

Podesta, John. (Winter, 2002). American Bar Association. *ABAnet.org.*

Police back on day-to-day beat after 9/11 nightmare. (2002–07–21). *CNN.* Retrieved on 2008–03–03.

Poole, Patrick S. (1994). *An Examination of Ex Parte Merryman.*

Poor info hindered 9/11 rescue. (May 18, 2004). *CBS News.* Retrieved on 02–22–08.

Post-9/11 report recommends police, fire response changes. Associated Press. (2002–08–19). *USA Today.*

Pradnya, Joshi. (2005–09–08). Port Authority workers to be honored. *Newsday.* Retrieved on 2008–02–20.

President Bush discusses NSA Surveillance Program. (2006–05–11). The White House. Retrieved on 2006–02–20.

Press Release from ACLU of Colorado. (2005–12–08). Retrieved on 2008–02–02.

Press Release: Federal Bureau of Investigation. (2001–06–21). Retrieved on 2007–12–26.

Protecting America against terrorist attack–A closer look at the FBI's Joint Terrorism Task Forces. (2004–12–01). Federal Bureau of Investigation website. Retrieved on 2008–09–11.

Public perspectives on the mental health effects of terrorism: A national poll. (2003–December). National Association of State Mental Health and Program Directors, the National Mental Health Association and the Consortium for Risk and Crisis Communications.

Quick Facts. Federal Bureau of Investigation. Retrieved on 2008–09–10.

Ramasastry, Anita. (2004–04–20). Reform the Patriot Act to ensure civil liberties. *Law Center,* CNN.

Raymond, Barbara, Hickman, Laura J., Miller, Laura, & Wong, Jennifer S.

(February, 2006). Police personnel challenges after 9/11: Anticipating expanded duties and a changing labor pool. *The Rand Corporation.* Retrieved on 2007–11–07.

Reeve, Simon. (2002–06–27). *The new jackals: Ramzi Yousef, Osama bin Laden and the future of terrorism.* Northeastern University Press.

Reform the Patriot Act–Do not expand it! *American Civil Liberties Union.* Retrieved on 2008–08–12.

Reuter, Peter, &. Truman, Edwin M. (September 2005). Money laundering controls and terrorist finance. *Financial Regulator* (10), 2, 35–37.

A Review of the Tools to Fight Terrorism Act (Senate Hearing). Statement of Chairman Kyl (September 13th, 2004). United States Senate Committee on the Judiciary, Subcommittee on Terrorism, Technology, and Homeland Security.

Robinson, Jeffrey. (2004–08–13). The money trail: How petty crime funds terror. *The International Herald Tribune.* Retrieved on 2008–02–15.

Rockwell, Jr., Llewellyn H. (2001–12–19). The Attack and its Aftermath. *The Free Market (19),* 12. Retrieved on 2008–01–19.

Roll call 414 for H.R. 3199, July 21st, 2005.

Roll number 258, June 15th, 2005.

Roll number 339, July 8th, 2004.

Saad, Lydia. (2004–03–02). Americans generally comfortable with Patriot Act: Few believe it goes too far in restricting civil liberties. *Gallup.* Retrieved on 2007–12–20.

Sanjuan, Pedro A. (2000–05–02). The Navy doesn't need Vieques. *The New York Times.*

Savage, Charlie. (2006–03–26). Bush shuns Patriot Act requirement: In addendum to law, He says oversight rules are not binding. *The Boston Globe.*

Schmidt, Jean. (2006–01–13). *Securing Our Nation.*

Schwartz, Paul. (2007–05–31). Reviving telecommunications surveillance law. *University of Chicago Law School Surveillance Symposium.* Retrieved on 2008–02–02.

Schumer, Charles E. (2002–05–23). Press Release: Schumer announces agreement to include families of 1993 of WTC bombing in Victim's Compensation Fund. Retrieved 11–5–07.

SE Asia unites to smash militant cells. (May 8, 2002). *CNN.* Retrieved on 2008–03–10.

Senate Roll Call 358 for H.R. 3199 (2005–12–16).

Sieff, Martin. Experts see Saudi as broker, not author, of terrorist acts. *The Washington Times,* 14 August 1998, p. A7.

Singel, Ryan. (2003–03–12). A chilly response to 'Patriot II.' *Politics: Law.* Wired News.

Shapiro, Howard M. (1994). The FBI in the 21st Century. *Cornell International Law Journal, vol. 28.* Retrieved 2007–11–29.

Shevitz, Tanya. (2003–09–01). Huge drops in foreign students on campus: Post 9/11 security discourages many from coming to the US. *The San Francisco Chronicle.* Retrieved on 2008–04–04.

Sneak and peek search warrants. (2002–09–11). *Flagpole Magazine,* p. 12.

Snyders, Matt. (2008–05–21). Moles wanted: In preparation for the National

Republican Convention, the FBI is soliciting informants to keep tabs on local protest groups. *City Pages.* (2008–05–21).

Special Registration. (2008–10–08). United States Immigration and Customs Enforcement.

Special report: A Review of the FBI's handling of the Brandon Mayfield Case. (March 2006). United States Department of Justice.

Special Report of the Select Committee on Intelligence, United States Senate, January 4, 1995 to October 3, 1996. (1997–02–28).

State v. Horn, 15 Kan. App. 2d 365 (rev. denied 248 Kan. 998 [1991].

State v. Vandiver, 19 Kan. App. 2d 786 (1994).

The Student and Exchange Visitor Program. (2008). US Immigrations and Custom Enforcement.

The Student and Exchange Visitor Program. (2008 February). US Department of State.

Sposato, Janis. (2002–09–18). *Implementation of the Student and Exchange Visitor Information System.* US House of Representatives Committee on the Judiciary Subcommittee on Immigration, Border Security, and Claims.

Stock, Margaret D. United States Immigration Law in a world of terror. (2003–12–1). *The Federalist Society for Law and Public Policy Standards.*

Sununu, John E. (2005–11–16). SAFE Act co-sponsors say Patriot Act Conference report unacceptable.

Suskind, Ron. (2006). *The one percent doctrine.* New York: Simon & Schuster.

Talanian, Nancy. (2002). A guide to provisions of the USA Patriot Act and Federal Executive Orders that threaten civil liberties. *Bill of Rights Defense Committee.*

Talley, Tim. (2006–04–17). Experts fear Oklahoma City bombing lessons forgotten. *The San Diego Union-Tribune.* Retrieved on 2007–12–20.

Temporary migration to the United States: Nonimmigrant admissions under US Immigration Law (January, 2006). United States Customs and Immigration Service.

Terrorism Act 2000. Office of Public Sector Information. Retrieved on 2007–12–28.

Text of Fatwah urging Jihad against Americans. Retrieved on 2007–11–02.

Thomas, Cal, & Becker, Bob. (2005–06–22). The Patriot Act's worth keeping if we rein it in. *USA Today.* Retrieved on 2008–10–10.

Thompson, Bennie. (June 2007). *America's unfinished welcome mat: US-VISIT a decade later.* Retrieved on 2008–02–02.

Ken Thomas-Associated Press. (2001–09–12). *Fed investigate links in Florida.* Retrieved on 2007–12–29.

Transcript: Senate Judiciary Hearing on the Patriot Act. (2005–04–05). *Washington post.com.*

Understanding Islamism. *International Crisis Group.* Retrieved on 11–04–08.

US divided on civil liberties and terrorism. (2006–08–07). *Angus Reid Global Monitor: Polls and Research.* Retrieved on 2008–02–24.

US Visit Program. (2003–05–23). United States Immigration and Customs Enforcement. Retrieved on 2008–02–02.

United States Department of Justice. http://www.usdoj.gov/dea.

Statement of Barbara Comstock. (February 7th, 2007). *United States Department of Justice* (Director of Public Affairs).

United States Department of Justice (February 14th, 2004). President thanks Attorney General Gonzales at swearing-in ceremony. *Press release.*

United States Department of Justice. (2001). *The USA PATRIOT ACT: Preserving Life and Liberty.*

U.S. Government Printing Office. S14424. (2005-12-22) *Congressional Record.*

U.S. House approves Patriot Act extension; Senate to vote soon. (2006-02-01). *Top Worldwide,* Bloomberg.

United States v. New York Tel. Co., 434 U.S. 159, 167 (1977).

United States v. Salinas-Calderon, 728 F. 2d 1298 (10th Cir. 1984); *United States v. Vasquez-Alvarez,* 176 F3d 1294 (10th Cir. 1999); and *United States v. Santana-Garcia,* 264 F3d 1188 (10th Cir. 2001).

USA v. Omar Ahmad Ali Rahman et al. 1995. US Southern District of New York, 1995-07-13.

USA Today/CNN/Gallup Poll results. (2005-05-20). *USA Today.*

Visa stamping from Mexico. Immihelp.com. Retrieved on 2008-06-21.

Warrick, Joby et al. (2001-09-25). Experts: FBI lacks staffing to combat terrorists. *The Seattle Times.* Retrieved on 2007-11-02.

WhatReallyHappened.com. *The Oklahoma City Bombing.* Retrieved on 2008-06-14.

Washington Times. Letter to the Editor of the *Washington Times,* August 18, 2005. http://216.109.125.130/search/cache?ei=UTF-8&p=Slade+Gorton+letter+ to+the+editor+in+The+Washington+Times.&y=Search&fr=yfp-t-501&u =www.washtimes.com/op-ed/20050817-101757-6420r.htm&w=slade+gorton+ letter+letters+editor+washington+times+time&d=MpOrsOrnO2Tp&icp=1&.int l=us|Slade Gorton - Retrieved on 2008-3-24.

The White House-Press Release. State of the Union Address. (2004-01-20).

The White House. President's statement on H.R. 199, the USA PATRIOT Improvement and Reauthorization Act of 2005. (2006-03-09). *Press release.*

Wolf, Paul. (2001). *COINTELPRO: The untold American story.*

Wright, Lawrence. (2006). *Looming tower,* pp. 322–331. New York: Knopf.

Zalman, Amy. 1773: Boston Tea Party: Terrorism in the United States. Retrieved on 2008-01-03. http://terrorism.about.com/od/originshistory/p/boston_teaparty. htm.

Zajac, Andrew. (2005-04-06). Debate on USA Patriot Act. *Chicago Tribune.*

INDEX